Caspar Wistar Hodge

Gospel history

A syllabus of Professor C.W. Hodge's Gospel history

Caspar Wistar Hodge

Gospel history

A syllabus of Professor C.W. Hodge's Gospel history

ISBN/EAN: 9783337283872

Printed in Europe, USA, Canada, Australia, Japan

Cover: Foto ©Thomas Meinert / pixelio.de

More available books at **www.hansebooks.com**

GOSPEL HISTORY.

A SYLLABUS

OF

Professor C. W. Hodge's Gospel History,

PRINTED—NOT PUBLISHED—EXCLUSIVELY
FOR THE USE OF STUDENTS OF THE

MIDDLE CLASS IN PRINCETON SEMINARY.

PRINCETON:
CHARLES S. ROBINSON, PRINTER.
1876.

PREFACE.

This volume originated in the desire to have in more permanent and satisfactory form, than the meager pencil-scratches of any ordinary set of notes, the substance of a highly-valued course of lectures. And it is but just to say that Professor Hodge is responsible for nothing here printed, since his manuscript was not consulted, and no part of the work was supervised by him. It may also be added that this Syllabus is not intended to be well understood except in connection with the full Lectures in the class-room, and also in connection with Robinson's Harmony and the small syllabus.

The preparation of these notes has been a very laborious task, so much so that the editors have no expectation that their labor and pains will be adequately appreciated. But before any one indulges in wholesale criticism, let him *first* sit down and prepare, from the various sources, the manuscript for only five of these printed pages, taking special pains to look up the different authorities and hunt down the various references. Then let him remember that all this work had to be done in addition to the regular, and in some cases the extra, duties of the Seminary course. To any student who will comply with these two conditions, the editors herewith give full permission to cut and slash to his heart's content.

ABBREVIATIONS.

Alf.	for	Alford.	Rob.	for	Robinson.
Ell.	"	Ellicott.	San.	"	Sanhedrim.
Gal.	"	Galilee.	Syn., Syns.	"	Synoptists.
Jerus.	"	Jerusalem.	Tisch.	"	Tischendorf.
Lich.	"	Lichtenstein.	Wies.	"	Wieseler.

The other abbreviations will be readily understood by the reader.

PRINCETON SEMINARY. FEB. 25th, 1876.

SYLLABUS OF GOSPEL HISTORY.

CHRONOLOGY.

1. Rationalists attempt to overthrow date of the Gospels, on external grounds; they give a later date.
2. Alleged discrepancies of the gospels are exaggerated. Two kinds: *general*, in which a different character of Christ is presented; *special*, one gospel being supposed to contradict another. If we can trace a gradual historical growth from beginning to end, we have in this unity of the gospels, most effective answer to opponents. Birthplace of Christ is beyond question, but the date of birth is unknown. It is assigned to 753, 751, 750 (C. W. H.) 749 (Rob.) 748 (Kepler) 747 (Ideler). No one is at liberty to dogmatize where there is so much diversity of opinion. Give gospels benefit of their own reticence. It does not vitiate their historical value. The Passion is variously assigned between 781—790. Positive chronology is the particular date. Relative chronology is the relation of events to one another, their succession. Absence of chronological precision shows it was not essential to the plan of the writer. It seldom disturbs the order; Matt. and Mark are less regular than Lk. and Jno. The year and the day of the nativity are to be determined. Present era was fixed in the 6th century by Dionysius, a Scythian monk who flourished in Rome 553—556 A. D. He assumed that year of Christ's birth was coincident with 754. If 750 be the correct date, our era begins 4 years too late. This era was 1st used in historical works by Venerable Bede, early in the 8th century, afterward was introduced in public transactions by Frank kings, Pepin and Charlemagne. Gospels give 4 data:

(1.) Time of Herod the Great, Matt, 2: 1, Lk 1: 5.
(2.) Census in Judea under Augustus, Lk 2: 1.
(3.) Star of the Magi, Matt. 2.
(4.) Age of Christ when beginning public ministry, Lk 3: 23.

Josephus (Ant. 17 : 8 : 1): "Herod died, the 5th day after he had caused Antipater to be slain, having reigned, since he had caused Antigonus to be slain, 34 years : but since he had been declared king by the Romans, 37." (Ant. 17 : 6 : 4) : "Herod deprived Matthias of the high-priesthood, and burnt the other Matthias, who had raised the sedition, with his companions, alive. And that very night there was an eclipse of the moon." Now Herod was declared king in 714 ; therefore his death would be from 1st Nisan 750 to 1st Nisan 751, acc. to Jewish computation, at age of 70. Astronomical investigation places this eclipse on the night of 12th and 13th of March 750. He was dead before the 5th of April, because the Passover of that year fell on 12th of April, and Josephus (Ant. 17 : 8 : 4) states that before this feast, his son and successor Archelaus, observed the usual 7 days' mourning for the dead. His death, therefore, must be placed between 13th March and April 4th, 750. (Andrews). How long before Herod's death was the Lord born? Matt. and Lk. relate events that occurred between his birth and Herod's death : circumcision, presentation in temple, visit of Magi, flight into Egypt, murder of Innocents. Whatever view may be taken as to order of these events, they can scarcely have occupied less than two months. This would bring his birth into Jan. or Feb. at latest, 750.

Luke 2 : 1-2 ; *a* all the world should be taxed.

b the taxing was first made when Cyrenius was governor of Syria.

OBJECTIONS URGED.

I. No such universal taxing under Augustus on record; the censuses of contemporary history are local; a clear case of inaccuracy, say the skeptics. *Ans.* : It is known from Suetonius and Ancyrian monument, that Augustus three times instituted a census, in 726, 746, and 767. The second only needs to be considered. It appears to have been a *census civium*, confined to *cires Romani*, and not to have extended to the provinces; cannot, therefore, have been the taxing of Lk. Some restrict οἰχουμενη to Palestine or Syria. It would be improbable and unnatural for Luke to make this restriction. A better answer is, that if Lk. mentions the census, that is enough. Other answers: 1. The omission of contemporaries has its analogy; an argument from silence is never conclusive. Various laws were established, of which we are informed by no historians, but by monuments. In year of Cæsar's death, there was a geographical survey of Rome, but historians do not tell us of it. Ancient historians omit to give a complete list of governors of the provinces. On this period, Suetonius and Tacitus are very brief. This argument from silence, if pushed, would compel us to believe that no important event took place in the long reign of Augustus, of which the few historians whose works remain have not made specific mention. 2. Probably the censuses referred to on the Ancyrian marbles were confined to Italy, and did not extend to the Provinces. But beyond question, the census did at times extend to particular provinces. 3. A considerable gap occurs here in Dion Cassius (Roman historian); from 747 to 757, the very period in which Lk. says the taxing was made. 4. In Josephus the names of several who were governors of Syria about time of Lord's birth are mentioned, but only incidentally, nor is the list complete. Being a professed Roman flatterer, he leaves out all that might excite the discontent of Jewish readers. He passes over as lightly as possible whatever testifies to degradation of his people.

A positive argument is this: In time of Augustus, there was strong tendency to centralization, and establishment of the military power. Tiberius read in Senate an autograph MS. letter of Augustus's, which showed resources of the empire, how many soldiers could be raised and how much money they could give. How did he know, unless he had tried it? The citizens of Ancyra had marble copies made of bronze tablets in which he recorded the chief events of his life. In these he declares he made a census of Roman citizens four times; shows that he was doing this kind of work and confirms Lk. indirectly. Cassiodorus says that a careful survey was made in all provinces where Roman sovereignty extended, that there were enrolment lists. His authority of itself would have no great weight; but he may have read many works unknown to us, on this period. Mommsen doubts his statement, but Zumpt accepts it. "Being a Christian, he might have drawn his information from Lk." (Lange). Suidas: "Augustus sent out twenty men of great probity into all parts of the empire, by whom he made an assessment of persons and estates;" has no intrinsic improbability, but is unsupported. Suidas, like Cassiodorus, was a Christian.

INDIRECT PROOFS.—1. Under the Republic, each province retained its own mode of taking census, and under the Antonines, there was a regular land tax.

2. Exemption from land tax in Italy (by *jus Italicum*) began with Augustus. The exception proves rule. The land and poll tax under Pompey must have been in full force, which presupposes a census. Here again is a difficulty. When was the census made?

II. Palestine was not yet a Roman province; a Roman census was ordered during reign of Herod Great. But Herod was a *rex socius*, who had to pay tribute to the Romans; and then, this census may have been for statistical and military purposes, as in the decennial census of U. S. Jews were first compelled to pay tribute to Rome in time of Pompey. From time of Julius Cæsar, certain tributes were levied in Judea for Rome.

III. Cyrenius was Governor of Syria for 10 years after the nativity, and made a registration of inhabitants, Acts 5:37. The trouble is, to find room for another census in Palestine under same Cyrenius and at time of Christ's birth. Tholuck: "This enrolment took place before ($πρωτη$) Cyrenius was gov. of Syria; $πρωτη$ in comparative sense as John 1:15. This solution is not impossible grammatically. The taxing in question was 1st, as distinguished from 2d, which took place during h s 2d administration. Neander takes $ἡγεμονευοντος$ in wide sense of "leader;" is confirmed by Tacitus who says this man was thus employed. Ebrard: $απογραφη$ means registration as well as taxation. $απογραφη$ has a double sense: (*a*) transcription, (*b*) enrolment. If passage be read, this was 1st taxing, in distinction from 2d, and took place under him as governor of Syria, but in fact he was not yet an interregnum of several weeks of dry weather generally occurs between middle of Dec. and of Feb., somewhat distinguishing the former rains of the season from the latter. Lightfoot: "The spring coming on, they drove the beasts into wildernesses, or champaign grounds, where they fed them the whole summer. The winter coming on, they betook themselves home again with the flocks and herds." The climate of Bethlehem is not unlike that of Jerus., though milder. Shepherds could have been pasturing their flocks in Dec. Barclay: "in this month the earth is fully clothed with rich verdure, and there is generally an interval of dry weather between middle of Dec. and of Feb." (Andrews, 32–35). Abia's course was 8th in the 24. At destruction of temple by Titus on Aug. 5, 823, the 1st class had just entered on its course. Its period of service was from the evening of the 4th of Aug., which was the Sabbath, to the evening of following Sabbath, Aug. 11th. We can now easily compute backward and ascertain at what time in any given year each class was officiating.

DATE OF THE CRUCIFIXION.—Lk. 23 : 54 ; Mk. 15 : 42 ; Mtt. 27 : 62. $παρασκευή$ was common designation of 6th day of the week. The Sabbath occurring on 2d day of the feast, the 1st feast day became the preparation, the day before the Sabbath. 1. That $παρασκευή$ might not be apprehended as the weekly one, referable to the Sabbath, but be regarded as connected with the feast day of the Pass., Jno. expressly adds $τοῦ\ πάσχα$ (19 : 14). 2. $παρασκευή$,—Friday in the passover season, or paschal week, as a day of preparation for the Sabbath. The true reference is to the paschal feast, coming in on the evening of the day, of which feast the first day fell, according to John, upon the Sabbath.

DAY OF MONTH.—Crucifixion was 14th or 15th Nisan. Was the last meal of Christ with his disciples, the regular Passover supper or did it anticipate it? *Ans.* The paschal lamb was usually killed 14th Nisan and eaten same evening. The meal, therefore, was on preparation day, Thursday, Nisan 14th, and the crucifixion on Friday, Nisan 15th. (Mk 14: 12; Lk 22 : 7)). According to Synopts., the supper was the regular Passover. But

John calls it the preparation of the Passover (19:14); speaks as if the paschal supper was legally upon the evening of Friday, and consequently the Lord, who ate it upon the evening of Thursday, ate it before the time. 4 apparently discrepant references: 1. John nowhere calls it the Passover. "Out of 9 times in which πάσχα is used by John, in 6 it is applied to the feast generally, and not to paschal supper only. The meaning in the other 3 is in dispute." (Andrews). 2. Jno. 13:1—"Before the feast of the passover." Does this refer to the supper of verse 2? Tübingen critics say yes. Therefore it must have been a supper of a private nature, and not the Passover meal which it preceded; and according to John, Jesus never ate the Passover, but only a private meal beforehand. Being crucified next day, it must have been on Thursday, thus directly contradicting Synopts, who make it fall on Friday. But the clause does not refer to the supper of verse 2; it refers to what immediately follows, "that Jesus knew that his hour was come." He knew it beforehand.

3. Jno. 18:28—They themselves went not in, lest they should be defiled; that they might eat the passover. Held: that on day of crucifixion, Passover was not yet eaten. As it was not eaten before 6 o'clock, i. e. at beginning of next day (the Jews' day commenced at evening) the defilement incurred in the morning would have ceased before the regular Passover. Probably "eat the Passover" is used here in more general sense of keeping the paschal feast, and is not confined to eating of the lamb. Their scruple could have had reference only to the paschal sacrifices offered during the same day before evening.

4. Jno. (19:14, 16) calls crucifixion day the preparation of the Passover. The point at issue decides the genuineness of John's gospel.

4 methods of meeting the difficulty:

1. Some follow John, as most accurate, and allow that the others made a mistake. Reasoning: Jno. was an apostle, an eye-witness, and his gospel written last; therefore he would correct their mistakes. Bleek holds that Christ anticipated regular time of Passover; he translates Jno. 13:1—"Before the feast, when Jesus knew

that his hour was come to depart out of this world unto the Father, having loved His own who were in the world (He did love them unto the end), when a repast was spread (or during supper)," &c. The sentence thus formed is intricate, unlike John's usual manner, and without necessity.

2. Some endeavor to reconcile Synopts. and John by explaining away the Synoptical forms. No success. The Synoptics are explicit.

3. Rationalists,(Bretschneider, Baur, Davidson), uphold the synoptical account vs. John, maintain the former is true history and John not genuine, think John wrote with dogmatic intent, not historically, and that the error shows he could not have been an eye-witness as he claims.

4. Hengst., Wiesel., Rob., (215–222) and a majority of harmonists hold that synoptical accounts can be made to harmonize with John. John nowhere calls the meal a Passover, and this has negative weight. But omits Lord's Supper, and that does not warrant the conclusion that no such rite was instituted. He omits other things designedly, because he possessed the Synoptists. The omission is a tacit reference to what they had written, and what needed no repetition. Thus answer 1st objection.

The 2d, by making $\pi\rho\grave{o}$ $\tau\tilde{\eta}\varsigma$ $\dot{\epsilon}o\rho\tau\tilde{\eta}\varsigma$ qualify $\epsilon\dot{\iota}\delta\acute{\omega}\varsigma$, or $\epsilon\dot{\iota}\varsigma$ $\tau\acute{\epsilon}\lambda o\varsigma$ $\dot{\eta}\gamma\acute{a}\pi\eta\sigma\epsilon\nu$. If $\epsilon\dot{\iota}\delta\acute{\omega}\varsigma$, the sense is: "Jesus, knowing before the festival of the Passover, that his hour was come," &c. In this way the passage has no bearing upon the present question. If $\epsilon\dot{\iota}\varsigma$ $\tau\acute{\epsilon}\lambda o\varsigma$ $\dot{\eta}\gamma\acute{a}\pi\eta\sigma\epsilon\nu$, it is equivalent to festival-eve, and here marks the evening immediately before the $\dot{\epsilon}o\rho\tau\acute{\eta}$ or festival proper, on which eve, during supper, our Lord manifested his love to his disciples by washing their feet. The 3d (18: 28), by extending meaning of $\pi\acute{a}\sigma\chi a$ to paschal festival, and remembering that "eating the passover" meant not merely the paschal lamb of the evening before, but sacrifices and unleavened bread of the whole Passover week. The 4th (19: 14), by interpreting $\pi a\rho a\sigma\kappa\epsilon v\acute{\eta}$ as referring to the Jewish Sabbath, which actually occurred next day. It was Friday in the passover season or paschal week.

BLEEK'S ARGUMENT.—1. According to John's account (19: 31) 15th Nisan, the great-day of the feast coincided *that year* with the weekly Sabbath, (our Saturday); and the day before (i. e. the Friday) would be the preparation day both for the weekly Sabbath and for the great feast day. He argues (*a*) that the Sanhedrim would not have sent an armed band vs. Jesus on the holy night after the eating of the Passover, because it was expressly forbidden to carry arms on the Sabbath; (*b*) that on such a night the Sanhedrim would not have sat in council to judge Jesus, for to hold a court of judgment on the Sabbath was expressly forbidden; that crucifixion could not take place Nisan 15th, for it must have been a glaring violation of the Sabbatical rest of the day, according to Jewish notions still in vogue. Yet Bleek admits that criminals were often arrested on the Sabbath, and of course, if necessary, by men bearing arms. In opposition to Bleek: the strict Sabbatical law was not applicable to the feast Sabbath. Besides fanatics would have caused them to kill Christ, whenever they had opportunity. (Lk. 23: 2, 18). If the law did govern feast Sabbath, the hatred of the Jews made them break the law. (Andrews, 457).

2. Luke 23: 26, 27, we read that Galilean women, when they returned from the sepulchre, prepared spices, and rested the Sabbath day according to the commandment, and returned again to the sepulchre when Sabbath was past. Now it would have been illegal for them to have prepared the spices on the day preceding the Sabbath, if that day was Nisan 15th. (Ex. 12: 16: Lev. 23: 7). The same argument applies to the burial of Jesus by Joseph of Arimathea on the day of crucifixion, and still more strongly to Lk. 23: 26; Mk. 15: 21. Simon would not have been in the fields at work, Nisan 15th. Opposed: Here all depends on the strictness with which the Jews observed the feast Sabbaths. Maimonides mentions bathing and anointing, as things that might be done on the feast days; and of course then everything necessary to prepare the dead for burial would be permitted. Multiplication of instances may show that the law does not apply.

3. The Synopts. had, as the basis of their narrative an account which represented the 14th Nisan, and not the 15th, as the date of Christ's death. By a misunderstanding, however, there came to be incorporated with this the notion that Jesus ate the last supper with his

so gov. until 760, we must cons'rue ἡγεμονευοντος as applicable to any one who rules. Thus Cyrenius may have been a joint or assistant ruler, as Josephus speaks of Saturninus and Volumnius as Presidents of Syria: or an extraordinary commissioner sent from Rome especially for this purpose. In all this, is nothing improbable ; it agrees with the fact that about that time he was in East and engaged in political affairs. Wieseler: "this taxing was before Cyrenius was gov. of S." Zumpt, in his list of Syrian governors, B. C. 30 to A. D. 66, thus fills the interval from 748 to 758:

 748—750 P. Q. Varus or 6—4 B. C.
 750—753 *Quirinus* or 4—1 B. C.
 753—757 M. Lollius or 1 B. C. to 3 A. D.
 757—758 C. M. Censorinus or 3—4 A. D.
 758—760 L. V. Saturninus or 4—6 A. D.
 760—765 "   " is succeeded by *Quirinus* (Cyrenius.)

If he be right, Quirinus was twice gov. of Syria. His fact is that because Cilicia, when separated from Cyprus, was united to Syria, Cyrenius or Quirinus, as gov. of the first mentioned province, was also really gov. of the last mentioned, whether in any kind of association with Saturninus, or otherwise, can hardly be ascertained, and that his subsequent more special connection with Syria led his earlier, and apparently brief, connection to be thus accurately noticed. Varus was in office at least till the summer of 750. But that he did not continue as gov. until 759 is probable from the fact that Augustus ruled that no one should govern a province more than five years. A coin of Antioch proves that in 758 L. V. Saturninus was gov. of Syria. Zumpt's list shows who filled this office 750—758, Varus till B. C. 4 or 750. No names are given till Quirinus A. D. 6, by Josephus. During interval he was on military duty near Syria. The triumphal insignia granted him prove him legate and in Syria. This taxing began a little before he became actual legate. As he had been proconsul in Africa, and as it was a rule that the same person should not be ruler over more than one of the consular or prætorian provinces under care of Senate, he could not have been gov.

of any of the provinces adjacent, Asia, Pontus, Bithynia, Galatia; he must then have been acting as gov. of Syria and legate of emperor. If he succeeded Varus, he may have completed taxing begun before, acc. to Lk. Tertullian says the census at the birth of Christ was taken by Lentius Saturninus. When then was he gov. of Syria? Most say 746—748; consequently the birth must be placed as early as 747. Mommsen adduces a marble recording honors to man who had been twice legate in Syria. Only two had been, L. Saterninus and Quirinus. Concerning importance of this investigation, we are not bound to establish any one of these views any more than Luke.

STAR OF THE MAGI. — Kepler has shown that in year 747 a three-fold conjunction of Jupiter and Saturn in the sign Pisces occurred, and that in spring of following year planet Mars likewise appeared in this constellation. He regarded it as probable that an extraordinary star was conjoined with these three planets, as in 1603. He thought this conjunction formed star of Magi. Ideler rejects the new star of Kepler, and looking only to conjunction, puts birth 747—thinks Christ was two yrs. old when the command of Herod was given. If this be true, the year would be 748, and agree with Kepler's conjunction. Hence the star had been seen by Magi two years before their arrival at Jerusalem. Wieseler argues correctly that we have no certain ground for believing that star of Matt. was this conjunction of planets. He mentions that the Chinese astronomical tables record appearance of a new star at a time which coincides with the 4th year B. C. Precise conclusions are not to be drawn, but confirmation of approximate date is secured.

DAY OF THE NATIVITY.—Up to 4th century, 6th of Jan. had been observed as day of Lord's baptism, and had been regarded as day of his birth, from Lk. 3 : 23, the supposition being that he was just 30 when baptized. In 4th century, under influence of western church, this was changed, and both churches observed Dec. 25th. This is good date, because it gives time enough for the records in Matt. to transpire. During Dec., Jan., Feb. and Mar. there is no entire cessation of rain for any long interval,

disciples at the hour legally instituted for the Jewish passover; and as we have the Synopts., both representations, though non-coincident, yet, unconsciously to the evangelists, now lie side by side.

4. The feast (Easter, paschal cont. of 2d cent.) about which the dispute was, was held in Asia 14th Nisan, at the hour in which the Jews celebrated their passover (i. e., on the night which, according to Jewish reckoning, began Nisan 15th); and hence Christians of Asia Minor who followed this practice were called *Quarto-decimani*. They were chiefly Jewish converts, and pleaded the authority of John and Philip. The western church, composed of Gentile converts, discarded the pass., and celebrated annually the resurrection on a Sunday, and observed the previous Friday as a day of penitence and fasting; pleaded authority of Peter and Paul. The Tübingen school (Hilgenfeld's *Paschastreit*, pp. 5–118) make inference vs. John and say that that Gospel was not ascribed to him by the East. church. Neander (Hist. I., 513) thinks that Christians of Asia Minor celebrated Nisan 14th *as day of Christ's death*, but he says that they kept the Jewish passover and included in it the commemoration of Christ's death. Bleek: "John's knowledge that Jesus had eaten the last supper with his disciples not on the day legally fixed, but a day earlier, could not have obliged him to refuse to keep the yearly pass., as he had been wont to do at Jerus'm, among Christians at Ephesus, who also were wont to celebrate it, for Jesus himself had kept the pass. in the earlier years of his ministry. It is likely too that the Christians of Asia Minor subsequently retained the custom simply because it had become a custom, and because of the opposition raised vs. it." Hengst., Thol. and Wieseler urge that, according to John, Jesus celebrated last supper with disciples, not on the day of the pass. (evening of Nisan 14th or beginning of Nisan 15th), but a day earlier, and therefore that John's account does not differ from that of Synopts. The harmonists find clear proof that eastern and western churches had all four gospels, proving they knew all the circumstances and saw no difficulty in the statements.

Wieseler: Nisan 15th fell on Friday, 783 or A. D. 30. The darkness at crucifixion could not have been caused by an eclipse, for it was then full moon. Phlegon, of Tralles, tries to show that it was caused by an eclipse which took place between July 785 and 786. But the astronomer Wurm, that the eclipse referred to took place 782.

DATE OF THE BAPTISM.—Six data are given in Lk. 3: 1-2: "Now in the 15th year (780) of reign of Tiberius Cæsar, Pontius Pilate being Governor of Judea (779—789), and Herod being tetrarch of Galilee (750—792) and his brother Philip being of Iturea and of the region of Trachonitis (750—787), and Lysanias the tetrarch of Abilene (———), Annas (759—767) and Caiaphas (778—789) being the high-priests." Luke's least carelessness or ignorance of the history would lead to a mistake. Yet his credibility remains unimpeachable. An anachronism is charged. Josephus mentions one Lysanias killed sixty years before. Therefore, it is said, that Lk. is sixty years too late. Lysanias was probably a family name. We can see clearly why Luke, writing after Abilene had been made a part of the Jewish kingdom, should have mentioned the fact, having apparently so little connection with gospel history, that at the time when the Baptist appeared, this tetrarchy was under the rule of Lysanias. It was an allusion to a former well-known political division that had now ceased to exist, and was to his readers as distinct a mark of time as his mention of the tetrarchy of Antipas, or Philip. This statement respecting Lysanias shows the accuracy of Luke's knowledge of the political history of his times, and should teach us to rely upon it even when unconfirmed by contemporaneous writers. Annas had been high-priest, yet Caiaphas actually was such when the Baptist appeared. The sovereign pontificate had fallen to a degraded condition. The office had become subject to removal. Dismissal from it happened almost every year (Jos. Ant., 15:3:1; 18:2:2; 18:5:3; 20:9:1, 4). Caiaphas maintained himself longer than the rest (25—36); his three predecessors only about one year each. As a Sadducee and a priest he was animated with double hatred to the Saviour. (Andrews 131—138). Lightfoot sup-

poses that Annas was the sagan, or vicarius of the highpriest, the next in order to him, in his absence to oversee, or in his presence to assist in the oversight of the affairs of the temple, and the service of the priests (C. W. II.). Wieseler: The common explanation, adopted by Farrar, is that Annas was Nâsi or President of the Sanhedrim.

FIFTEENTH YEAR OF TIBERIUS CÆSAR.—Luke 3: 1, 23. Augustus died Aug. 767. The 15th year of Tiberius began Aug. 781. Christ's 1st Passover then would be in 782. But Luke 3: 23, "he was about 30 years of age when he began his ministry." As already seen, he could not have been born later than 750. He must have begun his ministry, therefore, 780, and been baptized in that year. Tertullian, however, gives the 15th year of Tiberius as the year of Christ's passion: "Christ suffered under Tiberius Cæsar, R. Geminus, and P. Geminus, being consuls, on the 8th day before the Calends of April," (25th March). He was followed by Lactantius, Augustine, and others, especially of the Latin Fathers. San Clemente so explains Luke from chronological necessity. He attempts to show that the 15th year of Tiberius is "not to be referred to the beginning of the ministry of John, nor to the baptism suffered by Christ in Jordan, but to the time of his passion and crucifixion, the evangelist himself being our leader and interpreter." This makes the whole ministry last but few months; Christ would be 32 years old at baptism, and John's account requires him to begin his ministry 3 years before, and before Luke makes Baptist's ministry to begin. Brown thinks that the heading of St. Luke's 3d chapter contains the date, not of the mission of John the Baptist, but of the year of our Lord's ministry, especially in reference to the great events with which it closed. Wieseler refers Luke's words to the imprisonment of John, not to the baptism of Christ; holds that Christ was baptized 780, John was imprisoned 782, and Luke 3: 1 is anticipatory, and chapter following goes back to period prior to John's imprisonment. The exegesis is violent. The usual solution (started by Zumpt) is that 15th Tiberius dates from the time he was made associate emperor (765) by the Senate, 2 years before the death of Augustus (767). This would bring 780 for the year of baptism and solve the difficulties. There are various dates for computing the reign Augustus, according as he increased in power. The same is true of Tiberius. This increases the difficulty. Certain Egyptian coins date from the connection of Tiberius with Augustus. Tiberius obtained full control in the Provinces in 767. His 15th year then, 779, or first passover 780. Luke 3: 23—(*a*) began to be or (*b*) was about 30 when he began, i. e. his public ministry.

The solution is confirmed by Jno. 2: 20. Herod began the temple in 734; to this add 46 (time of building) and the result is 780, the proper date.

RESULTS.

	ROBINSON.		WIESELER.		ZUMPT.			
Born	749 or 750	. .	750	. .	747	. .	Pilate,	779-789
Bap.	779 " 780	. .	780	. .	779 A. D. 26	. .	Herod,	750-792
1st Pass.			780	. .	781	. . 780 " 27	. .	Philip,	750-786
2d "			781	. .	782	. . 781 " 28	. .	Lysanias,	
3d "			782	. .		782 " 29	. .	Annas,	759-767
Cruc.			783	. .	783	. . 30	. .	Caiaphas,	778-789
						. .	Tib. 765 or 767-782	

DURATION OF THE PUBLIC MINISTRY.—3 views are held: 1. That it was 3½ years; 2. 2½ years; 3. 1 year or less. The Fathers, from Is. 61: 2, held that it was 1 year. But the word year is to be understood as the poetical parallel of day, or hour. The opinion of Fathers is also based on tradition of crucifixion 15th Tib., 782, combined with Luke's putting baptism same year. (Lk. 3: 1). Brown holds that the ministry was 1 year, doubts the text (of John) even though it says the feasts were passovers. The Synopts. seem to give an entirely different account from John; they say Christ went to Galilee and only after a considerable time went to Jerusalem and the Temple. John says he went to Jerusalem and the Temple immediately, cleansed the latter, &c. The Synopts. make no feast till crucifixion; inference, that ministry was 1 year or less in length. John makes scene Judea, and mentions 3 or 4 Passovers. The Synopts. were aware of Judean ministry: Mtt. 4: 25; 27: 57. When Saviour wept over Jerusalem, they mention it. There is no explanation except that he had worked in Jerusalem. Attempts to overthrow this argument do not succeed. Baur: that Jesus wept over the Jews in particular. B. had to give this up. Strauss: that the words are per-

sonified wisdom and are quoted from lost writings. Schenkel: that Jno.'s mention of Passovers all refer to one. Lk. 10: 38, another reference to Judean work. It is impossible that a pseudo-John should represent the course of the Life of Christ so differently from the Synopts., when the latter were duly accredited. He wrote with a dogmatic purpose, and would not expect to be believed. On other hand John was aware of the Galilean work. (7: 6-9.) He implies that Galilee had been the chief scene of our Saviour's visitations. He allows all the time necessary for it and on several occasions leaves it to be inferred. Jno. 6: 2, multitudes went with Jesus because of His miracles, but the miracles are not related. Jno. 6: 66, many of his disciples went back from him, but Jno. had not told us of the formation of a band of disciples. Jno. 6: 70, the 12 are mentioned, but there has been no account of their calling. Between chapters 6 and 7, there is an interval of 7 months. To reconcile Synopts. and Jno., all that can be required is to give a good reason for their differences. The Synopts.' plan includes active life in Galilee. Matt. seeks proof in miracles for Christ's Messiahship. Luke gives biography of Christ in his active work. Jno. came later, when doctrinal points were discussed, particularly the person of Christ. Jno's purpose is to give His own discourses so that they may know what He claimed concerning Himself. It was not in Galilee, in parable, that these profound Christological statements were made. It was among the educated, cultivated Pharisees of Jerusalem. Renan: "I dare defy any person to compose a consistent life of Jesus, if he makes account of the discourses which John attributes to Jesus."

John's feasts: 1. "the Jews' passover," (781) (Jno. 2: 13); 2. "a feast of the Jews, (782) (5: 1);" 3. "the Pass. nigh," (6: 4); 4. "Before Pass.," (12: 1); 5. "feast of Tabernacles," (7: 2); 6. "feast of dedication," (10: 22); (Bible Dict. for Pass., Pentec., Tabern., Dedic., and Purim.) Of these feasts 4 were Passovers, if Jno. 5: 1 be so interpreted. We gain or lose a year here. Pentecost occurred this year (782) on the 19th of May. No special argument in its favor; was not so generally attended as Passover or Tabernacles, and no reason appears why

Jesus should have omitted Passover and gone up to Pente. Tabernacles followed, Sept. 23d. Chief argument in its favor: it brings feast of 5:1 into close connection with that of 7:2, and thus best explains 7:21-23. But some months more or less are not under the circumstances important, for the miracle with its results must have been fresh in their minds even after a much longer interval. If He had not in the interval between these feasts been at Jerusalem, as is most probable, His reappearance would naturally carry their minds back to the time when they last saw him, and recall both his work and their own machinations vs. Him. The great objection to identifying the feast before us with that of Tabernacles is that it puts between the end of ch. 4, and beginning of ch. 5, a period of 8 or 9 months, which the Evangelists pass over in silence.

FOUR OBJECTIONS VS. PASSOVER.— 1. Jno. 6:4, "passover nigh." Christ did not attend. If not, then he was not at any feast till Tabernacles (7:2), a period of 18 mos.; was absent from Jerusalem for that time. Argued: as a strict Jew he could not have been so long away. Ans.: that Jesus should have absented himself for so long a time from the feasts is explained by the hostility of the Jews, and their purpose to slay Him (Jno. 5:16-18; 7:1). We know He would not needlessly expose Himself to peril. To the laws of God respecting the feasts He would render all obedience, but with the liberty of a son, not the scrupulosity of a Pharisee. He was Lord of Sabbath; so He was of the feasts. He attended them or not as seemed best to Him. Chief argument in favor of Purim is, that it is brought into such close connection with the Passover (only 7 mos. absent). Ellicott: "If the note of time derived from Jno. 4:35 be correct, then the festival here mentioned clearly falls between the end of 1 year and the Passover of the one following (6:4) and therefore can be no other than the feast of Purim." That Jesus should have absented himself a long time from the feasts, is explained by the hostility of the Jews.

2. John does not here name the festival, whereas he seems always to specify it (2:13, 23; 6:4; 7:2; 10:23; 11:55; 12:1).

3. That if 5 : 1 and 6 : 4 are Passovers, there is a whole year of which Jno. gives no account. Ans. : this is in accordance with analogy of Jno.'s gospel. The Synopts. fill in this and Jno. confines himself to feasts. Andrews : "this is not the only instance in which Jno. narrates events widely separated in time, without noting the interval. Thus, ch. 6 relates what took place before a Passover, and ch. 7 what took place at feast of Tabernacles, 6 months after. In 10 : 22 is a sudden transition from Tabernacles to Dedication."

4. Accounts for Synopts. not mentioning feasts. His work in Galilee has reference to national salvation thro' the faith of those who should believe on him there. This may explain their silence in respect to the feasts which Jesus attended while in Galilee. Any transient work at Jerusalem, addressing itself especially to the hierarchy, had no important bearing upon the great result.

FOR PASSOVER.—1. Common text wrongly omits article, which would naturally refer to chief feast. Modern critics and best MSS., including Sinaitic, agree as to this. (Winer, p. 119 or 126). Lange : "The article is not absolutely conclusive, for in Heb. a noun before the gen. is made definite by prefixing article, not to noun itself, but to the gen., and the same is the case in the Sept." Ellicott : "The true reading appears certainly to be ἑορτή. It has in addition to secondary authorities, the support of three out of the four leading uncial MSS., and is adapted by Lachm., Tisch., and others." Tholuck : "Were the article genuine, we would be compelled to regard the Passover as meant. If it is not genuine, the Passover may be meant, but so also may some other feast." (Andrews, 172).

2. Phrase "feast of the Jews" is not applicable to Purim. P. was "not a Mosaic feast, nor of divine appointment, but established by the Jews while in captivity, in commemoration of their deliverance from the murderous plans of Haman. (Esther, 3 and 9). It was national and political, rather than religious. Why then should Jews go up from Jerusalem to this feast? Ellicott : "The view of the best recent harmonists and commentators is that feast was the feast of Purim." Lange : "Fanaticism in

the people naturally sought to make it a festival of triumph over the Gentiles (subsequently over the Christians also.) On this account, the particular feast was preëminently *the feast of the Jews* (with the art.) and the art. in C. Sinaiticus cannot be made to speak exclusively for pass."

3. Jesus went and found a crowd. P. was observed all over the land: had no reference to Jerus. No special services were appointed for its observance at the temple, nor does it appear that it was their custom. Each Jew observed it wherever he chanced to be. Lange: " Christ may have attended this f. as he attended other festivals, (7 : 2 ; 10 : 22) without legal obligation, merely for purpose of doing good."

4. No adequate motive is assigned for Christ's going to Jerusalem: he was not required to do so by the law. Ellicott : " In the year under consideration, Passover would occur only a month afterward, and our Lord might well have thought it was advisable to fix his abode at Jerusalem and to commence his preaching before the hurried influx of the multitudes that came up to the great yearly festival."

5. Healing of infirm man was on a Sabbath. The festival of Purim lasted 2 days, and was regularly observed on 14th and 15th Adar (March); but if 14th happened to fall on Sabbath, or on 2d or 4th day of the week, the commencement of the fest. was deferred until the next day. Purim was never celebrated as a Sabb. Lange: " The Sabb. spoken of 5 : 9 may have preceded or succeeded the feast."

6. Lk. 13 : 6–7. " These 3 years." Hengst. says the reference is to Jewish people, among whom Christ had wrought for 3 years. But we cannot draw argument from parable; not conclusive enough. Andrews : " It is doubtful whether the expression has any chronological value." Lange : " If one insists on having a def. time for God's work of grace on Isr., we may reckon the time from the public appearance of Jno. B., one-half year before the entrance of Jesus upon his office, up to the present moment, which altogether does not make up much less than three years."

7. Time needed for events. Otherwise we must compress into one month, what according to the other scheme took a whole year. It can hardly be conceived that he should have done so much in such narrow limits. The harmony will make Christ's ministry 3½ years (Rob.) or 2½ (Wiese. and Zumpt).

PREPARATORY PERIOD.

§1. Limits: from beginning of gospel narrative until entrance upon public ministry. Subdivision: (*a*) all preceding nativity; (*b*) all succeeding it until entrance upon public ministry. Mtt. and Lk. are authorities for nativity, and are supplementary to one another, in no case parallel. Matt. gives histor. proof that Jesus was the Messh. of O. T. Therefore he records his birth, genealogy, and other events connected therewith. Lk. gives events in order, and therefore goes back to annunciation and to his predecessor. Mk. portrays active life of Christ. John's design is to represent him as a historic person in his own words. The history differs from every other h. The facts have no parallel; naturally it should have none. The miraculous element predominates here as nowhere else. This is history written for a purpose. Charged: that it was written afterward. But we have, intermingled, the divine, angelic, and human. When the Son of God was to come, there must be peculiar circumstances. Unbelievers stumble here, and believers find proof for genuineness. Some believers, however, find their strongest difficulty here.

Classification of characteristics: (*a*) Events were to be so adapted as to form basis of our faith. If it be true that Son of God became S. of man, it is more than probable it was done in this way. We must have practical evidence of birth at the time of its occurrence. It would not do to attest it afterward, else it would be charged that it was an invention, or dream of an enthusiast. Ebionites and Socinians say he became Son of God first at baptism. Miraculous element, therefore, is inseparable from the hist. It grows out of it from the very nature of the case. Incarnation itself the greatest miracle. (*b*) Publicity must be secured; attention attracted. Chain of evidence was so good, as here written, that it was never doubted by enemies (primitively). (c) The child must be secured, so as not to appear a rival of civil rulers, and to prevent premature action by them. Yet witnesses must be numerous enough to identify Christ from birth; to show that babe of Bethlehem and Jesus of Naz. were one and same person. (d) While humility of Son of God was to be shown, yet from first moment, he must be attended with all dignity and honor due to divinity. He must bring heaven with him, angelic choir, homage of good men (Sheph'ds and Magi). As at cross, so at manger, humility is relieved by heavenly dignities. (e) Ante-typical; as life and death of Christ are the final facts of O. T., it must be shown he came to fulfill it. Unity of divine plan must be vindicated; his relation to the law be made clear. These things belong to this period as preparatory. If men had been left in doubt, they would have rejected Christ at beginning of his ministry. Hence we read repeatedly, "all this, that the Scriptures" &c.; we see express recognition of faithful few, in whom spirit of old economy was manifested. Gospel hist. is last ch. of old dispens'n. N. T. begins with Pentecost, where O. T. scenery, poetry, &c., find their fulfillment. (f) Typical; his life is type of every Chn. and of Church as whole. Old economy is typical bec. it points to the future, as it embodies what has been already realized. That very life in which the old is fulfilled is still a type of Chn. spiritual life. Impossible to interpret Gospels and Acts, without violating meaning, unless we believe facts are arranged purposely to embody the doct., the spiritual truth. Such were miracles, the fact that he carried his dealings beyond borders of Palestine (gospel for world). Why did he attend temple? why submit to circum.? to teach the evil of sin.

§2. Official character of John Baptist was necessary at outset. Ritualists claim Christ was disciple of John, that his work grew out of John's. Annunc'n of Bapt's birth prepared people and his parents to understand his mission, and how to treat him. Honor is done to O. T. in choosing priest of temple (1 Chron., 24), prophecy is fulfilled, type is given, in declaration that John was to be a Nazarite from the womb (as Samuel and Samson).

Spiritual meaning of incense is seen (prayer); Lk. 1:10. Emphasis is laid on character of parents (Lk. 1:6), they were observers of rites and exercised a lively faith. Ceremonial righteousness was their possession. Mass of the Jews corrupt. But some were willing to introduce new economy. Meaning of both names was explained and fulfilled by what happened to those who bore them: Zach. (the Lord remembers), Eliz. (God's oath). Hope of giving birth to the deliverer was common among Jewish women. 400 yrs. angelic visitation had been discontinued, now it is renewed. John as Nazarite (Numb. 6: 1-21) was to be a reformer. Mal. 4:6, the Jewish conception of this p'cy was that E. was to be the forerunner and hence had not died. This impression was to be corrected. Z's faith not strong enough at first; asks a sign, and is given one (dumbness, a punishment for his unbelief). "As faith is to be the chief condition of the new covenant, it was needful that the first manifestation of unbelief should be emphatically punished; but the wound inflicted becomes a healing medicine for the soul." (Lange).

Objections answered: 1. Z's treatment was not only punitive but was to confirm his faith, and to be a lesson to the people. 2. Strauss objects, that a name is given to an individual angel, wh. we do not find in O. T. until after the captivity in Danl. Obj'n is therefore that Jews had no doct. of angels before captivity, that they borrowed their ideas from Persians. If so, how came they to have Hebrew names? Furthermore (a) the O. T. is full of the doct.; and (b) we have no proof that Jews borrowed from Persians; (c) Tho' names are given to none until Dan.'s time, yet it is characteristic of O. T. to be progressive. Names of angels might be expected in an Apocalyptic book like Dan. (d) Doct. of angels was received and confirmed by Christ and Apostles. 3. Doubted, whether such definite names are borne in heaven. Gab'l represents ministries of angels toward man; Mich. is type and leader of their strife, in God's name and His strength vs. the power of Satan. In O. T., therefore, he is guardian of Jewish people in their antagonism to godless power and heathenism. Many Reformers embraced idea that Mich. is Christ. If true, some would represent name of Gab'l (man of God) in same way. Interpretation is inadmissible. Whenever angel Jehovah appears, it is always as God. We are never left in doubt.

Myth. theory holds that this was a myth'l age, that disciples believed Christ was raised from dead, owing to the enthusiastic statements of the women. Myth is a story or narrative, involving moral or relig. truth, in wh. narrative form and idea involved are blended. There is no conscious invention to give birth to a popular idea. This theory saves moral character of early disciples; holds that John became imp. after he began his public ministry, and these stories grew up in connection with both. Only question is, how much is mythical and how much historical? Practical application of the theory necessitates in many cases the charge of conscious deceit. *Naturalistic exp.* maintains that Christ worked great cures, but by nat. causes. He seemed to raise from dead, but the man was not dead. So here, Z. was paralyzed owing to excitement. *Tendency hypoth.* holds that there was a conscious falsification of history in accommodation to certain current ideas; hist. is rewritten to give currency to certain doctrines. Strauss (2d Life) came over to this theory: shifted his ground. *Legendary theory* (Renan) holds there is a basis of fact, but altered by blending of natural enthusiasm and pious fraud; very much like legends of saints in Rom. church. Renan adopts more of Gospels than others, because his romancing is not bound by so doing: his method is not so destructive as Strauss's.

§3. Six mos. after conception of Elizabeth, an angel (Gab.) appears to Mary and announces that she was to give birth to Messiah. Points of analogy and contrast with annunc'n and birth of John (Alexander):

1. Analogy:
(*a*) Both were announced by angel of God.
(*b*) " to be extraordinary.
(*c*) " named by the angel.
(*d*) " connected with prophecy.
(*e*) Offices of both were described.
(*f*) In both, a sign was given to strengthen faith of the parents.

2. Contrast:
(*a*) John's was communicated to priest in the temple; Christ's to humble virgin in small town of Galilee.

(*b*) John's announcement was more honorable than Christ's birth.

(*c*) Our Lord surrounded his messenger with pomp which he denied to himself.

The announcement must be made previously to his birth, that the woman may know what was happening to her. Is. 7:14 fulfilled in Mt. 1:23. A virgin betrothed should be chosen, partly that she might be protected by a good man in circumstances into which she was brought, partly that the heirship to the throne might be conformed to. Two points: 1. Whether both (J. and M.) were of house of David. 2. Whether Lk. 1:27 is to be confined to Jos. Angel tells M. that the child must be of h. of D. What meaning would this have to her before her conception, unless she knew that she was of h. of D.? Lange " The words relate solely to J. They by no means deny descent of M. from D." Announc'n was private to avoid notice of civil authorities and the jealousy of Herod. Lk. 1:32, Dan. 7:14, his kingship over Israel is promised. For M., intimate with O. T., this p'cy wd. contain essence of most remarkable promises (2 Sam. 7, Ps. 45, Is. 9, Mic. 5). Lk. 1:42, 44, the extraordinary conception of her kinswoman was a sign of more ext. c. of her own.

Objections: 1. That doct. of immac. conception is inadequate to account for sinlessness of Jesus. But he who was light and life of men must surely see light of day, not by carnal procreation, but by immediate exercise of divine power. How could he be free from every taint of original sin, and redeem us from power of sin, if he had been born by fleshly intercourse of sinful parents? The strong and healthy graft which was to bring new life into the diseased stock, must not originate from this stock, but be grafted into it from without. Miraculous concep. is a σκάνδαλον to those alone who will see in our Lord nothing but pure humanity, and who put his sinlessness in place of the real incarnation of God in him. Rationalistic explanation: that he was of ordinary birth, and that this view existed among the Jews, and contined until the 5th cent. By that time, gospels were embellished to give expression to current views, and the conclusion is the immaculate concep. Answ'd: (*a*) The relation in wh. Christ stands to his mother is emphasized, as compared with Jos. The latter is never mentioned except as protector of Christ's infancy. From the moment of the conception, the Holy Spirit continued to influence and penetrate mind and spirit of M., to suppress power of sin and make her body his consecrated temple. (*b*) Titles, " born of a woman," " made flesh," " son of man," the constant reference to mode of his origin, as well as the nature of his constitution show his relation to the woman was more important than to the man. (*c*) The doctrine is based on prophecy. 2. That in gospels he is son of Jos. (John 1:45; Lk. 4:22 and 2:48). Mary, in publicly speaking to her son of Jos., must say " thy father." Pressensé : " This assertion *son of Jos.* is always put into mouth of Jews as sign of unbelief or contempt. It is even so in the case of Nathaniel." 3. That the doctrine is not found elsewhere in N. T. Then we have no Saviour.

Naturalists and others indulge in different forms of blasphemous interpretation. They deprive Jos.'s bride of chastity and purity, her richest dowry. The notion was first conceived in brain of heathen (Celsus) who derides mother of Jesus as victim of seduction. Jewish version of this fable (*rationalismus vulgaris*) names one Panthera or Pandira as her seducer. *Myth. theory :* that this conception in cont. to hist. probability, that Jews did not sympathize with expression "sons of God," bec. polytheistic. It was a story invented to support church claims, referring to the religious feeling of ancients, who revered their great men so much as to make them sons of God (numerous in mythology.) So also, it is said, the Evangelists did with Christ.

§4. Visit of Mary to Eliz. Ebrard and others : that Jos. had taken his betrothed wife to his home, after a public solemnization of their nuptials, before this journey. Alford : " that as a betrothed virgin she could not travel alone." But that no unmarried female could journey to visit her friends is incredible. M. may have journeyed with friends, or under spec'l protection of a servant, or with neighbors going to Pass. Lange : " She told Jos. of visit of angel." But Jo's knowledge of her condition was subsequent to her return. M. leaves it to God to enlighten him as He had her. 3-fold design of visit :

1. To give occasion for exercise of the spirit of inspiration, to confirm claims of the 2 children.

2. To connect these extraordinary events in minds of people, before these persons were born. The children were brought together in the bosoms of their mothers.

3. To make known their relative dignity; Jesus over John.

Mary's hymn is modeled on Hannah's. (1st Sam. 2). It may be divided into 3 or 4 strophes, forming an animated doxology. The grace of God (Lk. 1 : 48), his omnipotence (49–51), his holiness (49, 51, 54,) his justice (52—3), and especially his faithfulness (54–5), are celebrated. It sounds like an echo of Miriam's and Deborah's harps; has characteristics of Heb. poetry, in tone and language, and can be rendered almost word for word. Historically, it is important as showing the Messianic hope, and the form of Messianic expectation. Lk.'s preface is classical Greek; yet this hymn is in best Hebrew. This fact confirms hist. proof of text. Obj'ns : Rationalists reject the supernatural and account for it on nat. grounds. Meyer rejects it on purely subjective grounds (M. could not go alone and Eliz. would not receive her). Strauss consistently rejects all, even the relationship bet. Jesus and John. Home of Zach.: "The supposition is that 'Ιούδα (Lk. 1 : 39) has been substituted for 'Ιούτα, and it is credible." (Lange.) Most common idea : that Hebron was the place, bec. in "the hill country." It was 17 miles S. of Jerusalem. (20 Rom. miles.)

§5. Birth of John. Effect was shown by the concourse at his circumcision. It was customary to name child on same day, as circumcision (Gen. 21 : 3, 4). Eliz. insisted on his being called John. Some say that Zach. had not told Eliz. of the name given in temple. Therefore this was new revelation. Most likely he had told her. From making signs to Zach., some have inferred that he was deaf as well as dumb. Others : it was to spare the feelings of mother. Zach. wrote on tablet that his name was John (already given and not open to change). The first N. T. writing opens with grace. Prophetic cycles accompanied great hist. epochs; there is an equal advance of proph. with hist. It comes at revolutionary periods : Moses, Joshua and Judges, the completed kingdom under David and Solomon; Isaiah, Hosea, &c., during Assyrian period; Jere., Hab'k, Zeph., during period of exile.

Zachariah's song was to Jewish witnesses a renewal of inspiration, the highest circumstance of the occurrence. For 400 years it had ceased. By its renewal, they regarded a new national change as intended. Like Mary's, it refers to fulfillment of O. T. prophecies, but is not based on any O. T. song, and is more national than individual. In Mary's there is a relative want of originality, and it is full of reminiscences. Lange: "The royal spirit is more expressed in her song: the priestly character in Zach.'s In his the O. T. type, in hers the New prevails." Mary's expectations of the Messiah (Lk. 1: 5) were not of a particular and exclusive, but of an universal nat. Zach's song (Lk. 1: 76, 78) is a striking proof of the prevalence of theocratic over paternal feeling, as the Mssh. is always placed in a more prominent position than his forerunner. Dayspring, Mal. 4: 2. Both songs breathe theocratic spirit of O. T.; show the expectation of Him who was to have spiritual rule. John dwelt by himself in wild and thinly peopled region S. W. of Dead Sea near his home, perhaps to show by his seclusion that he was uninstructed in ordinary way but by Holy Ghost. Renan: "the masses had become accustomed to look upon 'the man of God' as a hermit. They imagined that all the holy personages had their days of penitence, of severe life, and of austerities. It was readily conceived that the leaders of sects must be recluses, having their peculiar rules and their institutes, like the founders of rel. orders." Strauss and Meyer see in his seclusion, influence of the Essenes (myst. ascetics and devotees). But there is no analogy. N. T. does not mention them, Josephus does largely.

§6. Annunciation to Joseph nec., bec. a direct witness was needed to the person most interested, to show that her acct. was not a mistake nor a matter of mere enthusiasm. Her explanations were not believed and her faith was tested. Jos. determ'd to divorce her (privately). Milman: "Bill of divorce was nec. even when the parties were only betrothed, and where the marriage had not actually been solemnized. It is probable that the Mosaic law wh. in such cases adjudged a female to death

(Dt. 20 : 23–5) was not at this time executed in its original vigor." Joseph was δίκαιος (Mtt. 1 : 19), not kind, but legally just, merciful. A public divorce would be in writing from the priest, with the causes of it stated, else the woman could not marry again. Annunciation was at Naz. God appears 4 times to him in a dream (Mtt. 1: 20; 2: 13; 2: 19; 2: 22). Prophecy of Mtt. 1: 22 is uttered by the angel, from Is. 7 : 14. Strauss : it is not at all applicable to Christ; the Evgst. by mistake thought it was. Alexander: "the application of it to Christ is not a mere accommodation, meaning that the words originally used in one sense, and in reference to one object, might now be repeated in another sense, and of another subject; for this does not satisfy the strong sense of the passage (that it might be fulfilled), nor would such a fanciful coincidence have been alleged with so much emphasis by Mtt., still less by the angel. The only sense that can be reasonably put upon the words is, that the miraculous conception of Mssh. was predicted by Is. in the words here quoted. This essential meaning is not affected by the question whether the prediction was first fulfilled in the nat. birth of a child soon after it was uttered, and the subsequent deliverance of Judah from invasion, but again fulfilled in a higher sense, in the nativity of Christ; or whether it related only to the latter, and presented it to Ahaz as a pledge that the chosen people could not be destroyed until Mssh. came." Best resort is (Hengst.) that the prophecy applies to Christ, and is presented to Ahaz as the sign of deliverance.

Matt. gives annunc. to Jos. only; Lk. to Mary only. Objected: 1. That these accts. exclude each other. 2. That the child's name was given to Jos., after it had been given to Mary; therefore not nec. second time. The two accounts harmonize and confirm each other. Each supposes the same basis of fact. (*a*) Silence in one hist. does not contradict a statement in another. (*b*) Selection of incidents is acc. to their respective plans. Matt. giving Jos's genealogy, must show how Jos. took Mary as his wife. He is theocratic. Jesus is presented as fulfillment of the theocracy. Lk. supplements Matt. and gives what belongs to Christ's human relations; depicts the Son of Man appearing in Israel, but for benefit of whole race of man.

§7. Birth of Jesus was at Beth. In consequence of an edict that all the world should be taxed, Jos. and Mary leave Naz. to go to Beth. the city of Dav. to be taxed there. Pressensé: "The Jewish law laid no obligation on a woman to undertake such a journey, for the writing of her name was enough. But who can wonder at the young wife, situated like Mary, accompanying her protector? Besides, she was not ignorant of the prophecy which pointed out Beth. as the city of Messiah." Lk. dates from decree of Augustus, bec. it was the occasion that brought Jos. and Mary to Bethlehem. It suggests 1. That the Saviour was born during the reign of Augustus (the golden age of Roman history). 2. That the theocracy had sunk to its lowest possible level. 3. That the parents enrolled their names in the registration of the whole world.

Jewish law required the enrolment of women and hence this law took them to Beth. (See preceding quot. from Pressensé). Farrar: "Women were liable to a capitation tax, if this enrolment ($\dot{\alpha}\pi o\gamma\rho\alpha\varphi\dot{\eta}$) also involved taxation ($\dot{\alpha}\pi o\tau\dot{\iota}\mu\eta\sigma\iota\varsigma$)." The Roman law cared not where; it required, however, enrolment of whole world, and hence Mary is included. Lange: "The enrolment would naturally take place in Judea, in consideration of the claims of nationality. The policy of Rome, as well as the relig. scruples of the Jews, demanded it. For this reason, every one went to his ancestral city to be registered, though in other cases the Roman census might be taken, either acc. to place of residence or *forum originis*." Place of birth a manger; evidently so ordered to signify the voluntary self-denial of Jesus. Calvin: "descendants of the royal race were designedly, harshly, and inhospitably treated by Rom. officials." Lange: "that Jos. and Mary were poor." But we are not to understand that they were poor or oppressed by Rom. authorities. It was simply bec. there was no room for them in the inn. Justin Martyr places the birth in a cave. The khan wld. probably remain for long time in the East. "Land and Book" I, 533; (Thomson quoted, Andrews 81; Farrar I, 3-6; W. Hepworth Dixon's Holy Land, 1,

ch. 13). Matt. makes no reference to the home, but speaks as if they came to it for first time. Lk, represents them as living there beforehand. Rationalists deny that he was born in Beth., say that he was born in Naz. Strauss rejects both acc'ts. Renan: "It is only by an awkward detour that the legend succeeds in fixing his birth at Beth." R. says that the royal line from D. had become extinct, but that Christ's birth *must* be fixed at Beth., bec. of prophecy. Ans.: (*a*) The acc'ts are not contradictory but complemental. (*b*) Matt. calls attention to both places, simply to speak of the fulfillment of prophecy. Lk. gives the sequence of events.

§8. Design of annunciation to Shepherds, Lk. 2:17. Why announce his birth to them? 1. That attention might be called to this birth, in the press of business. 2. That witnesses, simple, competent, sufficiently numer- and disinterested, might see him. 3. This testimony must not be accomplished in too public a manner, in order not to foster the designs of Herod. 4. The attestation is miraculous, by angels. 5. New connection is made with O. T. hist. and types. These shepherds were feeding their flocks on the same hills where D., their father, had fed his. Christ, the new-born king, is typified, who should feed his flocks like a shepherd.

Lange finely heads this as "The first Gospel upon Earth." The sign (Lk. 2:12) is not supernatural, but sufficiently accurate, for among the children born that night in Beth., probably not more than one would have been in a manger. 3 ways of reading the doxology:
(*a*) Glory to God in the highest, and on earth peace, good-will toward men.
(*b*) " " " in (among) the highest, and on earth 'peace, good-will toward men.
(*c*) " " " in the highest and on Earth, peace among men of His good-will.

Here we meet with one of the most imp. readings which materially affect the sense. The altered reading, *among the men of His good-will* is equivalent to *the elect people*. Valcknaer: "men with whom God is pleased." Thus we have the truth that εἰρήνη was given to Jews that through them it might be a joy παντὶ τῷ λαῷ. Some contrast ἄγγελοι and ἄνθρωποι. The latter come in, after the former had completed their mission. Argued: that the publicity of this event ought to have prevented subsequent unbelief. Ans. Lk. 16:31. *Naturalistic* theorists, to get rid of the supernatural, say that the Shepherds were aware of the condition of Mary; they saw a bright light in the heavens, and mistook it for the glory of God. *Mythical* theorists (more naturally): All this was looked for bec. of prophecy, which required the scene at Beth. Wherefore, subsequent writers embellish it with honor given to Christ. The Shepherds were related to David, and therefore they were made use of more than other men. Strauss rejects the whole thing.

§9. *Circumcision and Presentation in the Temple.* The chronological order of events here is called in question. By law, circumcision was on the eighth day, and presentation on the fortieth day. Now, where and when can be inserted " the adoration of the Magi" and " Flight to Egypt?" 1. Tradition and ecclesiastical observance have placed them before the presentation. Obj.: Tradition not old enough. 2 Matt. 2: 1 seems to imply that the adoration soon followed the birth. But if the argument proves anything, it proves that it was on night of birth. 3. Herod was ignorant of the birth until the arrival of the Magi; but if presentation had occurred, he would have heard of it. This is merely gratuitous. He might have heard and paid no attention to it. The visit of the Magi awakened his suspicions, as they came from distant realms.

Obj.: (1). Time inadequate. Forty days required between birth and purification. This could not comprehend the coming of the Magi and flight to Egypt. (2). Presentation could not have occurred subsequent to the slaughter of the Innocents. Even after Herod's death, when Joseph heard that Archelaus was in power, he was afraid to return. Matt. 2: 22-23. (*a*)Hengstenburg gets over this by translating " he went there with fear." (*b*) Ritual view puts presentation between Magi's visit and flight. But 1, it is expressly stated that the visit of Magi caused alarm in Jerusalem, and excited Herod's fears. 2. It separates between Magi's visit and flight, which Matthew connects as cause and effect. Hence, both prove fatal to the Ritualistic theory. 3. Robinson,

Schaff, &c., put presentation first. Obj.: Luke gives no return to Bethlehem, and implies the return to Nazareth to be immediately after presentation.

Ans.: It is not a part of Luke's plan. He only maintains the consistency of his own narrative. From Bethlehem to Jerusalem only two hours journey, and therefore unimportant to mention. Negative critics hold these two lines are contradictions, but harmonists that each narrative flows on in its course, yet consistent, and forming one beautiful whole.

Presentation in the Temple.—The design is four-fold. 1. Showed obedience to the law by purification of the Virgin and redemption of first born. Obj.: Jesus was a priest, and therefore it was illegal. Argument of no force, as Jesus was not a Levite to whom the law was prescribed. Hence Jesus rendered no formal service as redemption of first-born was necessary. 2. A new opportunity for testimony to inspiration, given by Simeon and Anna. 3. It spread the report of his birth. 4. Recognition of the spiritual Israel. It is worthy of notice here, that these examples and testimonies are scattered the country over. Zachariah and Elizabeth in the south, Joseph and Mary in the north, Simeon and Anna at the metropolis. It is objected on the ground of discrepancy that ver. 24 gives the sacrifice as due from the mother, while ver. 27 does not mention the redemption-money for the child. Every woman at purification presented a lamb and a dove for sacrifice, but in case of poverty, an additional dove was substituted for the lamb. The latter having been made by Mary, betrays indigence. Ver. 22 makes αὐτῶν refer to *whom?* Not Joseph. But there is no difficulty in applying καθαρισμοῦ to Jesus, because He represented His people. It is not positively stated that Simeon was far advanced in years. Some suppose he was Rabbin Simeon. Some interesting points just here.

1. The fact of inspiration shown in the promise that he should see the Messiah. 2. The clear recognition in Simeon's words of the fact announced in the angelic doxology of the universal application of our Lord's work. 3. Prophecy verified. 4. His sufferings foretold. These four points teach three things: (1). Rejection by the Jews. (2). Calling of the Gentiles. (3). His sacrificial

character. We also infer that tribal relations were not all lost, as Anna is mentioned as belonging to the tribe of Aser. Fasting and prayer to be understood literally and not of an ascetic order, as they simply mean Anna led a religious life. The sceptical objections here are lame. The Mythists assert that the motive for miracles in the narrative was a desire to exalt Christ on the part of later writers. This alone they say was the cause for the multiplicity of miracles.

§10. *Adoration of the Magi.* Matt. 2: 1-12. According to the most approved plan, this belongs to verses 33-39 of Lk. 2. Its signification is the counterpart of the last. The time after presentation was brief, as Herod's death soon followed. The adoration of the Magi represents His acknowledgment by the Gentiles. They could not have been Jews. Their question was, where is He who is born King of the Jews? The salient change in the church at this time was the calling of the Gentiles. N. T. dispensation is of grace, hence universal, and not an accident of its condition, but an inward change in the essential character of the dispensation. O. T. preparatory and honored in its being superseded. Care was taken that He did honor to the law—the O. T. Likewise in the fulfillment of prophecy and calling of the Gentiles. Christ was apprehended by the Magi as the *king*, and they tendered Him royal gifts. This custom common to the East. Divinely guided, hence it is natural to infer that they cherished a real faith in the Son of God, but not so clear as was possible after the resurrection. By some it is thought the gifts were significant. 1. Gold significant of royalty, authority, sovereignty. 2. Frankincense of prayer and intercession, thus recognizing him as the hearer and answerer of supplication. 3. Myrrh, being a favorite anodyne and antiseptic, had reference to his sufferings and resurrection: hence the incorruptibility of his nature, and the promise that his body should not see corruption. The mother accepted the gifts as His due. Tradition has greatly embellished this event. The three donors represent three different races, viz: Shem, Ham, and Japheth. In pictures, one is represented as a negro. But more important than these traditionary views we shall observe 1. The Magi, called

μάγοι ἀπὸ ἀνατολῶν. Originally, a tribe of Medes set apart for priests, same as the Levites among the Jews. They embodied the learning of the people. Their knowledge consisted principally of astrology. 2. The country of their abode the text leaves uncertain. Three have been given, Arabia, Mesopotamia, Persia. The last best. Notice the change from ἀνατολῶν to ἀνατολῇ. Both forms are used as definite geographical expressions. Ἀνατολῶν is the far-east Persia. Ἀνατολῇ, east Babylonia. Observe the representatives of the race are chosen from the cradle of the race. The Greeks and Romans were too impure and familiar with the Jews, and treated them with contempt. Barbarians were too ignorant. The east chosen because the cradle of science. The writings of Zoroaster come nearer to the Holy Scriptures than any others. 3. What brought the Magi? Phenomena natural or supernatural? Prevailing belief, natural. To its being miraculous it is objected: (*a*) Nowhere taught in the text. (*b*) Magi saw the star in the East. If seen in the East it could not go before them. To remove this difficulty read ver. 2: "while we were in the East &c." (*c*) They were not led to X. but came to Him. Not guided to Bethlehem until they asked for the child. When directed again to Bm. they saw the star the second time. Popular tradition is that the star led them. Ans: Kepler the first to suggest the natural explanation in 1604. (See Andrews pp. 9–10). He observed in that year a conjunction of Jupiter and Saturn, in Pisces, in Dec. 1603. Mars was added in the following spring, and a new star of surpassing brilliancy appeared in the autumn of 1604. In 747 A. U. C. there were three such conjunctions of Jupiter and Saturn, and Mars was added in 748 A. U. C. Both of these conjunctions have been supposed to be the star of the Magi. Rabbi Abarbanel states that the same thing occurred at the birth of Moses, and also in 1463, which led him to look for the birth of the Messiah in his own day. Wieseler says it was a new star in 749 and 750, and finds it recorded in the Chinese annals. This clashes with Zumpt, whose theory is determined by the date that Cyrenius was governor of Syria, as previously stated. Ques: How is this star to be associated with X's birth? Ans: 1. They knew this was the part of the heavens which belonged to Judea. 2. A prevailing expectation at the time for a *Deliverer*, who should appear in Judea. (Vide Suetonius and Tacitus). 3. Collateral traditions from common sources of knowledge. Chinese sages, 33 years later, coming west, inquired for the long expected and common Saviour. 4. These were combined with Jewish expectations. Jews were scattered widely over the world, who spread knowledge of God and Messianic predictions. David and Daniel had prophesied of Him. In Num. 24: 17 and Is. 60: 3, he is spoken of under the figure of a star. Mary applies N. 24: 17 to X. Balaam's words may have been handed down outside of the church. These passages may have given shape to astronomical expectations relative to X. Hence the Magi were naturally led to observe heavenly phenomena. Hengstenberg objects. 1. $\alpha\sigma\tau\eta\rho$ is applicable to only one body, and $\alpha\sigma\tau\rho ov$ to a constellation. The former is true, but the use of the latter is wide. 2. Kepler has been reviewed by Pritchard. He says conjunction in no case was perfect. The stars always separated by two diameters of the moon between. Ans: Still, the phenomenon was very remarkable as well as the coincidence of his calculations. The two planets came together about three hours and a half before sunrise, and hence in the East. The first appearance would be seen in the East May 20, 747, just before sunrise. The second in Nov. five months later in the south, at 8 P. M.: hence star appeared toward Bm. The former indicated the birth, the latter the way to Bm. This involves those who claim 747 in all the chronological difficulty to which we have referred. Accordingly, the birth of X. is put three years earlier, and makes Him 33 years at Baptism. Therefore the Magi did not probably set out at the first appearance, but delayed some time. Again, the term of Quirinus was not earlier than 750, whereas this makes nativity three years before. But the taxing might have been four years earlier than 750. The only alternative for this naturalistic explanation is to adopt the theory of a *new star*, natural or miraculous. 3. Objections: Why should Herod slaughter 3 year old children? As the first star was only five months before, therefore we must agree that star at Bm. was a new star or a miraculous one.

Milton supposes a leading of the rays; Dr. Pritchard the going and standing of the star was in consequence of the Magi's journeying and arrival; Dr. Alexander that the words mean they saw the star again on the road to Bm. and thus confirmed their hopes, and hence it was a star seeming to go before them. 4. God would not use their false notions of astrology for such an end. Strauss asks, Is astrology wrong elsewhere but right in this case? Ans: God employs men as they are, bringing good out of evil. Also, astrology was then considered as associated with all true astronomy. It embodied true science. Astrology and Alchemy embraced all that was known of science. There are perplexing difficulties either way. Still, the astrological phenomena must have given corroboration to the expectations for the Messiah. Observed at the time of birth, and hence they furnish collateral evidence to the time of the nativity.

Mythists assert the whole to be a myth. Arabian merchants befriended the parents in their poverty. The magi were fixed upon, as they were astronomers; and star, because of O. T. passages referring to a great light, and which were literally understood. The gifts referred to Isaiah 60:6.

As to the general effect, Herod and the city were troubled. The wise men of the Jews called and questioned, and replied, "Christ was to be born in Bm." Mic. 5:2. Note the difference in reading between Micah and Matt. A striking illustration of two opposites meaning the same thing. Warned of God in a dream, the magi avoided Herod and returned home another way.

§11. *Flight into Egypt — Herod's Cruelty — The Return.* Matt. 2:13–23. Besides saving the child's life, it symbolically embodies the great truth that the Messiah was to suffer. Hitherto all peaceful. Except poverty and humility, nothing as yet indicated His suffering. The design of the flight is five-fold. 1. To introduce the suffering element. 2. Christ's kingly office set forth. Princely honors bestowed. 3. O. and N. T. typical relations established. Egypt was a refuge, being near and under Roman power. Moses was saved there, where also was the transitional state of the church from the family to the nation. Church came up out of Egypt when preserved. Now in danger church repairs there again. Christ is saved. 4. In Egypt, Hos. 11:1 fulfilled. Obj'n: misapplication. Ans: The calling of Israel from Egypt bears a typical relation to Christ. 5. New evidence of miraculous care observed for the child. Joseph conspicuous, as evidence for miraculous conception, and preservation. Hence he is too much underrated.

Massacre of the Innocents. Objections: 1. Herod defeated his purpose by inquiring of the Magi. Too cunning for this. Better accomplished by secret messenger, &c. 2. Silence of contemporaneous history. Could such cruelty escape notice? No, say negative critics. Josephus and Roman historians make no record of it. Answer: Whatever was unpleasant to Roman ears Josephus was careful to omit. Roman historians did not mention it because they had no sympathy with Jewish hist'y. Again, this was only as a drop in the bucket as compared with Herod's cruelties. Through jealousy he killed his wife and sons. When dying he issued orders to destroy his nobles, that there might be weeping at his death.

The wise men mocked Herod. Pride, ambition and fear caused him to kill all the male children, $\tau o\upsilon\varsigma\ \pi a\iota\delta a\varsigma$. No mention of secrecy. From two years old and under cannot be limited to those beginning their second year, nor can it be said Christ was two years old. If the child had just been seen by the Magi, why those two yrs. old and under? Herod would have killed enough children without extending his order to those two years old. Ans. Prophecy was thus fulfilled, Jer. 31:15. Objected again that the prophecy is misapplied. Rachel is poetically represented as rising from the grave, owing to the deportation of captives at Ramah, the descendants of Jos. and Benj. Here as rising to weep for the massacre of the innocents at Bm. Ans.: Typical connection between the two events. As to the number of children slaughtered, sceptics exaggerate. Voltaire says 14,000. Antiquarians estimate the population by measurement of space. This necessarily is liable to mislead. Variously estimated about 90, 10, or 12. Smallest most probable.

Mythists, &c., say all heroic persons passed through dangers during infancy and childhood. Romulus, Remus, Cyrus, &c. Hence the eventful infancy of Christ, or, it

was a pure invention to connect it with Moses and Heb'ws in Egypt. The place of sojourn is unknown. Traditions clash. Some, near Heliopolis; others, at Memphis. Nor is the duration of the sojourn fully known. Varies as the date of birth by different critics. The return was soon after Herod's death, as Jos. had not heard of his successor. We may note Math.'s agreement with contemporaneous hist. Period of intricate changes, yet no mistake is made. Herod's territory divided into three parts. Herod Antipas, tetrarch over Galilee and Perea; Archelaus: Judea, Idumea and Samaria. Herod had appointed Archelaus king, but Augustus allowed him the title of Ethnarch. Philip was allotted Trachonitis, Auranites. The gospel narrative moves through all these without a single blunder.

It was Joseph's intention to return to Bm. Warned in a dream to return again to Nazareth. Prophecy fulfilled, Jud. 13:5. That Nazareth is never mentioned in O. T. is based partly on the etymology of the word. Supposed to be from a Heb. word meaning *a twig*; others from a word signifying *a crown*. Allusion to Is. 11:1 compared with 53:3. Messiah to be a twig from the prostrate stem of Jesse, i. e., of humble origin. There is reference to the reputation of the town. "Can any good come out of Nazareth?" Christ fulfilled prophecy by living there. The return and settlement at Nazareth close the period of infancy.

The peculiarities of this first subdivision of the preparatory period are heightened by the silence that followed. 1. Matt. and Lk. combine to form a unit, fitting like a lock and key. 2. The supernatural and historical elements are one. If miracles, they must be received on historical evidence. Bleek says Christians cannot but expect Christ's entrance into the world accompanied by peculiar signs. 3. The attempt to discredit is based on subjective and rationalistic grounds, i. e., difficulty to believe, varying with the individual. Critics argue *in circulo*. The choice is between Matt. and Strauss. 4. The historical characteristics already justified in connecting with O. T. The typical and symbolical exhibited, and facts imply and embody truths, which were brought out.

Second Subdivision of Preparatory Period.—Its limits comprise the return and end of 30 years of quiet life at Nazareth, or settlement at Nazareth to commencement of ministry. Profound silence. No uninspired writer could refrain from his own interpolations. Hence the contrast between apocrypha and N. T. Design of the silence. 1. Essential to have a full account of Christ's origin, his ministry, public work and sacrifice. To this the gospels correspond. 2. Period of growth, not work. Just enough presented to maintain hist. connection. Silence a check upon those who would dwell on unimportant truths. More would have been gratification of curiosity to which sacred historians never descend. Otherwise the narrative would be impaired. 3. Such given as adds to our ideas of Christ. Two extremes to be avoided : (a) That Christ learned nothing in a natural way, but all supernatural, even to reading and writing. This view unwarranted by facts, and unnecessary to his divinity. (b) Naturalistic. This exalts his mental powers to the exclusion of the divine. This untrue, as the people wondered at his wisdom, having never learned. Narrative says " he taught not as one taught by the scribes." He probably lived and learned as other boys. Supposed to have learned his father's trade. Mk. 6 : 3. See Dr. Alexander.

Gospel Lessons.—1. Early life uneventful. 2. Growth, not action. Grew in wisdom and stature. 3. He grew in favor with unbelieving Galileans, who knew him best. His brethren the most difficult to persuade, and his townsmen sought twice to kill him. They were scandalized by his assuming superiority. There was no unnatural and repulsive precocity in him. He possessed a perfect human nature. Early Fathers say he had no personal beauty, based on Is. 53 : 2. Later view founded on Ps. 45. 4. The most important is the following :

§12. *Visit to the Passover.*—Lk. 2 : 41–52. This single paragraph presents the fact of his extraordinary powers. Were it not for this, there would be room for the assertion that Christ received no miraculous gift till Baptism. The event marks a transition in his consciousness. The growing boy, full of heavenly wisdom, seeking after knowledge, kind to his parents, obedient in all things. Olshausen beautifully says, " He was a perfect boy, perfect man." A marked arrival of fuller consciousness of his mission is also noticeable. Impressed with his desti-

ny. In analogy with human experience. Christ had a child knowledge of himself. Now a youth's experience, then the sudden mental changes, of which a youth is often conscious. Hence glimpses of a portentous future. How or when came to Jesus the consciousness of his Messiahship we are not told. It must have been gradual. A sinless being, with a knowledge of sin, yet pure, and conscious of difference between himself and others. Reading the law, and yet having perfect love to God; the types and prophecies of O. T. and conscious of their fulfillment in himself. A gradual conception of his Messianic character must have been wrought in him. There are evident traces however, when touching upon great truths, of modern flashes gleaming in upon his soul. This is one, and those at Baptism and on Mt. of Trans.

At this point the " Lives of Christ " open themselves. The authors show what is to be their theory of the person of X., upon which they explain the events of his life. Rationalists deny or explain away the supernatural. Orthodox writers vary. It is important to know the author's standpoint, and guard against misinterpretation of forms of statement. Ebrard, Pressense, and Beecher explain by the κέν ωσις theory, which is a self-limitation, or self-emptying of the Logos. Divine and human one and the same. Not two natures, but one. Distinction made between essential nature and attributes. X. was God essentially and potentially, but emptied himself of his Divine contents. A babe like any other babe. Void of ideas, was a bundle of germs which developed throughout his whole life, and at exaltation his Divinity fully restored. The human developed into the Divine: the Infinite having become finite, and the finite growing back into the Infinite. This theory denies the *real* humanity of X., robs him of human sympathy. X. is an undeified God.

Others lower X's humanity by separating it too much from his divinity. He possessed all of our humanity, but the converse is not true. Hence his was not ours, but his own. Yet ours touches his. For this view, two reasons. 1. He was sinless, therefore his capacities unlike ours. We do not know what sinless humanity is. 2. He was Divine, and two natures in his person, therefore *above* us. All he did was not as a mere man. The human influenced by the divine, and hence all he did was done by God. Illustration: A Christian is exalted, owing to the indwelling of the H. G. So X., though a man, is exalted, by a personal union with the Father and H. G. Hence as a man is infinitely above any other man. Paul maintains this in Hebrews, as the ground of the infinite value of his sacrifice. It is possible to so view X. as to conceive of him as sustaining a *double personality*. Most of the "Lives of Christ" are based on German theories, largely tainted with this speculation. This is growing common with the Baptists. We study him not merely as coinciding with our views of his nature, but as a *true man*, developing according to his nature, acting and acted upon.

Jesus went up to the temple with his parents. At 12 Jewish boys became "sons of the law," and took part in the feasts &c. The country was safe from former dangers. When X was about 10, Archelaus was banished to Gaul. The government in the hands of procurators, subordinate to governor of Syria, and thus Galilee, Samaria and Judea were under Roman protection. The parents returned from Passover but Jesus stayed behind. They had proceeded a day's journey before they missed him, thinking he was with his kinsmen. Failing to discover his whereabouts, they returned to the city. Found him the third day at the temple, "sitting in the midst of the doctors." "Sitting" does not necessarily imply equality. Strauss says it is unnatural that a boy of 12 should be instructing men, that a scholar would have stood. "Hearing and asking" imply instructing. Ans: Nothing in the narrative inconsistent with an intelligent boy, pure and curious for knowledge. Scholar standing was not customary. The mother's question shows their mutual relation. It is beautiful. τεκνον, τι ἐποίησας ἡμῖν οὕτως; The reply is variously interpreted. The grammar admits of two. Some supply ellipsis locally—"Why did you look elsewhere, did you not know I would be in my Father's house?" Better: "in my Father's affairs." and thus at the Temple, as the article is indefinite. The first recorded words of X., and an acknowledgment of God as his Father. Others affirm that at this juncture

the consciousness of his destiny became more *real*. Previously he had been passive, but not so now. Best humanitarians claim the words are expressive of penetrating insight into his divine mission. We may remark that the incident serves to enhance our interest occasioned by his miraculous birth. The parental anxiety, inquiry for a lost child, public place where he was found, were all calculated to arouse thoughts in the parent's minds.

Critical Objections. 1. Unnatural that his mother should lose him. Ans: He was old enough to take care of himself. Easily lost in a large crowd. 2. Unnatural that he should cause his mother so great anxiety, and then give her such a reply. Ans: Reply not rough, but a gentle admonition that her claims were subordinate to a higher duty. 3. If the circumstances of conception were true, the mother could not fail to comprehend his answer. Ans: Mary may not have fully known what he meant. 12 years could have glided by with nothing extraordinary. Hence the origin of the Mythical interpretation, based on Moses and Samuel. From the narrative, we learn that he returned to Nazareth and was subject to his parents.

Joseph's death. Supposed to have died soon after this. Not mentioned again. Apocryphal gospels say he died when Jesus was 19. Evidently dead at the time of crucifixion, as Jesus gave his mother into John's care.

Why Nazareth chosen as abode? 1. To fulfill prohecy. 2. It was his parents' home. 3 It afforded safety. Greater danger in Jerusalem. 4. Could gain more influence in Galilee than in Jerus. under the Pharisaic eye. 5. Isolated from Jewish instruction, he is supposed to have been taught of God. His wisdom given by inspiration. 6. Reared where the scenes of his public ministry were to be chiefly laid. Renan: "The whole Galilean ministry was within sight of his youthful home." Present Nazareth consists of 3000 inhabitants. It lies in a narrow valley, shut in between two rocks. North of the Esdraelon plain, the hill looks n. e. to Hermon. Therefore the view was familiar to him when looking towards the snow-capped Hermon, the northernmost point of X's work. The eastern view confronted by Tabor, west by Carmel and the sea. The southern by Gilboa and Samaria.

§13. *Genealogies.* Mth. 1: 1-17; Lk. 3: 23-38. The importance of these lies in the necessity to prove X's Messianic claims. The Jewish genealogies were sacredly kept and open to all. Strauss considers them fraudulent, and that they involve difficulties, being opposed to O. T. Hence no proof of Christ's Davidic descent. 1. On the contrary, the royal line could not be obscure. People would have guarded the royal seed as He was to descend from David. This was the promise. If Christ had been of Davidic descent, he would have been hailed as Messiah. Ans: No theocratic rulers on account of sin. 2. Birth at Bm. was not generally believed, nor does Jesus reply to this. John 7: 42. A Nazarene, and so he passes in Gospels and Acts. Ans: Nowhere else charged, not in Sanhedrim. Were the charge substantial, it would have been fatal to him. He was not ignorant of his lineage, as he calls himself *David's son*. Peter at Pentecost, the Acts and Epistles use it. Strauss says title is officially no real fact. 3. No concurrent testimony, no reference to Ebionites. Ans: Abundant proof without the genealogies. "The son of" or "begat" not limited to literal relationship of father and son. This true when line runs out. This remark clarifies Mth.'s genealogy. Remote ancestors called fathers when distinct line vanishes. Case: Math. says "Jacob begat Joseph." Lk., "Joseph was the son of Heli." No literalness here. Again, Mth. speaks of three divisions of fourteen genealogies each. Difficulty. But the most obvious way to remove it is to count David *twice*. Another difficulty. In second table four kings omitted which Chronicles supplies, thus making eighteen generations instead of fourteen. Therefore "so all the generations" must mean all given in Mth. Charge of ignorance absurd, as every child in Judea knew the royal list better than we do the Presidential, or the royal line of Gt. Britain. But why fourteen? 1. To aid memory. 2. Symbolic value of the number of letters, which were fourteen. David—14. D^1, V^6, $D^1 = 14$. 3. Periods chronologically equal. Untrue, because the first period is twice as long as the other two. 4. These periods of national history. This the most satisfactory, i.e., the theocratic descent. What names omitted and why? Amaziah, Joash and Ahaziah, occurring between

Joram and Ozias. Some say because they descended from Jezebel, and others because they were mere ciphers. Jehoiachim omitted as captivity began in his reign, or because made king by a foreign power. Objection to Mth. 1: 11. Jechonias had no brethren. Ans: Brethren may mean contemporaries. Again Jechonias had no children, hence not the father of Salathiel. "Write the man childless." Jer. 22: 23. Perhaps this meant he should lack in a direct line of successors to the throne. All these little difficulties sufficiently accounted for.

Discrepancies between Mth. and Lk. 1. Mth's genealogy opens the narrative and was probably copied. Lk's is introduced as a part of X's personal history. 2. Mth. descends while Lk. ascends. 3. Math. traces the royal line, Lk. the natural to Adam. 4. Lk. fuller than Mth., giving 42 names to Mth's 28. To David the lists agree. Difficulty: Between Salmon and David only three names occur for 400 or 500 years. Same dif. in Ruth, and hence another instance of contradiction. Ans: Names omitted. Said that Rahab was another line than Jewish.

Divergence of lineage from David downward. Mth. follows Solomon, Lk. Nathan. Two hypotheses: 1. Both Mth. and Lk. give Joseph's genealogy. 2. Mth. that of Joseph and Lk. Mary's. (1) current before Reformation, and now supported by many of the best critics, viz. Alford, Meyer, &c. (2) held by Wieseler, Ebrard, Greswell, Alexander, &c. If both of Joseph, why different? Ans: One through kings the other from father to son. How same names in two different lines, e. g. Salathiel and Zorobabel? Ans: 1. Two persons with same name. 2. A mere coincidence. Lines together in Salathiel, as direct line runs out and, Sal. nearest heir. This explains how Jechonias is Salathiel's father, while Lk. makes Salathiel son of Neri. Main obj: If both Joseph's, they only establish X's legal right to the throne, but no personal descent. Ans: Some say this was all that was required. But prophecy does not allow this as it is too definite. Compare 2 Sam. 2: 12 and Acts 2: 20; 13: 23.

Hypothesis of Jos. and Mary. First cousins relieves the objection. Grandfather of both one and the same person: Matthat and Matthan. Matthan had two sons. Heli and Jacob. Hence Jos. and Mary were first-cousins—

of Davidic origin. M. had sisters, but no mention of brothers. Tradition says M. was a ward of Jos. Thus a partial relief afforded if genealogies be of Jos. They give X's right to the throne personally and officially. Objections against Lk's giving Mary's: 1. Female line not recorded. Ans: This not female, but genealogy of woman through her father, and thus the *male* line of M's ancestry. 2. M. and Eliz. were cousins, and Eliz. of unroyal line, hence M. not of royal line. Ans: This could be on mother's side. Intermarriage allowed among the tribes. 3. M's name not mentioned in Lk's genealogy, but purports that of Jos. Ans: This not easily overcome, yet not absolutely fatal to the theory, as Lk. says, "who was supposed to be the son of," &c. 4. No other proof that M. was from David. Ans: Untrue—proved outside of genealogies that Christ was of royal line, which confirms the probability that list was M's. Lk. 1: 31–32. This prior to marriage and thus necessary that the child should have a *voluntary* father. This the light in which she could understand her union with Jos. if she were of the house of David. Lk. 1: 27. David may refer to the principal subject, as well as to the nearest antecedent, i. e. Jos. M. went to Bm. to enrol her name the same as Jos. Lk. 2: 4. So far then as she was not from Levitic genealogy, proofs contrary. All texts which prove Christ to be from David also prove the same for M.

This subject is beset with difficulties. Slight mistakes destroy certainty. Genealogical principles unknown to us. Much has been cleared up which critics deemed insurmountable, and hence reasonable to suppose that coming researches will remove all difficulties. (See Smith's Dict., Arthur Harvey, and Dr. Green on Colenso.)

§14. *History of John the Baptist.* Mth. 3: 1–13; Mk. 1: 1–8; Lk. 8: I–18. Ministry of John and Tempt. introduced Christ's public work. Lk. begins by formal transition of six dates. Mth. and Mk. begin with preaching of the Baptist. Prophecy groups the Baptism and entrance upon public work. Predictions of Malachi are now fulfilled. John began to preach in 749, a Sabbatical year by best chronology, which relieved the people from labor and thus afforded them leisure to attend John's ministry. "The word of the Lord came to John in the

wilderness," given to commence work directly, and hence he was inspired and divinely guided. Rationalists say this was useless, that John had a conviction that he was a man of God, and, seeing the condition of the people, undertook the work of reformation. But the scriptures show he was under divine guidance.

Design of John's Ministry.—1. Preparation for Christ. John represented O. T. economy, and was the last and greatest of O. T. prophets, being an embodiment of its spirit. Hence first design was to announce New Dispensation. Popular belief in external kingdom, which John proposed to remove. 2. Preparation of people by repentance. O. T. economy educated religious life without satisfying it and the people to expect the Messiah. But the majority of the people had lost the spiritual import of prophetic teaching. The Sadducees were sceptical and Pharisees self-righteous. The earnest Essenes had become fanatics. Hence the necessity of repentance to restore the spiritual, so that Christ might come in contact with O. T. religion in revived life and power, and not an effete religion. 3. To point out the Messiah in the person of Jesus of Nazareth, and hand over to Christ the O. T. Dispensation. " This was He of whom," &c. 4. To show both dispensations united in Christ, that the old yielded to him and withdrew.

John accomplished his designs, first by preaching. No new doctrine, but a return to the power and spirit of the O. T. Its character was severe, denunciatory, and replete with threatenings of wrath. Abounded in O. T. figures. Points out specific sins. Calls all to repentance, but never inculcates asceticism, yet wants them to observe the purity represented by it. Points to Christ as the lamb of God, advances upon Isaiah by pointing to the individual. His preaching more weighty because of the purity of his life. Personally fitted to revive O. T. religion, representing the formal and spiritual.

Design further shown by the rite of baptism. The people were wont to connect the spiritual with the symbolical. Baptism something new, not associated with the law. Its significance was the washing away of their sins, a restoration of the spiritual. John charged with having learned his baptism from the form of receiving proselytes. Ans: As an initiatory rite of Judaism it did not assume form until after the destruction of the temple. He received it from the washings of the O. T.

John's relations to O. T. 1. By birth, being of priestly origin. 2. By his fulfilment of Malachi's prophecy, 3:1, and Isa. 40:3. 3. By the place he frequented, viz., the Desert of Judea, or, as Lk. says, "the region round about Jordan," i. e. between mountains, lower Jordan and the Dead Sea. Boundary crossed where Israel entered Canaan. Symbolical of the moral and religious destitution of the people. So regarded in O. T. Hence John lived unlike his master, who sought men at their own homes. He must be found in the wilderness. His personal appearance was peculiar. Dress made of the cheapest and coarsest material, and had camel's hair which is shed yearly. But this raiment was not official, only assumed by Elijah and John to symbolize renouncement of ease and luxury. In 2 Kings 1:8 Elijah called a "hairy man." Comp. Zech. 13:4. Hence our conclusion. His food was locusts and wild honey. The nearest at hand. All these things were fit to mark him as a representative of O. T. dispensation.

Was John's preaching merely negative? Was his repentance a saving grace? Did baptism cleanse or simply symbolize? Rationalists affirm that repentance meant renouncing of sin outwardly. Some orthodox writers say no vitality in John's work. Answer: John taught all the grace and power of O. T. Hence real repentance and faith, as far as O. T. exhibited. He vindicated the relation between O. and N. T. "I baptize with," &c. Further said baptism was a mere external ceremony; others make the contrast between John and Christ, "I baptize in dependence upon him who," &c. Best: No allusion to Christian baptism as an ordinance. Eminent authorities hold this view. Christian baptism not yet established. Meaning then, "I baptize ceremonially with efficacy." Proposed to the people's faith— "He shall pour out the Spirit." Thus the distinction is in degree and not in kind. "He shall .... with fire:" 1. Reference to judgment fire. Next clause, "chaff, &c." 2. Purifying fire. Drs. Alexander and Schaff. Better: Holy Ghost, and therefore zeal.

The popular success of John was immense. Jerusalem emptied itself to the banks of the Jordan. Judea, Samaria and Galilee gathered there. Priests, scribes, lawyers and soldiers, all conditions thronged to hear him. Yet, success not enduring, as the masses only received him formally. His power enhanced by his peculiar position, as a voice from the desert. Had he preached in Jerusalem it is said he would have been powerless.

§15. *The Baptism of Jesus.* — Matt. 3 : 13, 14 ; Mk. 1 : 9-11 ; Lk. 3 : 21-23. John began six months before. Christ now ready to be brought before the excited crowd. It was the design of Christ's journey, to be baptized. "Τοῦ βαπτισθῆναι," which denotes purpose. The act anomalous, that the less should bless the greater. Matt. says John felt this and tried to hinder him. Christ's words peculiar: suffer now. Two things implied in them : 1. Something was to be allowed, suffered, although unusual. 2. Seemingly temporary. "Suffer it to be so *now.*" It is πρεπον, seemly to complete the law's obligation, what is right in a specific sense for the fulfillment of redemption. The refusal of John shows : 1. John knew and believed Jesus to be the Messiah. 2. Was subordinate, did as Christ commanded him. John baptized on Christ's authority. What was the design ? As John's baptism involved confession of sin, what relation did Christ's bear to this ? 1. Strauss : Confession of sin actual. 2. Others, it implied peccability, and hence Lange, it was ceremonial uncleanness. Too narrow a view. 3. Schenkel says it means sympathy with others. 4. True view. As the circumcision, it was expressive of his assumption of his people's sins. In the law's view he was a sinner, and therefore exhibited the necessity of the washing away of the sins assumed. As Messiah he was sin-bearer. Objection to last : Jesus confounded with the people ; they made confession, and might infer Christ did likewise for his own sins. Guarded : *Lest* they might think so, the divine and John's testimony intervened. The design is again shown as manifesting the unity of the two dispensations. The chief representatives of each meet. The O. T. covenant baptizes the N. T. covenant. Christ publicly gives authority to the work of John, and John confesses Christ to be superior to himself. John decreased, Christ increased.

Baptism served to inaugurate the work of Christ. Afforded opportunity to God to recognize his Son. This was the chief import of the baptism—ἰησοῦ βαπτισθέντος, the genitive absolute, Lk. 3:21. Main subjects the miraculous manifestations. Divine attestations necessary to the Messiah's coming. Wherefore Christ's arrival delayed till a great concourse had flocked to John.

At Baptism Christ was anointed for his work by the Spirit. Not only formal, but full of vital power. The person of Christ is acted upon. Holy Ghost the agent in making him a fit place for the indwelling of the Logos. John's baptism represented cleansing from sin which is the Spirit's work. In the case of Christ the gift confirmed by a sign of the Spirit's descent. The sign and descent go together. Lk. says "Jesus was praying"—a religious act, a real communication of the Spirit to Jesus. After baptism is the temptation, the trying of his gift. Conjecture: Christ now for the first time realizes his mission, the full consciousness of his sacrificial character. Ans: It is not given to penetrate so deeply into the mind of Christ. Certain: He did advance in knowledge of an important spiritual crisis. Always full of the Spirit sufficiently for his purposes, but now receives it immeasurably for his public ministry. Had it before in kind, not in degree, as now he is the organ of the Holy Ghost.

As a dove. 1. Motion of the dove—gliding. 2. Quickness. 3. Softness of the dove. But these are inconsistent with what Lk. says, σωματικῷ εἴδει; hence an appearance, a bodily shape, real dove shape, if language means anything. Why dove? 1. Reference to O. T. after the deluge. 2. Brooding, symbolical of new creation. 3. Purity. 4. Symbol of sacrifice, ceremonial associations. (3) and (4) combined the best. Represented the whole spirit of his ministry. 1. The salvation he preached was peaceful, pure and lovely. 2. A sacrificial work. 3. Productive agency of Spirit at creation—brooding dove. Difficulty: Mth. 3:16—"the heavens were opened αὐτῷ—to him;" Mk. 1:10—"He saw the heavens, &c.:" John 1:32—"I saw," i. e., John Bap. Hence the Baptist *must* have seen the Spirit himself. Ans: 1. This was the sign by which he could recognize Christ. Van Oosterzee considers the event as private,

and Spirit seen only by John and Christ. Obj: *a*. Nat. inter. deny the objective reality of the phenomena. The vision became so only in the spiritual world, and for the spiritualized. *b*. Discrepancy in the several accounts. Mth. and Mk. say "Jesus saw;" John—Baptist "saw;" while Lk. is general—"heaven opened and Spirit descended." 2. Dramatic representations, in the reconciliation between O. and N. T. Voice from heaven not confined to John and Jesus alone. "My beloved Son" founded on 2 Sam. 7: 12. But the expression does not imply that he became Son at baptism, because of his eternal relationship. Ps. 2: 25, 42 and "In whom I am pleased" from Is. 42. Lange says aorist, denoting an eternal act; Alexander—a definite act. The last best.

In this expression we have another attestation to Christ's Messiahship. This is the revelation of the Trinity in their personal agency in redemption. The first in conception. The Father at baptism declares the Son's Messiahship and the Spirit gives grace for the office. Minor differences in form of expressions made a subject of cavil. Mth: "This is my, &c." whilst Mk. and Lk. "Thou art, &c." Some think both are proper and that there were two utterances from heaven. Words were doubtless in Hebrew or Aramaic and here in an inspired translation.

Objections:—1. Shortness of time. If John began six months before there was not time enough for his success and influence. Ans: John's work not independent but an appendage to Christ's. Results accounted for by the condition and great state of expectancy of the Jews. Strauss makes John to have begun when about 20 years old, long before Christ came to him. 2. Inconsistency between John and Syn. Syn. say John knew Jesus whilst John says the Baptist did not know him. Again John represents the Bap. as recognizing Christ as the Messiah from the first, whereas Syn. affirm that he sent a deputation to Jesus from prison, saying "Art thou he that should come?" Strauss says John's gospel belongs to a later period, that John would not have said the "Lamb of God" as yet because he did not know him as the suffering Messiah. Had he understood him, he would have baptized him and given up his work. Ans: In baptizing, John obeyed. Strauss again: If the miraculous conception were true, Christ had no need of the Spirit at this time, and hence the event is a myth. Again: John an Essene, and he baptized and lived as the Essenes did. This gives a historical root of Christianity. John Baptist and Essenism are the germs of Christianity. John saw the necessity of a moral reformation, and if the people could be aroused, the Messiah would appear, and hence he proclaimed time for repentance had arrived. But John according to Strauss never acknowleged Jesus as Messiah. Later, Christ is baptized and indoctrinated into Messianic ideas. Jesus possessed a freer and clearer nature than John, and felt a lack in John's negative method. Hence he realized all those graces of his nature which resulted from his communion with God, and which were unatta'nable by ascetic methods. They looked upon each other as other teachers did. Strauss has three mythical stages of growth: 1. Church idea of the dignity of Jesus required that John should acknowledge his Messiahship. 2. Lk.'s story of his childhood. 3. John's account of a clear acknowledgment of Christ by the Baptist from the first. Strauss' canon: That account which tends to exalt the person of Christ is the mythical one. This rules out John's narrative altogether of the Baptist's recognition of Christ from the first. The remainder of John's gospel is assumed.

The residuum: 1. The relation of John to the Essenes, who were entirely different. Essenes were dualistic. Enjoined asceticism upon all, John on himself. 2. The ascetic washings were not baptisms but oft repeated. John's once for all. 3. Strauss: John founded a sect. Ans: Untrue, but called the whole nation to repentance. Asceticism taught purity consisted in mortification, but receivers of John's baptism did not belong to any such school. 4. It involves a long continuation of Christ with John which is inadmissible. Renan: Christ more independent than John. Before Christ came, John had formed a full idea of reformation. Likewise Christ had deferred doing good until he had seen John and improved on him. Schenkel says Christ and John were antagonistic. Christ at first sympathized with John, but afterwards regarded his influence injurious. Baptism of Christ

only a transaction in his soul, which he conceived to be his divine mission, and hence separated from John. Keim holds it was purely humanitarian. Relates with reverence. Christ merely a man. Outward signs unreal, but baptism a consecration to a work which John had begun.

§16. *The Temptation.*—This is a great mystery, as it involves the doctrine of his person. Follows baptism. Hengstenberg holds that there is not room enough in 40 days for Bap. and Tempt.

Designs: 1. Typical. The heads of the Messianic and evil kingdoms brought face to face. Jesus, full of the Spirit, is subjected to a trial of strength with Satan, and triumphs in the complete overthrow of his adversary. Tempt. recalls the history of redemption, that of a conflict between the kingdoms of light and darkness. "Seed of the woman" in O. T. now fulfilled. Christ overcomes for his people, therefore, in connection with baptism and before his life work. 2. Had Messianic designs. (*a*) It formed a part of Christ's humiliation. (*b*) All the temptations proposed false views of the Messianic work. What could be accomplished only through suffering, Christ is urged to do at once by unlawful means. 3. Personal reference to his own inward experience. Spends forty days in prayer and fasting, and thus by outward means he was prepared for his work. 4. Exemplary. It shows us how to triumph, by prayer, fasting and the Holy Scriptures. Christ's practical sermon on "Resist the devil and he will flee from you." A complete circle of temptations, addressed to his whole nature, so that he was tempted "in all points like as we."

"Led by the Spirit." 1. His own mind. 2. The devil. 3. The Holy Spirit. Probably the last who led him to conquest over Satan in the wilderness. The desert was the Quarantania mountain near Jericho. "With wild beasts" indicates a contrast with Adam's situation. "Forty days fasting" has O. T. associations. Obj: Impossible—too long a time. Ans: 1. Supernatural power. 2. Power of spirit over body exalted to an eminent degree in Christ. 3. Abstinence only from ordinary nourishments. Lk. 4: 2: οὐκ ἔφαγεν, thus making his abstinence total. Typical import in the number forty. Moses interceded for his people forty days; punishment consisted of forty strikes; Ninevites fasted forty days, Ezekiel's sin-bearing forty days, and purification same length. Hence connected with confession of sin. Mth. and Lk. differ. One puts tempt. at the end of forty days, the other says he was tempted all the time. Most natural explanation that he was tempted in thought.

Character of the Temptations. I. "If thou be the Son of God" refers to God's words at baptism. Satan wants proof. "Command these stones, &c." Stones numerous. *a*. Tempt. to gluttony. Improbable, because to eat bread after forty days fasting would not be gluttony. *b*. Tempt. to distrust Providence, and escape suffering inseparable from the character and mission which he assumed. Not exclusively applicable to Christ. His sufferings were representative. Jews looked for the Messiah as an embodiment of plenty to supply their wants. (See feeding of 5000.) Wherefore Christ was tempted to do by one stroke what was to result from his death and universal law of love among men. Ans: Deut. 8:3. Misinterpreted as referring to truth. No reference to truth but to manna, as truth can not feed the body. Idea: Man must look to God to supply all his wants, not primarily either to ordinary or extraordinary means.

II. Directly opposed to the first. A presumptuous distrust in God. As if Satan said, "If God is to support you, try him." Imitates Christ by quoting Ps. 91:11–12. πτερύγιον τοῦ ἱεροῦ. *a*. Roof of Solomon's porch. *b*. Royal porch. *c*. Double pitch of roof like wings. *d*. Wing, as we use it. He is urged to forego suffering. Again Christ takes suffering as the appointed means to fulfill his mission. He quotes Deut. 6:16. Double meaning. (1.) Thou shouldst not tempt me who am your sovereign. (2.) I should tempt God by so doing.

III. "All kingdoms." Not Palestine. Did Satan own the world? Then he had a right to give. Called and is the prince of this world. The world and Messiah antagonistic. Not Christ's kingdoms now, though they are one day to be Christ's. Falseness of his claim lay in regarding his power as superior to Christ's, whereas all his power is allowed him for the good of the church. The supreme sin in the temptation is the worshipping of Satan. Question whether (*a*) civil homage due a sovereign or (*b*)

religious worship is demanded here. The two are inseparable. To acknowledge Satan would be to receive from him. Tempt. was to secularity and idolatry. Jews especially exposed to this, adapting themselves to surrounding nations by adopting their idols. Satan proposed to give the kingdoms of the world immediately. This was just the object of Christ's coming, i.e., to establish Messianic sway over the whole earth. The people expected this, but Christ chose the spiritual and suffering instead of the temporal. The humiliation and suffering are seen to be his choice rather than his accepting the proffer of Satan. From Deut. 6: 13, "Thou shalt &c." Signal honor put on Dent. (Especially assailed by late critics.) Thrice quoted by Christ under the usual form: γεγράπται.

Remarks: The three temptations were a summary of his life sufferings. His triumph a token of final triumph. Three things. 1. Rebellion vs. God. 2. Denial of Christ's supreme Divinity. 3. Subjection of the same to Satan. Not vulgar seductions of sense, but are addressed to an enlightened, lofty nature. Hence they are the highest conceivable forms of sin. Addressed to the whole nature, corresponding to the different periods of life, the sensual (childhood), intellectual (youth), and imaginative (manhood). The three temptations are therefore comprehensive. As to their order, Mth. and Lk. differ, hence the Rationalistic cavils. Mth.'s order is preferred. 1. Because it exhibits the contrast between the first two. 2. Lk.'s "get thee behind me Satan" more fitting for the closing scene. Not easily ascertained what determines Lk.'s order.

When Temptations ended "the devil departed from him." Ἄχρι καιροῦ, till a fixed season, i. e., to be renewed at times. Some refer it to Gethsemane, but properly his whole life was a temptation. Following the departure of the devil "angels ministered unto him," διηκόνουν is serving food, and hence appropriate.

Nature of the Temptation. How was Christ approached? Owing to difficulties, sound, sober critics have taken refuge in the symbolical rather than the literal, e. g., Pressense and Lange. Doubtless it was something akin to humanity because of the "worshipping him." Grounds: 1. Bodily appearance of Satan without analogy in scripture. Ans: S. can assume the form of an "angel of light" if he wishes. 2 Cor. 11: 14. Why not that of man? 2. Unimaginable that S. could transport Christ through the air, &c. Ans: These cavilers admit S. has power over the soul which is far greater, then why not over the body? Dr. Alexander: No compulsion. Verb means "they went together," and thus a part of Christ's humiliation in allowing himself to be tempted. 3. If Christ did not know S. he was not omniscient, if he did he would not have conversed with him. 4. He could not see the world's kingdoms at once without a miracle and if he did Satan performed a miracle. Ans: Who knows Satan's power—how much divine power God had given him? Jεικνύσιν is "causes to see." Many believe S. caused all this to pass before the mind's eye. If this is so say some critics this surrenders the literal inter'n. Not so. It is deciding whether the literal or metaphorical should be applied to the passage. 5. Strauss: Satan too cunning to make such a proposal. Again: If Christ could be tempted he was not sinless, if so, no temptation. (Lange and Pressense: Christ had but one essence and that divine.) If it be necessary to suppose that Christ could sin in order to be tempted, then the divine essence could have sinned. Ques. of middle ages since Augustine: Can we conceive of Christ as peccable? Now, we must hold two things. 1. Christ's tempt. not merely an external act. His struggles fierce and internal. They shook his very soul. "In all points." 2. "Yet without sin." Wherefore he was sinless.

Diverse views of the occurrences. 1. Strauss declares it to be a myth. Meyer says there was a conflict between the kingdoms of light and darkness. 2. Schleiermacher: A parable given by Christ, and mistaken by his disciples. Intended to teach them how to escape temptation. 3. Nat: External occurrence uttered in symbolical language. Lange. 4. An ecstatic state of mind brought about by fasting. Origen and Cyprian, with Olshausen in modern times. 5. Simply a conflict in Christ's mind produced by imagination. Therefore Christ was necessarily sinful. Literature on this is immense. Vide Trench's Studies on the Gospels.

PUBLIC MINISTRY.

Early Judean Ministry.

Preliminary: Synoptists and John now differ. I. As to limits of the period, Syns. speak of Christ as leaving Judea for Gal. immediately after the Temptation and there teaching. They mention no public work in Judea, previous to His going to Jerusalem, toward the close of His ministry. John (chs. 1–4) supplements their account, mentioning a brief visit to Galilee, then a going to Jerusalem to His first Passover, and a subsequent tarrying and baptizing in Judea. Hence, John chs. 1–4, may be termed History of Early Judean Ministry.

II. They differ as to Christ's teaching, its nature and manner.

1. According to Syn. substance of Christ's teaching is "kingdom of God," its nature, design, conditions of membership. (Sermon on Mt., Parables, etc.) In John the phrase occurs in but two chs. (3: 3–5, 18: 36).

2. Syn. Christ silent as to Messianic claims, suppresses popular Messianic enthusiasm and refuses Messianic titles. In John His Divine Person is the main theme. (Nicodemus, Woman of Samar.)

3. Syn. say little of His sacrificial death. In John it is predicted from the first. (Vide. 1: 29, 2: 19–22, 3: 14.

4. In Syn. Christ teaches universality of gospel only toward close of His life. John records it among His earliest utterances. (Vide. 4: 21–23).

Sceptics, exaggerating these difficulties, reject John, begin with Gal. Ministry, and adopting Syn. account, allege:

1. At first Christ had no consciousness of Messiahship, but was driven to assume Messianic character to accomplish His plans.

2. Doctrine of a sacrificial mission grew up in His mind gradually. Strauss says both these ideas conceived late in life while in Cæsarea Philippi, when He saw death was inevitable.

3. Idea of a universal gospel did not originate until after His rejection by the Jewish nation.

To reconcile these differences is the great problem of gospel harmony. This may be done by showing 1st.

That there is no inconsistency in the accounts, or 2. That their combination yields historic unity. (1.) These accounts involve one another and are parts of one whole. The idea of king and kingdom are supplemental. (2.) Syn's teaching as to Person of Christ is not so meagre as sceptics claim. Messianic titles are suppressed, because of false Messianic notions. From the outset authority is claimed which is irrational unless divine.

The critical view requires the rejection not of John alone, but also of a great portion of the Syn's account. (Baptism, Temptation, Synag. at Nazareth, Sermon on Mt., Parables.)

(3.) In John, Christ does teach "the kingdom." (To Nicodemus 3: 3-5. Before Pilate 18: 36.) In Syn. there are passages teaching divinity (Matt. 11: 25-30.)

(4.) A progress is marked in the self-revelation of Christ in Jno. as well as in Syn. In public it is enigmatical; direct declarations are private. (Cleansing temple. Discourse with Nicodemus and Samaritan woman.)

Historical reason for this difference: Christ owed a duty to the Jews as a nation, first. They could not be rejected until they had rejected Him. Jno's plan is to record instances of Christ's declaration of Messiahship in Jerusalem. When rejected there, He goes to Galilee, prepares for the founding of a church, with its officers and government, as is related by the Syn.

Jno. 1-4: 45 in the harmony are inserted between Matt. 4: 11 and 12 (Vide Scheme.) To justify such insertion, it must be shown:

1. No real contradiction exists between the two accounts. 2. The portion omitted was not in the plan of the individual writer. 3. Combination furnishes a consistent view. 4. Many undesigned coincidences evince that the accounts presuppose one another.

Reasons for insertion *here*:

1. Mt. and Mk. indicate space between Temptation and Galilean Ministry, by saying that Christ went to Galilee because of the imprisonment of Jno. Bap.

2. These four chaps. Jno. record interviews between Jesus and Jno. Bap. They must have occurred before Jno. was imprisoned. They must have occurred after the Baptism—as it is referred to as past (Jno. 1: 32),

and if later than the Baptism they must be subsequent to the Temptation, as nothing intervened between these events (Mk. 1 : 12). Four chs. of Jno. at least should be inserted here as the narrative is unbroken. Some harmonists insert five—thus changing the time of the beginning of the Galilean ministry.

Length of this period is inferred from §25. Jno. 4 : 35. Four months till harvest. Harvest time was the middle of Nisan, i.e. beginning of April.

Four months previous brings us to December, eight months subsequent to the first Passover (ch. 3), and one year after the Baptism. Hence duration of Judean ministry is estimated as one year. (So Meyer, Wieseler). The exegesis of some assigns to this verse merely the weight of a proverb—(1) Gratuitous. No evidence of such proverb. (2) Force of ἔτι forbids (so Meyer vs. Alford and Gieseler). These minor differences do not essentially affect the events of the period.

Designs of the events of this period :

1. *Primary.* Offering Himself to nation as the true Messiah—by, *a.* Testimony of Jno. Bap. *b.* Cleansing Temple—showing supreme authority in House of God. *c.* Miracles. *d.* Teaching spiritual nature of His kingdom.

2. *Secondary.* Preparation for Galilean ministry, in consequence of foreseen rejection by Jewish hierarchy—by, *a.* Brief visit to Galilee. *b.* Choice of disciples irrespective of existing theocracy. *c.* Stay in Judea, teaching and baptizing with Jno. Bap., until his imprisonment.

Series of first things is given in Jno.: viz. first gathering of disciples, first miracle, first Passover, first teaching, &c. Jno. records a week's history—day by day.

1st day 1 : 19–28, 2d. 1 : 29–34, 3d. 1 : 35–42, 4th. 1 : 43–51, and 2 : 1, τῇ ἡμέρᾳ τῇ τρίτῃ, i. e. the third day after starting on His journey, making seven days in all. Compare Jno's record of last week of Christ's life.

§18. *Testimony of John Bapt. to Jesus.* Such testimony, naturally to be expected at this period, historically occurs. Sanhedrim send from Jerus. a deputation of Priests and Levites to inquire into the meaning of John's work. Their arrival at the Jordan coincides with Christ's return from the desert of the temptation (v. 27.) (Others however place Christ's return at v. 29 on the day following).

This deputation evinces the extensive impression produced by John's work. The mission was authoritative, sent out by the highest ecclesiastical court of the nation, whose duty it was to investigate all religious movements. It was not necessarily hostile at first. Had they found John easily influenced and a courtier (Lk. 7 : 25), they would have favored his views and used him as an instrument in furthering their own designs. (John 5 : 35); but having heard his testimony to Christ, they charge him with "having a devil." (Lk. 7 : 33). Their questions show acquaintance with the prevailing belief that the Messiah was at hand, and exhibit the state of popular Messianic expectations. Art thou the Christ, or Elias (Mal. 4 : 5), or that prophet. (Deut. 18 : 15.)

Does not John's denial that he is Elias, contradict Christ's express statement, Matt. 11 : 14? Ans: John denies he is Elias in *person;* admits he is in *spirit* by quoting prophecies referring to Elias, as referring to himself officially.

Jews of that day, seem to have made a false distinction based on Deut. 18 : 15, between Christ and "that prophet." (John 4 : 19, 25, 6 : 14, 7 : 40, 41).

To these questions, John returns an abrupt "No," wishing to keep himself in the background, while he brings Jesus forward. He defines his own mission and character, by simply quoting Is. 40 : 3.

Points of interest are 1. Extent of John's influence. 2. Excited Messianic expectations and their character. 3. Providential care that rulers should be brought into contact with Christ, and receive ample proof of His claims, from the very first. 4. Humility of John Bap. Lange notes analogy between temp. of Christ and John, a temptation to external power.

Place. Text. Recpt. εν Βηθαβαρα, (John 1 : 28), critical reading, Βηθανια. Location, now unknown. Probably e. of Jordan : a ford near Jericho. Renewed testimony, (v. 29). "Lamb of God." One of the most striking passages of scripture. It embodies the great truths of both Testaments and declares the fulfillment of prophecy. The theme of the O. T. is one to come. John says 'Behold Him,' "He is here."

Hengstenberg confines his reference to the Paschal Lamb, as being the true sin-offering. But John uses "Lamb" as representative of all O. T. sacrificial types.

Reasons for selecting "Lamb" as a title of Christ are, 1. Fulfills Is. 53 : 7. "Lamb to the slaughter," which Jews recognized as Messianic. 2. Expresses the spirit of Christ's ministry. (Comp. Rev. 5 : 6.)

Some critics deny a sacrificial reference, others object, 1. That John in here teaching vicarious death of Christ as Son of God, for the world, displays a knowledge of doctrines not then current, but which were the after development of advanced theology.

Ans. *a*. Objection based on subversion of history. These conceptions of Messiah's work were fundamental: they had died out of the popular creed and John's mission was to revive them.

b. John speaks as a prophet and was himself surprised at the manner in which his prophecies were fulfilled. (Lk. 7 : 20).

2d Objection, John 1 : 33 "I knew him not" contradicts Mt. 3 : 14, which presupposes knowledge of Jesus, both as man and Messiah.

Ans. *a*. Distinction between knowing officially and personally. (Rob. Gk. Harm. p. 187, §18. Note.) John Bap. was aware that Jesus of Naz. was Messiah of prophecy. "But he knew not Jesus personally" before His baptism, when the spirit descended as sign upon him. This is not an explanation. If he did not know him personally, why refuse to baptize him (Mt. 3 : 14). To explain by dignity of Christ's personal appearance (Farrar I. p. 114 seq.) is unsatisfactory.

b. Better explanation. οὐκ ᾔδειν has only relative force. John Bap.'s previous knowledge was subjective, now possessing a new knowledge based on testimony from heaven, he makes an official declaration. (Comp. relative use of terms by John in chs. 2 : 11, and a further and increased belief based on testimony of miracles, also 7 : 5).

§19. *Jesus gains disciples.* Had the writer of the fourth gospel been an impostor, John Bap.'s testimony would have been succeeded by the abandonment of his separate work, his following Christ as a disciple, going with him to Jerus. and testifying to His Messiahship before the

Sanhedrim. Multitudes would have accepted and followed Him. On the contrary, the gospel narrative informs us that but few believe, that John Bap. recognizing the independency of his own ministry keeps aloof from Christ and continues bearing testimony to Him as the Messiah.

Design of Christ in gathering disciples. 1. To lead people to Him gradually. 2. He thus begins to lay the foundation of that church which was to continue after He had been taken away, an action based on foreknowledge of His death. Although submitting Himself to the people for their rejection, He acts as knowing the result.

v. 35-37. Next day at tenth hour i.e. 4 P. M., two disciples of John follow Jesus: first converts: their address "Rabbi" the first recognition of Christ as a teacher.

Of these two, one was Andrew, the other is argued to have been Evangelist John, from, 1. His habitual silence as to himself. 2. The minuteness of the details proves the narrator to have been an eye witness. 3. Syn. mention John among the first disciples.

41 v. Twofold exegesis,—$\pi\rho\tilde{\omega}\tau o\varsigma$:

1. Andrew and John seek each his own brother: Andrew finds his *first.* (So Meyer and Alexander).

2. Both seek Peter: Andrew is first to find him.

43 v. The next day Philip, being called, brings Nath. commonly understood to be Bartholomew—because 1. John never mentions a Bartholomew nor the Synops. a Nathaniel. 2. Time of his call, while journeying through Gal.: (Barthol. resided at Cana of Galilee). 3. When Christ showed Himself to His disciples after resurrection at sea of Tiberias, Nath. was of their number. (John 21: 1, 2.) 4. Philip brought Nath.: and the names Philip and Bartholomew always together in the catalogues of the Twelve. 5. Bartholomew is a patronymic, son of Tolmai, by which name he was probably better known than by that of Nathaniel. (Vide. Farrar I. p. 152 and Note). Thus 6 disciples are called in the first week.

Objection: In Mt. 16: 18, Peter's change of name is connected with his confession, thus contradicting John 1: 42. Ans. Name Cephas is here *given;* in Mt. Christ *confirms* and *applies* it.

Note the character of those called; religious-minded men: come to Jordan to hear John; meet Christ; listen to Bap.'s testimony concerning Him, and are convinced of the validity of His claims.

Rationalists allege that Syn. (Lk. 5: 1-11) represent disciples as following Christ because of miracles He performed. John says (1. 35-51) they were impressed by His personal influence. These accounts are not inconsistent. According to both, Christ furnishes evidence of His Messiahship. Here He calls Philip with authority, shows divine knowledge in reading mind of Nath., claims to be the connecting link between heaven and earth. (Comp. Gen. 28: 12.)

Note the only recorded words of Jesus up to this point. At 12 years of age to His mother, Lk. 2: 49. To John Bap. Mt. 3: 15. To Satan, Mt. 4: 1-11. To His disciples, John 1: 39.

§20. John 2: 1-12. *Marriage at Cana.* John here emphasizes the fact of the "*beginning* of miracles." Ch. 2: 11. Cana of *Gal.* mentioned, not to distinguish the town from another of the same name, but to show that the beginnings of Christ's work were in *Gal.*

Why in Galilee, and before in Jerusalem? 1. Prediction (Is. 9: 1, 2, quoted Matt. 4: 14) that Gal. should be first to receive spiritual light, is thus fulfilled. 2. John, who confines his account to Christ's Judean work, thus shows his knowledge of the work in Galilee.

Christ went to Galilee at this *time*, both as a preparation for the coming Gal. ministry, and to produce a simultaneous impression in different parts of the country by his appearance in various places within a short time, giving opportunity for judgment upon himself and work. This visit is an episode in Judean Period, pointing forward to the next.

Farrar identifies Cana with Kefr-Kenna. (Vide Vol. I. Note, p. 161. Andrews, p. 149.) Robinson prefers Kana el Jelil.

That the marriage was among Christ's relatives has been inferred from Mary's prominence at the feast; as to the parties themselves conjecture is fruitless. Joseph being unmentioned, it may be assumed he was now dead. Jewish marriage feasts usually lasted 7 days (Judg. 14: 12). Festivities had begun when Jesus arrived.

Objections: 1. How did Mary know he could perform miracles, if this was first? especially as the occasion did not demand it. Wine might readily be purchased. *Ans:* Some, he wrought miracles in private; some, she looked to him naturally for aid; others, from circumstances of his birth, she had come to believe in his divinity; others, knowing his work had been inaugurated by his baptism, she looked for a speedy fulfilment of her hopes.

2. How reconcile Christ's working the miracle with his statement, "My hour is not yet come," v. 4. *Ans:* Mistaken idea in her mind as to character of Messianic kingdom, viz., time of material plenty. Christ shows that human motives, even the most urgent, were not to be the cause of the manifestation of his glory as Messiah. Comp. Lk. 2: 49.

3. Amount of wine produced. Each firkin or *bath* (Heb.) contained from 7 to 9 gals., hence each jar held about ⅔ of a barrel. (Vide Farrar, Vol. I., p. 166, note 2.) *Ans:* Some argue from v. 8, that the water became wine, as drawn, or was a handsome wedding gift for a poor household. The large quantity is significant of Christ's giving without measure. It precludes all possibility of collusion.

Designs. 1. To manifest his glory. 2. To relieve want and embarrassment of host. 3. Teaches true morality; contrasts John the ascetic with Christ, who did not withdraw from the world, but lived above it. 4. Enforces the sanctity of the marriage tie. It is analogous to feeding the multitudes: but here, substance is changed, there multiplied. (On this miracle, vide Princeton Review, July and October, 1865.)

From Cana, Christ goes to Capernaum (emended text, εἰς Καφαρναούμ), probably to join a caravan there making up for the feast. From Lk. 4: 23 it has been inferred that Christ at this time wrought miracles there. It is preferable to refer this allusion to healing nobleman's son, Jno. 4: 46–54.

§21. John 2: 13–25. *First Passover. Temple Cleansed.* Christ finds the Temple polluted by the presence of cattle and doves for sacrifice, and of money changers, exchanging foreign coin. Although Christ used a scourge, the force employed was moral and spiritual rather than

physical. Πάντας (v. 15) refers to men as well as cattle. Some infer from v. 16, *said, etc.*, leniency toward dove-sellers. Captious cavil. Command is given, because doves could not be scourged.

V. 16, "make not," etc. Comp. stronger utterance Matt. 21 : 13,—quoted from Is. 56 : 7,—employed at second cleansing of the Temple. V. 17 quot. from Ps. 69:9.

Significance of the act: 1. Teaches lesson in repentance, and need of reformation. 2. Symbolic expression of Messianic claims. Declares God his Father (v. 16), assumes supreme authority in temple (fulfilling Mal. 3 : 1–3), refers to Temple as type of his body (v. 19), God's permanent indwelling, typically represented in the Temple, being literal in his life. Christ in public declares Messiahship thus enigmatically, because, 1. People are not ready to receive him; false Messianic notions prevail; more explicit statement would lead to popular outbreak. 2. Bible an oriental book. Jews an Eastern nation. To them an enigmatic act needed no interpretation. That the Jews understood him is evident from their demanding a sign, v. 18. This shows they were knowingly rejecting Christ, although possessing evidence of John Bapt., of prophets, and of Christ's miracles. By *sign* they denoted an outward manifestation coinciding with their idea of Messiah. Sign given v. 19, afterwards called sign of Jona, contains indisputable reference to his resurrection (v. 21). This is only occasion of Christ's predicting his resurrection on third day. That his enemies understood him is seen from their allusion to it after his death. (Matt. 27 : 63.)

Critical Objections. 1. Unhistoric expectation and prediction of his death. He could not yet foresee this issue: people and disciples could not understand him. [Neander and Olshausen, denying any reference to resurrection, interpret, 'Persist and destroy this national temple, and I will found a spiritual church.']

Ans: Not necessary for Christ to limit his discourses by what others could understand. True exegesis uses ναὸν, v. 19, in typical, not double sense.

2. *Obj.* Boldness of act would enrage the Jews and excite opposition.

Ans: The suddenness and justice of the act combined with the air of Christ's personal authority (Cp. John 18 : 6) account for no popular disturbance.

3. Syn. record a similar scene in Passion Week; could not have occurred twice, hence both are mythical.

Ans: Why not twice? Appropriate at beginning and end of ministry. A first and last opportunity of accepting him. John, who above records the early Judean ministry, mentions the cleansing occurring in that period, and to avoid repetition omits the second, contained in the Syn. Strauss understands cleansing as a real act, but in opposition to Judaism and the entire sacrificial system.

V. 23 alludes to further miracles. None recorded, John introducing miracles only for sake of the connected discourses. Verses 23, 25. Effect. "Many believed," with evanescent faith, founded only upon the miracles. (Comp. επιστευσαν, v. 23, επιστευεν, v. 24. "Many trusted him. He did not trust himself to them.")

§22. John 3 : 1–21. *Discourse with Nicodemus.* Nicodemus, member of Sanhedrim, on evidence of miracles believes Christ to be a divinely appointed teacher. He is mentioned (Comp. 7 : 50), Tabernacles, also (ch. 19 : 39) burial. "Coming by night" shows odium already attaching to Christ. Being a Pharisee and ruler, his visit shows that Christ's influence was not confined to a single class.

Jesus teaches, 1. Nature, necessity, source of the new birth. 2. Spiritual nature of kingdom of heaven. 3. In order to regeneration there is necessity for faith in himself, as only revealer of the Father, and sacrifice for sin. Christ declares his pre-existence; displays foreknowledge of the atonement.

Perplexity of Nicodemus evinces total loss among his class, of spiritual meaning of O. Test. Christ's rebuke (v. 10) shows that he is teaching no new doctrine.

Objections to genuineness of the Discourse. 1. These doctrines not developed until later. 2. Terms and ideas are those of heretical school in early church, especially such phrases, "Christ the only revealer of the Father," "new birth," etc. "*Regeneration*" not a N. T. word. Verbal form occurs 16 times; peculiar to John. Only allied form in N. T. is παλιγγενεσια, Mt. 19 : 28, Tit. 3 : 5.

Strauss regards whole discourse as fiction, bearing impress of Pseudo John's mind. Nicod. an ideal character introduced as offset to the reproach that all first converts were from the poorer class.

Bauer. All allegory; Nicodemus representing unbelieving Judaism, seeking a sign, a counterpart of the woman of Samaria, who represents believing heathenism.

Sceptical Inferences. These doctrines, peculiar to John's gospel, are those of Gnosticism. Hence the fourth gospel must have been written as late as close of 2nd Cent. by a Gnostic, probably a Valentinian.

Ans. 1. Terminology alone is peculiar to John. Both Testaments teach these doctrines. Comp. O. T. expression Ps. 51: 10 "clean heart;" also Paul's phrase "$\varkappa\tau\iota\sigma\iota\varsigma$" Gal. 6 : 15. 2. True relation of Gnosticism to N. T. doctrine. *a.* Sceptics exaggerate the resemblance; more difference than likeness. *b.* Gnosticism a heresy arising within the church. Its ideas and terms are borrowed from John. *c.* Alexandrian philosophy of which Gnosticism was an off-shoot was imbued with O. T. ideas. N. T. was the development of these ideas. Hence both drawing from a common source employed to some degree similar modes of thought and expression. *d.* Christ dealt with the philosophical questions of His time. *e.* John, writing when Gnostic speculation had begun to disturb the church, like Paul, (Cp. Eph. and Col.) writes against it, using its nomenclature. Christ's teachings now are clearer than those subsequently given in Galilee, because, 1. His great purpose of offering Himself to the Jews as their Messiah necessitated lucid statement of nature and, blessings of His kingdom. In Galilee His audiences were popular and His aim was to establish the church. 2. This was private interview, with a well disposed inquirer. (Cp. Woman of Samaria.)

§23. John 3: 22–36. *Jesus remains in Judea and baptizes.* Some conjecture, without reason, that Christ returned from Jerus. into Gal. Christ leaves Jerusalem, not on account of open hostility, but because after offering Himself to the Jews, he had been rejected. He tarries in Judea (v. 22). 1. National promises must be fulfilled: offer of Himself be made more general, not restricted to a single feast. He may have attended

Pentecost and Tabernacles during this period. 2. John's testimony having not yet ended, the Galilean Ministry could not properly begin.

Meagre description of Christ's work at this period, no miracles, no long discourses, leads to inference that little was done. His work is same as that of Bap. 1. Facts show likeness. Christ employed the same rite as John, with same import, for as no subsequent mention of baptism occurs until Pentecost, *Christian* baptism was not instituted until after Christ's death. 2. Christ's early teaching in Galilee, evidently similar to that in Judea, and John Bap.'s work, are described in the same language. 3. As Christ's work and John's are parallel in time, both would naturally pursue the same line of teaching. There would not be two different baptisms in same period of development. Remarks: John Bap.'s hold on the masses gradually transferred to Christ: His work thus growing out of John's. They do not unite, for that would destroy their proper relation. Christ stands aside as Messiah. John points to Him. They do not separate widely, either in place or teaching, lest they should be mistaken for rival prophets. v. 24. "John was not yet cast into prison." From fourth gospel alone no exegetical reason can be assigned for this statement. John however wrote with Syn. before him. They make no mention of Judean ministry but date Christ's work in Gal. from the imprisonment of John Bap. John shows that his narrative of Judean work does not conflict with any Syn. statements because Christ had not at this time entered upon Galilean ministry " for John was not yet cast into prison i. e. Bap.'s testimony was not yet ended, it was not yet time for Christ to leave Judea. Ænon near Salim probably in Valley of Jordan Western side, near Jericho. (Farrar I. p. 202, Note.)

v. 25. Question started as to purifying, between John's disciples and *a Jew* (Emended Text v. 25. *Ιουδαιου*.) Bap.'s disciples complain to him of Christ's baptizing. He bears additional testimony to Jesus; declaring that not to accept Him as Messiah, means condemnation. (v. 36.)

v. 31–36. Some say without good reason that these are words of Evangelist, rather than of John Bap. for they display an acquaintance with doctrines not then revealed.

Points of interest. 1. John Bap. still had a body of disciples. 2. John still regards his ministry subordinate to Christ. 3. Clear views of John concerning Christ.

§25. John 4:4–42. *Woman of Samaria—Sychar.* This name occurs nowhere else in scripture. Common view, that it is nickname for Shechem, meaning "drunkard," or "liar" is based on, Is. 28:1–7, where Ephraimites are called, *shiccôrim* "*drunkards;*" Hab. 2:18 *môreh sheker* "teacher of lies" which is said to refer to Moreh, the original name of district of Shechem; and habitual use by John of λεγομενος (v. 5) to denote a soubriquet (cp. 11:16, 19:13–17.)

Some say Sychar was suburb of Shechem. Jacob's well, near entrance of valley, mile from present city, "one of few spots identified with Christ's presence." 6th hour i. e. noon.

Different tone of woman and Nicodemus. Nicodemus, sober, grave, and earnest, regards Christ as teacher. Woman, sprightly, conversational, looks upon Christ as traveller. Christ varies His teaching to suit each case. With Nicodemus an instructed Jew, He dwells on technical topics of religion e. g. doctrines of new-birth. To the woman He speaks of a supply for the soul—thirst common to all.

Two views of Samaritans. 1. Common view. Entirely heathen; no descent from Jacob, no right to O. T. privileges. 2. Mixed race—remnants of 10 tribes and heathen settlers—looking for Messiah as a prophet (John 4:25). They stand in N. T. as a link between Jews and heathen. Not regarding them as chosen people, Christ does not pursue ministry among them Mt. 10:5. Although non-Judaic, they were not pagan (v. 20).

A historical import of this incident, prediction of the universal spread of the gospel,—the natural sequel of discourse with Nicodemus. To him Christ taught the spiritual nature of His kingdom. If spiritual it must be universal, and all formal barriers be done away.

Samaritans believed on hearing Christ's words (v. 41, 42). Jews disbelieved though beholding His miracles.

Sceptics object: Christ here makes distinct claim to Messiaship, "I am He," but few days later, in Galilee, forbids any allusion to his divinity, even among disciples.

Ans: Christ is in foreign country. His statements would provoke no hostility from the rulers. This is no real advance on His teaching to Nicodemus or John Bapt's testimony concerning Him. But now He assumes title of Messiah for first time.

Distinguish in this period between private and public teaching. His utterances in private are unrestrained, in public, symbolic.

GALILEAN MINISTRY.

Ministry in Eastern Galilee.

Gal. Ministry extends from the close of Judean until the three last feasts. The Feeding of 5,000 divides this Ministry into those of Eastern and Northern Gal. Its commencement and duration depend upon two questions. 1. Is Syn. journey (Mt. 4: 12. Mk. 1: 14. Lk. 4: 14.) Same as that of John 4, or subsequent to John 5? 2. Was feast of John 5. 1. Passover, Pentecost, Tabernacles, Purim? Wieseler has attempted to settle question first by historically making time of John Bap's imprisonment coincident with feast of John 5.

Discussion of Ques. First. I. Those identifying, journeys argue. 1. Motive assigned by Syn. and John for Christ's leaving Judea is similar (§24. Mt. 4: 12, Mk. 1: 14. Lk. 4: 14. Jno. 4: 1–3). Syns. say it was imprisonment of John. John says he was aware that Pharisees knew that He "made and baptized *more* disciples than John" (ch. 6). John had been imprisoned by Herod through Pharisaic intrigue. Hence Jesus, as being born a greater object of hatred than John, departed into Gal. to avoid persecution. Two obj's: *a.* Syn. do not mention Pharisees as concerned in John's imprisonment. Ans: True; but if not, why does Jesus leave Judea? A *private* quarrel between Herod and John is no sufficient reason. Jno. (3: 25 certainly implies Pharisaic hostility evinced by endeavors to stir up differences between John and Jesus. Jesus' saying (4: 44) that "a prophet hath no honor in his own country" (i. e. Judea) declares hostility to himself and hence to John as they were engaged in the same work. Objectors cannot say that Jesus departed *merely* to begin His Gal. work, for according to their own theory the Gal. Ministry does not begin till

after next Passover. *b.* If John was imprisoned by Herod, how did Christ escape persecution by going to Gal., Herod's kingdom? Christ's mission being religious, not political. Ans: He feared Pharisees, acting upon Herod's example, rather than Herod. His care even in Gal. where their influence was slight, to repress Messianic enthusiasm and His reserve as to his Messiahship, show his apprehension of their hostility.

2. Journey of John 4: 43 is emphasized as though a formal leaving of Judea, while the return to Gal. after feast of John 5 is passed over without mention. Gess. characterizes John 4: 43 as comm. on Mt..4: 14.

3. The discourse with Sam. woman (John 4) precisely accords with this view. Christ, rejected by the Jews, and about entering on His Gal. ministry, discloses the universality of the gospel.

4. Reception given Christ in Gal. (John 4: 45) implies a formal beginning of His work there of which John gives a specimen 4: 46-54. If His work did not commence at this time, if the Syn. account be not inserted here, four months from this arrival until feast of John 5: 1 are unaccounted for, a single miracle alone being recorded. 5. At feast of John 5, John Bapt.'s ministry is referred to as past (v. 35 "*was* a light"), hence his imprisonment and Christ's consequent entering upon the Gal. ministry must be placed before John 5.

II. Those holding journeys of Syn. and John 4 to be different, argue: 1. The exegesis of John 4: 1 implies that John was still at large (vide Aud. p. 162; Wies. 161; Gres. II. 212.) *Ans:* Best comm. explain, "John was not as successful as Jesus."

2. From John 4: 54, "this is again second miracle," etc., which mention seems to indicate that this miracle, like the first at Cana, was something out of the ordinary course of events, it has been argued that the regular Gal. ministry had not yet begun. *Ans:* The emphasis lies upon ἐλθών, i. e., second miracle performed by Christ *coming out of Judea into Galilee.*

3. Hostility of Pharisees undeveloped until charge of Sabbath-breaking at feast (John 5). *Ans:* Hostility in its effects is certainly spoken of in ch. 3: 22 and 4: 3.

4. Unless Syn. account be introduced after John 5, we are obliged to bring in after this time a Passover not

mentioned by Syn. *Ans:* This argument does not hold (*a*) *in measure*—Syn. omit other feasts, e. g., Tabernacles and Dedication—nor (*b*) *in mode*—it is not their plan to record feasts at Jerusalem.

Arguments *pro* and *con* nearly balance. Compromise view is held by Ellicott and Tischendorf, influenced by Wieseler's chronology, who say Syn. journey and that of John 4 is identical, yet Syn. *history* does not commence till after John 5. *Ans:* The statement of Lk. 4:14, "Jesus returned in *power of Spirit* into Gal." is irreconcilable with this view of four months of inactivity. Also statements intimately connected must be forcibly separated. (Tisch. in later editions makes retractions from Wieseler's scheme of chronology.) Result. Weight of authority places John Bap.'s imprisonment at John 4, and thus identifies journeys (So Lange, Gess, Farrar, Robinson, Greswell.)

Discussion of Ques. Second. What was feast of John 5:1? (Vide. Chronology on Duration of Public Ministry also Farrar, Vol. I. p. 368 and Vol. II. p. 467 Excursus VIII.). If the feast be not Passover the Gal. ministry will be shortened by one year. The method of combining these two central points determines the entire Chronology of Gospel History, and a knowledge of it is a key to the understanding of any harmony. Adjustments of different harmonists:

1. *Robinson* identifies the journeys; feast of John 5, he considers Passover: hence, ministry in Eastern Gal. 16 months, in Northern Gal. 6 months, total Gal. ministry 22 months.

2. *Andrew* places Syn. journey after John 5.: considers feast Passover; hence E. Gal. 12 months, N. Gal. 6 months, total Gal. ministry 18 months. Christ inactive in Gal. 4 months before John 5:1.

3. *Lichtenstein*—places Syn. journey after John 5; considers feast Tabernacles (in Oct. 6 months later): hence E. Gal. 6 months, N. Gal. 6 months, total Gal. ministry 1 year. Christ inactive 10 months.

4. *Wieseler*—places Syn. journey after John 5.: considers feast Purim (one month before Passover John 6:4 according to his scheme second Passover): hence E. Gal. 1 month, E. Gal. 6 months, total Gal. ministry 7

months. Result of this plan is demonstration of its falsity, giving but one month to E. Gal. to which other schemes give six or twelve. This was most active period of Christ's life: time is needed for development of Pharisaic opposition, for change of popular sentiment, for growth of faith, for falling off of the merely curious. Mission of Twelve alone would occupy more than one month.

5. Lange, Gess, Farrar—identify journeys; consider feast Purim; avoid Wieseler's brevity in E. Gal. by beginning Gal. ministry between John 4, and 5, thus lengthening E. Gal. to 5 months. They synchronize John 5, and Mt. 11, also John 6. (Second Passover according to their scheme) and Mt. 14.

6. Ellicott, Tischendorf, vide supra. "Compromise view."

General Result. Harmony shows no contradiction invalidating the Gospel narratives. Note. 1. Robinson's scheme, identifying journeys, making feast John 5: 1, Passover, gives needed time in E. Gal. and accounts for facts. Individual bias eliminated, we come back to this scheme.

2. In no respect do these different schemes affect apologetic importance of Harmony. Same periods, with same relations, intentions, and order, occur in all. They differ only as to time of beginning Gal. ministry, its length, and rapidity of its development.

Order of events during this period of ministry in E. Gal: Narrative gathered from three Syn. who are sometimes parallel, sometimes supplemental. In obtaining chronological order, positive statements, when occurring, are to be followed, in other circumstances probabilities are to be considered. The order is more irregular because of activity and great number of events, but the commencement (imprisonment of John) and close (feeding 5000) are fixed. Nothing following the passover of John 6: 4 is to be included in this period, for no interchange of events between periods occurs in several gospels.

Robinson arbitrarily takes Lk. 11–13 : 9 belonging to last journeys to Jerusalem and, breaking up, inserts, in E. Gal. Mk.'s and Lk.'s order scarcely disturbed; only deviations Mk. §§ 24, 58, Lk. §§ 29, 58. Matt. much disturbed in adapting to their order. To justify, note

1. Mt. makes no statement as to sequence in portions changed. *Tote* often used loosely as connective, when no consecution is intended.

2. Mt.'s gospel is topical, e. g., Teaching, 5–7; Miracles, 8–9; Parables, 13. Chronological order *general*; after Feeding 5000, consecutive.

Characteristics of this period, are 1. Activity, frequent journeys, development of plan, miracles and teaching. Christ's greatest success is achieved; opposition is aroused. 2. Preparation for founding the church, rejection of Jews as a nation being not yet final. Christ renews the offer of himself at feast of John 5.

Relation of Gal. to Judean work. Jesus' Messiahship and the future church are the subjects of both periods, but in different order. In Judea the prominent theme is his Messiahship, in Gal. the church, also sacrificial element enters from succeeding period. This blending of the period as record of a single life, the best answer to sceptical objection of irreconcilable discrepancies.

Four successive subjects of this period twice repeated are,

1. *Organization.* Call of apostles, that there may be witnesses of Christ's work, who shall found and guide the church after his ascension. 2. *Miracles.* Attestations of Christ's divinity. Not arbitrary works of power, but a regularly developed system. 3. *Opposition.* At first secret, it increased until Christ was driven from Capernaum, after which it became the main feature of his life. 4. *Teaching.* a. Extended discourses. b. Parables. (Andr. divides arbitrarily by "circuits.")

These topics are interwoven; e. g. call of apostles (organization) is connected with miracles; miracles not only attest divinity, but teach spiritual truth; opposition is linked with teaching (John 10,) and parables (Mt. 21 : 23–46.) Teaching to some extent linked with all. Christ is set forth Prophet (teaching), Priest (propitiation), King (organization). 2nd Passover divides ministry in E. Gal. into two parts of 4 and 12 months. Smaller period, during which Christ's place of work is laid down and developed, is basis of Gal. ministry.

Characteristics of 4 months period. Choice of apostles. Miracles, selected as specimens of important classes. Miracles predominate over teaching. People are first aroused, then taught.

§26. John 4: 43–45. Mt. 4: 17. Mk. 1: 14, 15. Lk. 4: 14, 15. *Arrival in Galilee.* Reception Christ was cordial, Galileans having witnessed Christ's miracles in Jerus., (John 4: 45), John 4: 44 "his own country." Meyer. Alford and Andrews (p. 168) say Gal. is meant; others Nazareth, (Farrar Vol. I. pp. 219); best opinion is Judea, his native country. Supplemental character of John's gospel is seen in calling Judea Christ's country, though not mentioning his birth there. Subject of Christ's teaching: Kingdom of God *at hand*, (Mk. 1: 15.

§27. John 4: 46–54. *Nobleman's son at Capernaum, healed.* Only event recorded by John between Christ's leaving Judea to begin work in Gal., and his return to 2d Passover. (5: 1). John inserts to contrast faith of Galileans—and unbelief of Jews.

v. 54. Emphasis on ελθων, showing Christ wrought this cure "*as he was going*" to Gal. Hence insert before Syn. narratives.

Strauss. This miracle same as that Mt. 8: 15 circumstances being the same; but the differences are contradictions, hence both are false, mere myths based on Naaman's being healed at distance by Elijah. Ans: The differences of time and place, plainly prove two distinct miracles (Trench on Mir. p. 100).

§28. Lk. 4: 16–31, Mt. 4: 13–16. ANNOUNCEMENT, *Rejection at Nazareth.* Do Lk. 4: 16, Mt. 13: 54, Mk. 6: 1 as Lange, Farrar and Lich. say, refer to the same event? Robinson and Andrews hold that these passages record distinct occurrences, because 1. Mt. mentions Christ's removal from Naz. to Cap. prior to Mt. 13: 54 and Mk. 6: 1, Lk. 4: 28–31, assigns his rejection at Naz. as the reason. 2. Lk. 4: 29, 30, after discourse in synagogue, Christ escaped death miraculously; Mk. 6: 5, mentions Christ healing sick at Naz. after discourse thus showing there was no tumult.

3. Two visits not impossible. Would most probably make his own countrymen more than one offer. (Comp. Andrews, p. 198.)

Reason for Visit. Christ first proclaimed his mission at Jerus., the religious centre of God's chosen people. So at the outset of Galilean ministry he affords his own kinsmen earliest opportunity of accepting him. Driven from Nazareth, he goes to Capernaum (Mt. 4 : 13), rejected there, he returns to Nazareth a second time. (Matt. 13 : 54.)

Synagogue usages. (Farrar I. p. 220.) Only instance of Christ's reading, usually addressed the people. (Cp. Acts 13 : 15.) Christ's intentions were not revolutionary. He conforms to Jewish habits. Sacraments are first innovations. First time Christ applies prophecy to himself. Is: 61 : 1, describes work and character of Messiah. Christ declares the passage refers to himself.

Contrast. Christ's rejection at Jerusalem following an act symbolizing judgment (cleansing temple); at Nazareth after proclaiming the gospel. Gospel preaching, severe or mild, to natural man displeasing. Hearers become suddenly enraged, because Christ taught the coming rejection of Jews and calling of Gentiles, illustrating this truth by O. T. facts (1 Kings 17 ; 2 Kings 5 : 14). Blind, impulsive, uncontrollable rage, not to be explained by proverbial rudeness of Nazarines, for Christ's allusions to national rejection.

Was escape miraculous? Not so, some. Impressiveness. (Farrar, I., p. 227.) But as occurred among those familiar with him supernatural escape more consistent. Similar escapes, comp. John 7 : 30 ; 8 : 59 ; 10 : 39.

Lk. 4 : 23. *What miracles?* 1. Cross reference to John, either 2 : 12 (some suppose miracles wrought while on way to 1st Pass.), or, 2. Nobleman's son, John 4 : 46—54.

Settled at Capernaum for at least one year with Peter or his mother. Selected because central, populous : Roman garrison ; commerce in fish ; on caravan route ; sufficiently distant from Tiberias, Herod's capital. Vide. Farrar, I., p. 178.) Mt. 4 : 13, 14, records this as fulfilling Is. 9 : 1, 2, " by way of sea."

Site of Capernaum: It lay in plain of Gennesareth, which was 4 miles in length. Exact locality is unknown ; either Khan Minyeh (Robinson) or Tell Hum (Farrar, p. 181 ; Andrews, pp. 203–220.) Unmentioned in O. Test.

Josephus carried there when wounded. He lays stress on fountains (Jos. iii. 10, §8) and fish. Same fountains at Khan Minyeh, some say. Name Capernaum (Kefr, Nahum, i. e. Village of Nahum) favors Tell Hum. Tell, hill, substituted for Kefr, village: Nahum abbrev. Lake called in O. T., Chinnereth, Josh. 13 : 27. "Harp shape," (Farrar, I., p. 175, note.) Sea of Galilee, of Tiberias, Lake of Gennesaret, 14 miles long, 6 broad, 600 ft. below Medit'n, shut in by hills, abounds with fish. Shores thickly settled, 9 populous cities. Tiberias and Magdala alone remain. Climate varied, both temperate and tropical; vegetation luxuriant, fruit continuous.

§29. ORGANIZATION. Lk. 5 : 1–11; Mt. 4 : 18–22; Mk. 1 : 16–20. Call of Peter, And., James, John, first act of Gal. ministry, that from *beginning* Christ may have witnesses and teachers.

Two theories of call. 1. Naturalistic. Simply adhered to Christ from choice as Bap.'s disciples. Gradually, more devoted and enthusiastic attached themselves more closely to his person. Ans: Contradicts gospel narrative. Call is earliest act of Christ, showing foresight in selecting men best qualified for his work. 2. Mild rationalists admit early call, accounting for it by, *a*, Christ's natural sagacity; *b*. his natural discernment of character. Ans: Inadequate to account for historical phenomena.

Circumstances. *a*, Public, Lk. 5 : 1, so validity of call is attested. *b*, Selected, not from educated, prejudiced class, but simple hearted, best adapted for Christ's work. Their knowledge was to come from inspiration. Extreme poverty erroneous; in good business, partners, had "hired servants." Mk. 1 : 20; "left all" no sacrifice unless something left. Subsequent poverty voluntary. Blunt: Zebedee very old at this time and soon died. Comp. Mt. 8 : 21 " bury my father," Mt. 20 : 20 "*mother* of Zebedee's children." Last, unnatural if Z. alive. *c*. Miracle proved authority of call: illustrated office and work to be undertaken: toil, patience, ultimate success depending upon God, then labor and God's power to coöperate. (Trench, miracles, p. 106.) Some symbolize minutest details. Canon of allegorical interpretation: Those facts alone significant, originally intended to be such. Lk. places call after miracles at Cap. (Lk. 4 : 33–41.) other Syn.

before. Lk. wishes to contrast rejection at Naz. on one Sabbath, enthusiastic reception at Cap. on the next.

Differences. 1. Mt., Mk. record no miracle, Lk. omits Andrew's name, hence some say calls are different. But omissions are not contradictions, and *a* incidents in each are same, *b* after call both accounts say they left all and followed Christ. Lk. records miracle wishing to show deep impression on Peter's mind.

2. Lk. says, called while in boat, one call for all. Mt., Mk. on shore, mending nets, each pair of brothers called separately. Harmonize by making these acts successive. Order. Christ's discourse, miracle, beckoning to other boat for aid, call of Simon and Andrew, Christ afterward walking on shore finds Jas., John mending the broken net and calls them. (Smith's Dict. Peter. p. 2447, Andrews, p. 228.)

3. Syn. apparently contradict John who puts call year previous (John 1 : 35) hence, say sceptics, both accounts mythical. *Ans.* Syn. don't say first call; "at *thy* word" implies previous acquaintance, readiness in leaving business shows minds made up. Gospels give distinct stages of organization in calling of the apostles. *a.* John 1, call at Jordan to be learners, not required to leave home or relinquish business. *b.* Lk. 5. To be witnesses, in constant attendance on Christ. *c.* Mk. 3 : 13, 14. Prior to sermon on Mt. Definite organization of Twelve. *d.* Lk. 9 : 1–6. Temporary commission conferring authority to preach and work miracles. Full apostolic authority, not until Pentecost. *Miracle* is an event in external world due to immediate agency of God. (Hodge's Theol. Vol. I. p. 618.)

Some argue effect here might be produced without divine interference, by union of second causes and divine prescience, hence analogous to prophecy. Supernatural element just as great but strictly miraculous element, i. e. immediate exercise of divine power, does not enter. (Comp. *stater* in fish's mouth Mt. 17 : 27. Comp. Ps. 8 : 8). Trench insists on this distinction : allow second causes where we can. But, 1. These two cases belong to class of events where Divine efficiency is intended to be set forth. Ordinary reader makes no distinction. 2. Impression on mind of eye witnesses opposes this dis-

tinction. 3. Symbolical import of miracle overlooked by this view. It teaches, God not only foreknows, but his power coöperates with human.

MIRACLES. 1. *Classification.* Some speak of miracles of knowledge, of power, of love. But such classification is objectionable, for, according to definition, all miracles are acts of power. If they are not acts of Divine power immediately exercised they are not miracles. The expression " Miracle " should be kept distinct and applied to a special class of events. Regeneration etc. should not be termed miracle. Power, love, etc. may however be used to distinguish the main design of the miracle.

2. *Various names.* (Vide Trench p. 75). Gospels speak of *a. σημειαν*, a token of presence and working of God. *b. τερας*, a wonder, astonishment of beholder transferred to the work. *c. δυναμεις*, powers i. e. of God. *d. εργα*, works i. e. of Divinity.

3. Twofold design, and proof of each. *a.* Attract attention and impress; for always in the presence of witnesses; cases of popular sympathy; impression always recorded. *b.* Relieve suffering; for same *are* might have been produced by miracles of different characters, i. e. of judgment. Fig-tree cursed is the only miracle of this class. Destruction of swine work of demons, not of Christ. *c.* Teach truth: they are *dramatized parables*, each teaching some aspect of truth.

They teach: *a.* Christ's power and willingness to save souls; *b.* Sinner's condition and way of approach, by prayer and faith. Disease and death are parts of the penalty of sin inflicted by the curse of the law; hence when these are removed a prrt of the punishment of sin is removed. Mt. 8: 16, 17 quoted from Is. 53: 4. The atonement also is thus taught, Christ bearing *our* sins. *d.* Attest Christ's claims; for Christ says (Lk. 5: 23, 24) " whether is easier " . . . " but that *ye may know* " etc. Vide also Mt. 11: 3–5. Rationalists say, "if these miracles were real, why disbelieved? Ans: Abraham's answer is sufficient, Lk. 16: 31.

Christ's miracles *contrasted* with those of O. T. and of Apostles. 1. His were performed by his own power. Others were wrought in his name or that of God. It is no fair exception, as Rationalists declare, that Christ is said to sometimes work " by power of God," " by spirit of God," " by finger of God." There were special reasons for Christ's procedure on these special occasions. Sometimes also Christ's true humanity is expressed by his faith. 2. O. T. miracles were punitive, those of Christ were miracles of mercy. 3. O. T. miracles largely confined to the sphere of nature; Christ's were performed in all spheres, the larger portion on man. 4. O. T. miracles wrought with delay, wrestling in prayer; Christ's were performed with ease, instantaneously.

The number of Christ's miracles must have been indefinitely great; as the cases recorded are mere specimens. Vide Mt. 4: 24, 8: 16, 11: 5, 14: 2, 15: 30. We may imagine that no cases which could be brought to him were not brought. Wherever Christ went disease and death disappeared. Thus was signified the fulness and sufficiency of Christ's salvation.

A selection from this vast number is made upon the principle that each case shall make prominent some new phase of truth. When repeated it is because of a difference in method of cure, or the effect upon the subject, or on account of some new development in the work of Christ.

Number recorded. Some include those of which Christ was the subject, e. g., birth, resurrection, escape from populace. Others include also the case of Mary Magdalene, although it is not mentioned in detail. Omitting these the number may be given as 35. 9 on external nature, 26 of healing. Mt. records 20, Mk. 18, Lk. 20, John 8. Only one is common to all evangelists, viz. feeding of 5,000. Eleven are common to three, viz. 10 to Mt., Mk. and Lk.; 1 to Mt., Mk., John. Six were common to two, viz., 3 to Mt., Mk., 2 to Mt., Lk., 1 to Mk., Lk. Mt. records 3 alone, Mk. 2, Lk. 6, John 6.

Various principles of classification. 1. With reference to *power* displayed and sphere of exercise; upon man; upon nature; inanimate and animate; upon spirit world. 2. By truths embodied. *a.* Christ a Savior with almighty power. *b.* Character of sinner, blind, polluted, disabled. 3. By faith of recipient, whether personal or intercessory, strong or weak, that of a Jew or Gentile. 4. Mode of working, at hand or at a distance, by word or touch. It is impossible to make a perfect classification.

Theories. 1. Rationalistic. Miracles are impossible. Those seemingly miraculous occurrences alone took place which may be explained naturally. A distinction is made between miracles of healing and those in which nature is the subject of Christ's power. The former are admitted because they may be naturally explained; the latter are denied because inexplicable. Their presence in the narrative is accounted for upon the *mythical* hypothesis. Paulus: Jesus was a physician, having acquired his art from the Essenes; he gave prescriptions; a list of medicines is enumerated from contemporaneous authors. Celsus: Christ performed miracles by means of magical arts learned in Egypt. Renan: Christ performed miracles against his will. Popular expectation as to the Messiah compelled him to become a wonder-worker. Hence his miracles were mere deceptions.

Ans: The Scripture narrative represents Christ as working without means, and producing by word alone instantaneous effects.

II.. Psychologico-Ethical. Christ's miracles the result of animal magnetism; due simply to the influence of mind over the bodily condition. The theory is based upon observed facts, proving *a*, a mysterious influence of mind over mind, and, *b*, the influence of mind and will over body. In support of this view, 1. They argue from Scripture, that faith was required in all cases in the recipient or the cure could not be performed, e. g., no miracles in Nazareth "because of unbelief," Mt. 13:58. In Gal. generally the people were in sympathy with him, hence he could perform miracles. 2. Stress is laid on Christ's human sympathy, his commanding presence, his superior spirituality. Thus he projected himself into the consciousness of others. Some miracles, e. g., raising of dead, healing of congenital blindness, cure of leper, cannot be thus explained. Hence some are rejected. As to others, it is said that Christ merely declared a cure already wrought.

Strauss: Derogatory to make Christ's success depend not on teaching but on momentary power. Character of Jesus is weighted down with these cures. O. T. records cures, therefore Christ performed some, but only when he could not avoid so doing." Stress laid on "sign" being asked for, hence no miracles performed. "Sign of Jona" referred to the preaching of Jonah. Christ commanded the discip'es of Baptist to report to him the spiritual results of his work—not real miracles—when he said "the blind see," etc., Mt. 11:4, 5.

Strauss rejects all miraculous cures; all miracles with accompanying conversations; miracles introduced later to explain the conversation; all mentioned as occurring twice; all to which there are analogous parables—the allegory transformed by later writers into a miracle. Thus the number is reduced, the residuum is explained away.

All such writers are involved in the following dilemma: either Christ is a mere enthusiast, not above the people, or a conscious deceiver. In either case how could Christ be a moral teacher, the author of the Christian religion? Yet this they hold.

§30. Mk. 1:21-38. Lk. 4:31-37. *Healing Demoniac in Synagogue.* Lk. says Christ's first Sabbath in Cap'm: next after rejection at Nazareth. Taught in Synag. with *authority:* during service healed demoniac. Miracles of dispossession peculiar to N. T. δαίμων, δαιμόνιον, in Homer θεός; in later Gk. (Plato) beings intermediate between God and man; Philo and Josephus, souls of men, especially the wicked; Socrates, good spirit, tutelar divinity; LXX., heathen idols, hence Paul (1 Cor. 10:19), heathen sacrifice to δαιμονια. E. V. "devils" incorrect, for in N. T. but one διάβολος. His servants are *demons.* (Smith's Dic'y, Demons. p. 583.) (Demoniacs, Trench, p. 125. Neander's Life Christ, pp. 145-151.)

Design of this class of miracles is to exhibit man as by nature the helpless bond-slave of Satan, and Christ as the only one able to effect his deliverence. While Christ was upon earth peculiar license seems granted to evil spirits. His power over them, besides attesting his divinity was fulfillment of the Protevangelium. Gen. 3:15. Seven curses (including Mary Magdelene) of demoniacal posession are recorded.

Objections. 1. Phenomena of possession contradict consciousness. Will is free. It cannot be so wholly controlled by an unseen being much less could several demons possess one man. *Ans.* We must not look to

consciousness for information respecting facts outside the sphere of consciousness. Scripture teaches Satan has access to minds of men, to lead them captive at his will. Possession must have accorded with their nature and ours.

2. Possession not recorded elsewhere in Scripture and does not now occur: *Ans.* Latter position cannot be proved. Special propriety of such cases at time of Christ: culmination of the conflict between the kingdoms of good and evil. Saul is an instance found in O. Test. 3. No curse of this kind mentioned in John but all are in Gal. *Ans.* Silence proves nothing. John does introduce the obnoxious doctrine. John 8 : 48. "hast a devil," 13 : 27 "after the sop Satan entered into him." John records only miracles introducing long discourses, hence these omitted. 4. Demoniacal possession is analogous to mania, idocy, epilepsy, etc., hence mere nervous affections controllable by will power. Jesus, possessing great personal magnetism, wrought these apparently miraculous cures. *Ans.* Mythical theory here is inconsistent; aiming to prove the gospels myths, it admits that narrative of these cures relates actual, historical events, hence becomes Naturalistic. Dogmatic theory of Baur. Victory of Christ over heathenism set forth under this symbolic form. Accommodation Theory. Spinoza: Christ, though not sharing popular superstitions, accommodated himself to them, by acting as though the cases of possession were real, while he knew they were only apparent. Christ's literal words are parabolic. *Ans:* a, This view irreconcilable with Christ's character, as portrayed by those who hold it. It charges him with conscious deception. b, Christ's language is not hypothetical, but explicit. Separate personality of demons is evident, for Christ distinguishes demon from person possessed, addresses them, they answer, when cast out man becomes as other men, they enter herd of swine, &c. (Vide. Ebrard, p. 251, Farrar, I., p. 236, note.)

Christ silenced ($\varphi\iota\mu\omega\vartheta\eta\tau\iota$=be muzzled) demon's testimony (Lk. 4 : 34, 35) because, a, He would not accept testimony of such a witness. b, To permit such a title, "Holy One of God," at this stage of his work would have precipitated Pharisaic hostility. Prominent features of dispossession: loud voice, crying, bodily prostration.

Effect: Christ's authority established; his fame spread abroad; attention attracted to his preaching. (Mark 1: 27-28.

§31. Matt. 8:14-17; Mk. 1:29-34; Luke 4:38-41. *Peter's Wife's Mother.* This miracle wrought same day as preceding. Mt.'s plan being topical, not chronolog'l, this is grouped with other miracles in ch. 8. Disease, *great* "fever," πυρετῷ μεγάλῳ being medical phrase, it has been inferred Luke was physician, and had personal knowledge of the case. Fever probably signifies general disability of sinner joined with burning restlessness of sinful desires. Mode of cure: Christ stood over her (Lk.), took her hand, lifted her up (Mk.) and rebuked the fever (Lk.) Note completeness of cure; no weakness, nor gradual convalescence, but " immediately she arose and ministered unto them." (Trench on Mir., p. 192.)

Sceptics argue from " *rebuked* fever," either possession is ordinary disease, or fever is possession. Ans: Use of figurative language is overlooked. This is an isolated case—fever personified; it does not answer or cry out. Comp. Christ's command to winds, " Peace, be still."

This is first time Peter is distinguished above the other apostles; miracle worked in his own family. Compare "*wife's* mother," Mk. 1:30 and 1 Cor. 9:5. Mk. 1:32, 33, says at sunset, whole city brought sick to Christ. Some say, waited until evening, because unlawful to heal on Sabbath, but that objection not yet raised. Observe that it is first proposed by Pharisaic emissaries from Jerus'm. True explanation, cool of evening proper time to move the sick. This Sabbath a specimen day. Crowds seek him next morning. Note " all that were diseased," contrasted with "them possessed with devils," Mk. 1:32. Hence possession differs from ordinary disease.

§32. Mk. 1:35-39; Lk. 4:42-44; Mt. 4:23-25. *First Circuit in Galilee.* Mk. 1:38, 39, contains Christ's first intimation of future plan of labor. Taken in connection with disciples' statement v. 37, it teaches his work was not stationary, Cap. being selected merely as headquarters. It is conjectured this circuit very brief, but a week, a single miracle being recorded. Christ's work itinerant and thorough (Mk. 1:39, " synagogues in *all* Galilee"). Christ's method, teaching in synagogues; his doctrine,

"kingdom of God," "gospel of the kingdom." Note Christ's habit of private devotion, Mk. 1:35.

§38. Mt. 8: 2–4; Mk. 1: 40–45; Lk. 5: 12–16. *Healing Leper*. Ebrard, Trench, Lange, follow Mt.'s order; Robinson, Lk's, who more carefully observes chronolog. sequence. Ten lepers only recorded cure of this disease Lk. 17: 12). These two instances are only specimens, Comp. Mt. 10: 8; 11: 5; Lk. 4: 27; Lk. 7: 22. Josephus notes current slander that Jews driven from Egypt because of leprosy. Two kinds of leprosy. *a*. Elephantiasis. (Job). *b*. White Leproys, kind mentioned in Leviticus and gospels. Ceremonial law, Lev. 13. Sufferer clothed in mourning, with head bare and garments rent. When pronounced clean, ceremonies occupying a week were requisite and all classes of sacrifice. Import of these requirements. Two views. 1. Michaelis and Rationalistic School say were civil acts to prevent spread of contagion, and for social protection. Ans: *a*. Disease was hereditary, but probably not contagious, e. g., Naaman, general of Syrian army. (2 Kings 5: 1) Gehazi conversed with king of Israel (2 Kings 8: 5). (Trench on Mir. p. 174). *b*. This view does not account for the religious rites, or sense of moral impurity attaching to this disease.

2. True view. Leprosy selected as most appropriate type of nature of sin; hereditary, spreading from single spot over entire body, incurable by human agencies, loathsome. Lepers were thought smitten by God. Hence Vulg. renders Is. 53: 4 "*quasi leprosum*" giving rise to idea that Christ was to be a leper. (Farrar Vol. I. p. 149). So Talmud and early church, hence disease in honor.

Christ healing leprosy typified his ability to save from sin. Symbolic nature of this disease is seen in form of leper's request, to be *cleansed*, not healed and in, Christ's answer "Be thou clean." Christ *touched* the leper, although contrary to Mosaic law. Lev. 13: 24–46; Num. 5: 2. Shewing that in his saving work he shrinks from no man however polluted. (Farrar Vol. I. p. 275).

Leper commanded to shew himself to priests (Lev. 14: 4). *a*. To gain official recognition of cure. *b*. To exhibit his relation to the law. Christ enjoins secresy

(Mk. 1: 44). Objection—cure wrought in presence of multitudes, hence secresy impossible. Lange, Farrar, Andrews, cure wrought in presence of but few. Grotius, Bengel, Alexander, injunction limited to time between cure and shewing himself to priests. (Trench on Mir. p. 180). Better opinion: Christ intended to repress fanatical enthusiasm, which would hinder his work. He would subordinate works to word. He would not attract people as mere miracle-worker, but as Saviour. (Andrews p. 235. Farrar Vol. I. 277). Man disobeying and spreading report, (Mk. 1: 45). Christ was forced to avoid all centres of population because of undue popular zeal. Supposition that Christ's retirement was caused by ceremonial uncleanness, is fanciful. Naturalistic view. Schenkel. Leprosy could not be healed by will power; hence man was nearly well, Christ observing this, simply announced it.

§34. OPPOSITION. Mk. 2: 1-12; Lk. 5: 17-26; Mt. 19: 2-8. *Healing Paralytic* on Christ's return to Cap'm after Gal. circuit. Read Mt. 9: 1 as conclusion of ch. 8 and follow Mk.'s order. Mt. grouping miracles places this as though wrought upon Christ's return from country of Gergesenes.

This class of diseases exhibits the helplessness of sinner. In healing them Christ always commands patient to move the part paralyzed, thus setting forth nature and power of true faith. Christ's command "Be clean," in last miracle, emphasizes pollution of sin, "arise and walk," its power. Mk. 2: 1, ἐν οἴκῳ, "at home," not "in the house." Observe new step in teaching, by miracles. Christ addresses man, "Thy sins be (correctly, *have been*, ἀφέωνται, Doric perf. pass., not subj.) forgiven thee," thus directing attention away from mere external result to its spiritual signification.

Some falsely infer from Christ's address that the palsy was due to sinful indulgence, or that Christ accommodates himself to idea that all suffering was direct punishment of specific sin. Scribes and Pharisees secretly charge Christ with blasphemy. They were right in supposing God alone could forgive sins, wrong in not accepting proofs of Christ's divinity.

Emphasis of Christ's reply (Lk. 5: 23) rests on "*say*" i. e. claim to be able. The former claim any one might

make, the latter is more difficult of proof. At Christ's word the man is healed. People are astonished and glorify God. v. 24. Revelation of conscious divinity. New element: Pharisaic opposition. While people welcome Christ with enthusiasm Pharisees, for first time, raise opposition in Gal. This opposition was due to influence of Pharisees at Jerus. and though not officially sanctioned by them, shows they were carefully watching Christ's movements.

§35. Mt. 9: 9; Mk. 2: 13, 14; Lk. 5: 27, 28. *Call of Matthew.* Call of Mt. to be Christ's apostle is related to development of Pharisaical opposition, in the fact, Mt. was publican and specially obnoxious to this sect (Andrews p. 238.) The feast of Levi (Mt.) did not occur at this time because 1. Twelve were with Christ at feast, at call Mt. All not yet chosen. 2. Feast interrupted by message of Jairus. Raising of Jairus' daughter occurred subsequent to Christ's return from Gadara. Mt.'s call previous to this. 3. Breach with Pharisees too marked for this early period.

Mk. and Lk. relate under exactly similar circumstances, call of Levi, yet in their lists of apostles mention no Levi, but Matthew. Levi was probably original name, changed upon becoming apostle. Comp. Simon changed to Cephas. (John 1: 42.) Matthew—'gift of God.'

Publican hateful to Jews, being constant reminder of Roman domination, and taking advantage of his position to practice great extortion. Humility of Mt. seen in fact, he alone records his name as " the publican." Mt. 10: 3. (Farrar, Vol. I, p. 245.) For sceptical inferences. vide. Ebrard, p. 265.

§36. John 5: 1–47. *Second Passover.* Galilean work is here interrupted by a brief visit to Jerus. to attend feast. Hostility of Pharisees compels Christ's speedy return to Gal. not going again to Jerus. for eighteen months.

Reasons for inserting John 5, here. 1. Lk. §37 gives note of time viz. $\sigma\alpha\beta\beta\acute{\alpha}\tau\omega$ [$\delta\varepsilon\upsilon\tau\varepsilon\rho\sigma\pi\rho\acute{\omega}\tau\omega$]. Text here is doubtful, interpretation uncertain, the adjective never occuring elsewhere. Wieseler suggests the reference is to " *first Sabbath* in the *second* of the cycle of seven years, which completed the sabbatical period." Wetstein, " the first sabbath of the second month."

Andrews explains with reference to annual feasts. First Sabbath after Passover was *first* first Sabbath ; first after Pentecost was *second*—first Sabbath ; first after Tabernacles was *third*—first Sabbath ; Comp. modern usage—first Sunday after Epiphany, first after Easter, first after Trinity, &c. (Andrews, p. 241.)

Scaliger, Ewald, Keim, Robinson, etc. suppose this sabbath to be the first after the second day of Passover, from which the fifty days to Pentecost were counted; the Sabbaths of this interval being numbered, the first Sabbath after second day, third Sabbath after second day, etc. (Andrews p. 240. Lightfoot on Mt. 12: 1.)

Last view is to be preferred, it being the only explanation appealing to popular usage; likely that such a term would be current with the masses. 2. Agrees best with season of year. Standing corn ripe enough to be plucked and eaten. This could not be before Passover, being the time for offering first fruits. 3. Results obtained. The occurrences of this feast, if introduced here, harmonize precisely with Syn. narrative. The agreement amounts almost to demonstration. A connected account of the development of Pharisaic opposition, is furnished, three successive instances being noted, viz. its outbreak, at the healing of paralytic, §34, its growth at Christ's call of the publican, §35, its increasing definiteness at Passover, §36. At the feast of John 5: 1, for the first time, Christ is charged with Sabbath breaking. In the Syn. narrative the same charge is taken up and pressed by his enemies in Gal. The inference is unavoidable, that John 5 should be inserted here. The supposition that *at this time* Christ went up to the Passover and was there openly charged with being a Sabbath-breaker, by the Jews, Pharisees, the highest religious authorities, gives the best and only adequate explanation of the introduction *at this point* by the Syn. of the same charge, as preferred against him by the Pharisees of Gal. Christ had previously wrought many cures in Gal. on Sabbath, and even in the Synagogues, without Pharisees making slightest opposition, but their bitter persecution of him on this ground, henceforward, admits of easy explanation, when we find from John 5, that Jerus. Pharisees attempt to kill him because of a Sabbath cure. 4. Gal. ministry

began after John 4. Where can John 5, be inserted? This the only place.

Site of Bethesaida cannot be accurately determined. It was near Sheep Gate (i. e. market), which was toward the N. E. of the city. Robinson identifies with small intermittent spring called fount of the Virgin. Objected to, as not large enough for the five porches, and multitude of "sick folk."

Weight of authority rejects v. 3 (latter clause) and whole of v. 4. Wanting in, B, D, and Sinaitic. Internal arguments against its genuineness are, 1. Never alluded to elsewhere. If such spring existed, its fame would be world wide. 2. Wholly out of analogy with miracles of O. and N. T. No spiritual truth is connected with it, to be believed or attested. Angelic agency never recorded as working miracles elsewhere. (Farrar Vol. I. p. 372. Note.) In favor Text Recpt, Owen on John, in loco. Reference to angel is variously interpreted.

1. *Literal*. The text accepted with all its difficulties, on ground, that narrative is not impossible. 2. *Naturalistic*. Hengstenberg, Robinson. Spring simply medicinal, its properties due to angelic agency, but the cure not always immediate, nor all cured.

3. *Allegorical*. Take ἄγγελος in etymological sense, "messenger," then spring is spoken of figuratively as God's messenger. 4. *Best*. Reject the doubtful verses, and the difficulty vanishes with them.

Sabbath observance was test question. By it the Jews were distinguished from Gentile nations. It was the chief mark of their national and theocratic fidelity. At time of Christ the ascendancy of mere ritual was such, that its spiritual observance was scarcely known. Innumerable, minute and absurd regulations, had taken the place of the Mosaic law. It was with this dead formality, that Christ came constantly into conflict, and on account of it was so repeatedly charged with Sabbath breaking. (Farrar Vol. I. p. 430, §5). vv. 16-18. Jews "sought to slay him." Many regard this as official sentence of Sanhedrim, and Christ's discourse (v. 19-47) a defence delivered before them. No evidence that this was the case; the murderous purpose to kill Christ is now found, a pretext on which to base it is obtained, but the formal decree to slay him is made some months later.

Christ's discourse contains clear and profound statement of his relations to the Father. In Syn. he presents only popular arguments. Lessons of the discourse: 1. God works ceaselessly. Sabbath commemorates rest from creation not cessation from all work. 2. Christ's work identical with God's, not mere imitation, and is based upon his immediate perfect knowledge of the Father. 3. Christ the source of life, and the judge of all. Resurrection and judgment referred to. Eternal generation taught. 4. Necessity and responsibility of exercising faith in himself; rejecting him is to reject God. Rage of Jews aroused because he claimed God as his Father, "making himself equal with God." The Pharisees, therefore, understood Christ as claiming divinity.

Strauss alleges discrepancy in the gospel narrative of the development of opposition to Christ on the ground, that Syn. make its growth gradual, occasioned by Sabbath-breaking, while John traces it to Christ's teaching concerning his person, causing sudden outbreak.

Ans: This discrepancy much exaggerated. All four evangelists make the origin of organized opposition, Sabbath-breaking. All difference in their accounts of its development is due to the characteristic difference of Christ's ministry in Judea and Gal. In Judea his great design was to manifest himself plainly to Jews as Messiah: in Gal. to instruct believers who should organize the church; in Judea he had to deal with the rulers, his enemies: in Gal. with the people who heard him gladly.

Christ's allusion to John Bap.'s testimony as already past (v. 35) strengthens the view that Gal. ministry began previous to John 5.

§37. Mt. 12 : 1–8; Mk. 2 : 23–28; Lk. 6 : 1–5. *Plucking Corn on the Sabbath.* This incident occurred first Sabbath after Passover, while Christ was travelling, either to visit different synagogues, or more likely, hastening from Jerus. back to Gal. to escape impending persecution.

Conduct of Pharisees now changes. Hitherto their hostility had been secret, henceforward their emissaries follow Christ, striving to harass him, and destroy his influence. Plucking the corn was sanctioned by Mosaic law (Deut. 23 : 25.) Christ replies to the charges of the

Pharisees with five arguments. 1. David's eating shew bread. (I. Sam. 21 : 1–7.) Point of comparison between this case and Christ's is the breaking of law. Law of Sabbath and law of sanctuary derived their authority not from their essential holiness but from God alone, and if in certain circumstances it was just for a man to break the one, why might it not be lawful to break the other. 2. Law itself required of the priests more arduous toil on Sabbath than on other days, in performing temple services.

3. Hos. 6 : 6. "I desire mercy, not sacrifice." The design of the law was blessing; by their formality Pharisees had made it a curse. 4. Sabbath designed for man. Analogous to 3d. Sabbath instituted for man's good, and not to be so burdened with observances that his higher interests become subordinate to them. 5. Christ's supreme authority ; " Son of man, Lord of Sabbath" ; Sabbath law could be altered by him with same authority as by God. Observe supplemental character of gospels : of these five arguments, but two are common to all the evangelists. Note increasing self-revelation of Christ recorded by Syn.; he is greater than temple; has authority over law equal to God. Thus Syn. and John differ, not as to Christ's personal consciousness of Messiahship, but merely as to his mode of manifesting it.

§38. Mt. 12 : 9–14 ; Mk. 3 : 1–6 ; Lk. 6 : 6–11. *Healing withered hand on Sabbath.* Occurred after Christ's return to Galilee. Mk. uses definite article, *"the* synagogue," probably the one in Cap. Wieseler's chronological scheme giving him too many Sabbaths, for this month, he makes this Sabbath and the preceding, consecutive days, one the weekly Sab. the other a feast Sab. Pharisees watch Christ to find pretext for persecuting him. Christs asks them " Is it lawful to do good on the Sabbath-days or to do evil ? to save life or to kill ?" Some say this question is unfair ; the Pharisees never held it was right to do wrong. Ans. Christ takes extreme case. Their forbidding attendance on sick on Sabbath day, involved serious responsibility, possibly loss of life. Not to do good was to do evil. Christ had also in view their purpose to kill him, hence uses this *ad hominem* argument : He intended to relieve suffering, they were conspiring to murder him; which kept Sabbath better? He also argues from their practice. They would never hesitate to pull a sheep out of a pit on Sabbath, yet forbade healing a crippled man. Talmud now forbids such help to animals, but the injunction was perhaps occasioned by Christ's argument, as there was nothing of the kind in force then. Effect of this miracle was not as formerly, to excite admiration of all, but filled Pharisees with rage and led them to counsel with Herodians against Christ.

Herodians. 1. Westcott's view. (Smith's Dict. p. 1054.) Those who saw in the Herods a protection against direct heathen rule, and those who looked with satisfaction upon such a compromise between the ancient faith and heathen civilization as Herod the Great and his successors aimed at, as the true and highest consummation of Jewish hopes. 2. Common view. Herods mere tools of Roman gov't, and the Herodians mere sycophants, favoring Roman rule. Their union with Pharisees, politically their opponents, is a great step in the opposition organizing against Christ.

§39. Mt. 12: 15-21; Mk. 3: 7-12. *Success*. Christ's popularity, despite increasing opposition grew so greatly, that multitudes follow him from all parts of the country, Gal., Judea, Idumea, beyond Jordan, Tyre and Sidon. So great are the crowds, he is forced to enter a boat "lest they should throng him." Multitudes typify final success of the gospel and were fulfillment of Is. 11: 10; 42: 1, which predict the Gentiles as sharers in Messianic blessings.

The first stage of development of opposition is now ended, and the subject of teaching becomes prominent. The people having been aroused and drawn to him, they are prepared to hear his words.

§40. ORGANIZATION. Mt. 10: 2-4; Mk. 3: 13-19; Lk. 6: 12-19. *Appointment of the Twelve*. This is third step in organization, first at Jordan, second at Sea of Galilee. Mk. and Lk. clearly connect this, with Sermon on Mount; Mt., however joins it with their temporary mission. Lk. 6: 13. Note, different classes of followers distinguished, disciples in general and apostles chosen from these. Nature of office. 1. To be with him as witnesses. 2. To preach. 3. To work miracles. Mk.

3 : 14, 15. These qualifications preclude the permanency of this office. In gospels name *apostle* occurs but nine times, Mt., Mk. and John once each, Lk. six times, in Acts more than thirty times. They were "learners" until Pentecost, after that fully apostles. Their miraculous power was not coequal with that of Christ but was limited to healing sick, raising dead, demoniacal possession. They had no power over nature, only over man, their cures being illustrations of their saving work. Number twelve, significant of perfection (Lange on Mt. in loco.) Comp. 12 sons Jacob, stones of Jordan, High Priest's breast-plate, 12 spies, 12 foundations of New Jerus., 144,000, perfection perfected, the church in heaven (Rev.) There are four lists of apostles; three in gospels, one in Acts 1 : 13. Each contains three classes of four each. Peter heads the list. Each class invariably begins with the same name. Iscariot is always last. Lebbeus (Mt.,) Thaddeus (Mk.,) and Judas the brother of Jas. (Lk.) are commonly considered as referring to same person. (Farrar Vol. I., p. 251.)

§41. TEACHING. Mt. 5: 1 to 8: 1; Lk. 6: 20–49. *Sermon on Mount.* Contrast in point of simplicity, profundity, grasp of principles, and authority, between Christ's teaching and that of heathen philosophers or Jewish schools, affords clear proof of his divinity. Four forms of Christ's teaching. 1. Long discourses in John relating to his person. 2. Long discourses in Syn. concerning kingdom of Heaven, involving his person and sacrifice. Longest are, Sermon on Mt., and denunciations of woe against Pharisees. 3. Parables, setting forth the nature of kingdom of heaven, the duties and relations of its individual members. 4. Short sayings, pithy statements often repeated. Self-testimony of Christ in John, is contained in long discourses; in Syn. it consists in the titles he assumes (e. g. Son of David, Son of Man, Son of God), and claims which he makes, (e. g. to forgive sins, to raise dead, to judge, &c.)

1. *Son of God.* Expressions most frequent in John. Theories. *a.* Lowest, Pantheistic. Strauss and Baur. Great truth of Christ's teaching was universal fatherhood of God, as contrasted with the vindictive Jehovah of O. T. Christ's conviction of God's love to man and man's

dependence upon God, raised him to his high plane of thought, but being unacquainted with Pantheistic philosophy, he erred in conceiving of God as a personal being. As most vividly apprehending the fatherhood of God, he is styled son of God. *b.* Ewald. By this title Christ claimed nothing divine. Only higher, purer, religious union with God. To him was given a perfect divine communication, making him conscious (1) that there was to be a perfected rule of God upon the earth, (2) that he was to introduce it as its king. *c.* Orthodox view. Christ, Son of God, by eternal generation.

2. *Son of Man.* Expression occurs 78 times in gospels, and but 4 times out of them. Christ's chosen term for himself. It is applied to him by others but twice. Theories. *a.* At first, expressive merely of essential humanity and humiliation, of the fact that Christ's sympathies unite him as a brother, to all men.

Change occurs toward close of his ministry and the title is used as containing Messianic force. Comp. Mt. 24: 30; 26: 64 with Dan. 7: 13, 14, a Messianic prediction. *b.* Title denoted Christ was ideal man, nothing superhuman. Gess remarks, this view irreconcilable with Christ's constant claims of divine attributes. *c.* Orthodox. "The Son of Man," above other men, distinguished by some peculiarity, which may be discovered by considering what is predicted of him, viz., divine honors, prerogatives, etc.

Why does Christ employ this title? 1. Ans: *Incognito* to hide his real divine nature till men should be prepared to accept him. So Ewald, Bleek. 2. A mere circumlocution for Jesus, with which it is interchanged. 3. Used to set forth Christ's Messiahship. The title "*Messiah*" could not be employed because of the false ideas of the people respecting it. Had he assumed this title men would have expected him to fulfill their wrong conceptions. Jesus would not be called Christ until late in his life. Only once did he call himself "the Christ;" and that was at his trial and led to his condemnation. The title evidently contains the two ideas of exaltation and humiliation. After the Resurrection it was not used by the disciples. It is evidently based on Ps. 8, and Dan. 7: 13, 14. Gess sees a reference to the Protevangelium, Gen. 3: 15.

The expressions "kingdom of heaven," "kingdom of God," should also be noticed. "Kingdom of God" is employed by Mk., Lk. and John. Matt. used the phrase but twice. His expression is Kingdom of Heaven (τῶν οὐρανῶν, plur., Heb. form, alluding to different spheres.) Some regard the two expressions as identical. Heaven is put for God as being the place of his dwelling. This, however, does not explain Matt.'s exclusive use of one. Others, therefore, say the phrase "kingdom of heaven" is used by Matt. to contrast the new stage of God's rule with that of O. T. theocracy, i. e. gospel is heavenly fulfillment of God's rule on earth. "Kingdom of God" is equally applicable to both dispensations. The same essential idea is, however, involved in both. Diff. views held as to what Christ intended to do in establishing "the kingdom": 1. Infidel. Christ attempted to establish an earthly kingdom, to free the Jews, but perished in the attempt. 2. Rationalistic. *a*, He aimed at political regeneration. Seeing that social reform was necessary to this, he became a moralist. *b*, Christ at first held the same view as Pharisees. Gradually his mistaken ideas were corrected, and he sought to carry on a spiritual work. Renan : Christ vacillates between these two views of his work, the Pharisaic and Spiritual. 3. Accommodation--Schleiermacher, Schenkel : The aim which Christ had in his mind was simply to found as a teacher a moral, spiritual system. He however accommodated himself in his instructions to the popular misconceptions of the people with regard to the theocracy. Either he, like the people, was blinded by misunderstanding, or he made use of their false notions to elevate them.

Sermon on the Mount. Christ now gives a fuller and more orderly arranged specimen of his teaching than he had previously afforded the people. The time has now come for a more complete revelation, that friends and foes may be separated and the gospel system somewhat consolidated. *Place.* According to tradition the Mt. of Beatitudes, a lime-stone ridge 7 or 8 m. S. W. of Cap'm, called Kurn Hattin on account of its two peaks. To this identification Robinson objects that the Mt. is too far distant from Cap'm to be consistent with Matt. 8 : 5 and Lk. 7 : 1. The tradition, also, is only in the Latin church and from the 13th century. Matt. and Lk. differ. As to *place*, Mt. says, "went up into a mountain and sat;" Lk., "came down and stood in the plain." Mt. however uses τὸ ὄρος in a wide sense—a mountain district. Christ "went up to pray," (Lk. 6 : 12) and came down, i. e. part way, to the level plain between the two peaks, and taught. As to *time*, Mt. places it at commencement of Gal. ministry; Lk. puts it some months later in connection with the call of the Twelve. The miracle following in Mt. is healing of leper; in Lk., healing of centurion's servant. In *length*, Mt. gives 107 verses; Lk. but 30. The accounts *resemble* one another in the facts that both are mountain sermons occurring early in Gal. ministry; that the beginning and close are alike in both, and the drift of thought is the same. *Theories of the relation between the two.* 1. Two accounts of the same sermon, blurred and distorted by tradition. Some follow Mt. as most complete, others Luke as presenting fewest difficulties. 2. Conscious selection lies at base of differences; one discourse purposely varied by Evangelists; Lk. omits what was special to Jews. This coincides with differences, but does not offer an adequate explanation. 3. *Common.* One discourse; Lk.'s account historical as Christ gave it; Mt.'s an amplification by additions grouped from other discourses, analogous to Mt.'s plan in parables. A specimen of Christ's teaching. Objection to this is the unity of Mt.'s account. Calvin and Neander hold that both Mt. and Lk. give specimens of Christ's teaching. 4. Two discourses on same occasion, the one esoteric (Mt.'s) to the disciples, the other exoteric (Lk.'s) to the multitude. (So Augustine, Lange). Objections: There is nothing esoteric in Mt. Christ makes no distinction of this kind in his teaching. 5. Two distinct, yet similar discourses. Christ repeats the same truths because the circumstances and the wants of the people were the same. (So Dr. Alexander.) The choice lies between the third and fifth view. At all events, Christ gave a discourse at the time of calling the Twelve.

Design of the Sermon, and Connection with the History. The design of the discourse was to show the nature of the Messiah's kingdom. Christ came preaching a kingdom

and repentance. Naturally it would be asked, what is this repentance, what this kingdom, what its relations to Pharisaic ideas and to O. T. economy? There was need of explanation, that the people might know to what they were committing themselves. Christ in this discourse gives it, removing all erroneous views and false interpretations of his work. Some have mistakenly thought that Christ here sets forth a system of theology, others, a system of Ethics. The sermon was related to Pharisaic errors in teaching in opposition to them that membership in God's kingdom was dependent not upon external circumstances but upon personal character; that the Law was to be observed not in a formal manner but in its spirit. *Three main divisions:* 1. Ch. 5 : 1–16, character of members; characteristics required, spiritual. 2. Ch. 5 : 17–6. Claims of kingdom, *a*, 5 : 17–48, moral requisitions : *b*. ch. 6, religious requisites. 3. Ch. 7, exhortations to true life ; temptations and dangers, how avoided. The effect was astonishment (Mt. 7 : 29) " for he taught them as one having authority." Sceptics view this discourse as genuine, making an exception in its favor. They regard Christ as teaching an ethical and religious system. They draw a contrast between its free tone and the later dogma of Paul and other Apostles. Hence Christian dogma was a late invention. Christ taught morals, not doctrine. Such is true Christianity, love to God as our Father, to our brother-man as to ourself. Ans: 1. Discourse was not intended to be a full system, but adapted to the comprehension of the people. 2. Adapted to its position in history of redemption. Revelation corresponds to the period in which it is given. 3. Completed Christian doctrine is based, on life, death and resurrection of Christ, hence could not be brought forward at this stage. 4. Unity of truth is always preserved, although it is more definitely stated from time to time. O. T. and Christ's teaching involved all fundamental doctrines. In the Epistles, however, they assume a more analytic form.

That the discourse is *Evangelical* not Ethical, as Skeptics assert, is seen : 1. Because its standard of spirituality is so high that supernatural aid is required. Need of forgiveness is shown. Christ must be sought and this search is to be by means.

2. Righteousness is distinguished from moral right because it is connected with Christ's kingdom. His person is involved in his work. His disciples are spoken of as those having purity.

The discourse was an evangelical restatement of Law of Moses, and a preparation for the gospel.

§42. MIRACLES. Mt. 8: 5-13; Lk. 7: 1-10. *Healing Centurion's servant. Capernaum.* §42, 43, resume the subject of miracles. All centurions mentioned in N. T. appear in a favorable light. Mt. 8: 5, he loved Jewish nation and built a synagogue. Though a heathen Christ declared of him, "I have not found so great faith, no not in Israel." Comp. centurion at crucifixion (Mk. 15: 39; Lk. 23: 47.), Cornelius (Act. 10: 1.), Julius (Acts 27: 1.) (Smith's Dict. p. 406.) Legion contained about 6000 infantry, with a varying proportion of cavalry. It "was subdivided into ten cohorts ("band," Acts 10: 1), the cohort into three maniples, and the maniple into two centuries, containing originally 100 men, as the name implies, but subsequently from 50 to 100 men, according to the strength of the legion." (Smith's Dict. Army p. 162.) Gal. was garrisoned with Roman soldiery; Herod's bodyguards, and those farming imperial revenues.

New features in this miracle. 1. Intercessory faith. Master prays for his servant. 2. Striking greatness of faith. 'As his servants obeyed his word, so disease would obey the *word* of Christ.' 3. It was a Gentile's faith. This is first recorded instance of individual healing, outside the chosen people, hence intercession of Jewish elders is sought. (Lk. 7: 3.) Christ praises this Gentile's faith, as greater than any in Israel, and applies this fact by declaring 'Many Gentiles shall be called, many children of the kingdom cast off' (Mt. 8: 11-12.) Objections. 1. Mt. says centurion came in person to Christ: Lk. he sent through the elders, then through friends, but had no personal interview. Ans. "Qui facit per alium, facit per se." "What one does by his agent, he does himself." Mt. dwells on mere fact of miracle as displaying great faith; Lk. goes into detail. (Robin. Gk. Harm. p. 198.) 2. Christ lacks either sincerity or foreknowledge. He starts for house, but does not go to it; either did not intend going and practiced

deception, or changed his mind, because ignorant of what he was about to do. Ans. This assumes Christ was bound to disclose all his intentions. No inconsistency in Christ's not knowing things about to happen. To his human consciousness things came as to ours.

§43. Lk. 7: 11-17. *Raising son of widow of Nain.* Lk. 8: 1-3, narrates a second general circuit of Gal. Some hold this refers to prospective journey, undertaken near close of ministry. Common view (Andrews, Wieseler,) the reference in Lk. is retrospective, summing up the events narrated in §§ 43-47. Exegesis favors this interpretation. " Nain, the modern Nein is situated on the northwestern edge of the ' Little Hermon,' where the ground falls into the plain of Esdraelon." The entrance must always have been up the steep ascent from the plain, and here, on the west side of the village, the rock is full of sepulchral caves. (Smith's Dict. p. 2058.) Christ approaches Nain attended by many disciples, and much people. Style of gospel description simple, beautiful, impressive " *only* son of his mother, and she was a *widow.*" This was only time Christ was ever in plain of Esdraelon.

This class of miracles manifest Christ's power over departed spirits and attest his claim to be source of life, physical and spiritual. Three cases of this kind are recorded, each exhibiting more striking power than the preceding, viz., Jairus' daughter, from death bed; Widow's son, from the bier; Lazarus, from the tomb. Chronological order. Widow's son, Jairus' daughter, Laz. *Sceptical theories concerning these miracles.* 1. *Naturalistic.* Cases of suspended animation; death only apparent: pretended miracle, only resuscitation.

2. *Mythical.* Mere inventions of early church to make Christ's life accord with O. T. prophecy, and type.

Effect: all feared, glorified God, saying " Great Prophet has arisen," " God has visited Israel." Christ's fame spread not only through Judea, but through whole " region round about."

§44. OPPOSITION. Mt. 11: 2-19; Lk. 7: 18-35. *Message of John Bap.* In this section renewal of opposition is occasioned by Bap's disciples, and continues to §50. Mt. places this narrative after sending out the Twelve, but this is too late, for during absence of Twelve, John was beheaded; Mk. 6 : 30; Mt. 14 : 13. Lk's order is therefore best. The report of Christ's miracles was the occasion of Bap's message. John was imprisoned at Machaerus, " on the borders of the desert, N. of Dead Sea, on frontiers of Arabia," " identified with the ruins *M'Kauer*." Fathers say John did not doubt himself, but sent to Christ that his disciples might be satisfied. But that Bap. was, at least to some extent, staggered and perplexed by Christ's method of developing his work, is evident from fact of Christ's answer being addressed not to disciples, but John himself. Message expresses impatience mingled with distrust. He was languishing in prison, multitudes of others were being relieved and blessed by miracles; he, the forerunner, was forgotten, " was this really the Christ, or should they look for another?" (Farrar Vol. I., p. 289.) Christ's only reply is reference to his miracles, thus showing estimate he put upon them: His works were equivalent to assertion of divinity. John Bap. was greatest prophet because of his position as ———— "index-finger of O. T."

Christ received by the people, but Pharisees and lawyers doubted (Lk. 7 : 29.)

§45. Mt. 11 : 20–30. *Upbraids the cities.* Disciples of John having returned to him, Christ gives his estimate of the reception he had met in Gal. The same, or a similar denunciation of woes is recorded in Lk. 10 : 13, in connection with sending out seventy. Exact location of these cities is unknown; probably W. shore Sea of Gal. Their rejection of Christ contrasted with ancient heathen opposition to theocracy, viz., Tyre and Sidon, Sodom and Gomorrah. There is no record of a single miracle, wrought in Bethsaida or Chorazin, yet the Evangelist says these were the cities " wherein *most* of his mighty works were done."

§46. Lk. 7 : 36–50. *Anointing by a woman.* This took place at either Cap., Nain, Magdala. It differs from the case recorded by Mt., Mk., John as this is early in his ministry; that, in last week of his life. Romish tradition considers this woman the Mary Magdelene, mentioned a few verses later (Lk. 8 : 2) and makes her the representative of penitent frailty. This idea is based wholly on mere juxtaposition, there being nothing definite to

show that these are necessarily the same person, or that seven devils were demons of impurity. This incident contrasts with Christ's previous treatment, (§45,) is associated with new instance of opposition, and gives rise to Christ's first parable : the two debtors. (Farrar Vol. 1., p. 296.)

§47. Lk. 8 : 1–3. *Second circuit in Gal.* General statement, summing up results of the journey, begun §43, giving Christ's mode of living and travelling, and his household, viz. the Twelve, and certain women, Mary of Magdala (W. of Cap.,) Joanna of Herod's household etc. Connection ; Love and devotion of these attendants contrasted with rejection and opposition of Pharisees and masses. Christ was supported by free-will offerings.

§48. Mk. 3 : 19–30 ; Mt. 12 : 22–37 ; Lk. 11 : 14, 15, 17–23. *Healing blind and dumb demoniac.* Events of §§48–56 occur during a single day, the great day of parables, which opens with cure of demoniac. Lk. records this cure in ch. 11. during period of last journeys to Jerus. Two methods of harmonizing with Mt. 1. Cases are the same. Then must follow Mt's order because he gives distinct note of time, ch. 13 : 1. " that *same day*." 2. Cases are analogous. (Andrews p, 365.) Historical result is unchanged by either method. Collision with Pharisees did occur at this time, and only question is, was it repeated? Note intense excitement that was prevailing. Mk. 3 : 21, Christ's friends think him insane, endeavor to put him under restraint ; ordinary meals interrupted, multitudes coming together " so they could not so much as eat bread." (Mk. 3 : 20 ;) Christ goes to sea-side, is compelled to enter a boat to address them ; crowds ascribe to him Messianic titles. " Is not this the Son of David ?" Pharisees alarmed, unable to gainsay the miracles, impute them to agency of Satan. Mk. 3 : 22 " the scribes which *came down from Jerus.*" shows Christ was being watched by Jewish authorities, and the present opposition was official. Beelzebub, name of Philistine deity, meaning " Fly god," Pharisees change to Beelzeboul, i. e., " Dung god." Christ's reply. 1. *Ad hominum* argument, " If I by Beelzeboul cast out devils, by whom do you?" Reference to incantations and exorcisms of Rabbinical Schools. 2. Parable of

Definition of *Parable*—an illustration of moral or religious truth derived from analogy of common experience. It differs from the Fable in that " in the latter, qualities or acts of a higher class of beings may be attributed to a lower (e. g. those of men to brutes); while in the former, the lower sphere is kept perfectly distinct from that which it seems to i'lustrate." Neander: It differs from the Myth " in being the result of conscious deliberate thought, not the growth of unconscious realism, personifying attributes, appearing, no one knows how, in popular belief." It differs from the Proverb in that " it must include a similitude of some kind, while the Proverb may assert without a similitude, some wide generalization of experience." It differs from the Allegory, in that the latter really involves no comparison. Parable may be wholly fictitious or partly based on real events.

Three great groups, distinctly marked in gospels: 1. Seven in Mt. 13, illustrate nature of kingdom of Heaven. 2. Lk. Chs. 12-18, set forth immediate, personal relations of the individual believer to God. 3. Mt. 25, those pointing to Judgment and consummation of the kingdom. These groups are supplemental in their relation to one another. First group contains five fundamental truths. 1. Sower and seed. Varied reception of gospel truth, by different classes of hearers. 2. Tares and wheat. Evil springs up among the good. 3. Mustard seed, Leaven. Growth of church externally, internally. 4. Hid treasure, Pearl of great price. Value of kingdom, necessity of sacrifice. 5. Net. Gathering of all kinds; mixed condition of visible church until end of world. Skeptics reject Tares, and Net. because they imply conscious divinity of Christ, and contain the late ideas of imperfection in the church. They assert Mk.'s parable of seed growing secretly, is derived from that of the Sower. Bengel says these Parables form outline of Church History. Lange carries this idea to extreme, viz. Sower, Apostolic Age; Tares, Ancient Cath. Church; Mustard seed: State church under Constantine; Leaven, Mediæval Church: Hid Treasure, Reformation; Pearl, Christianity vs. world; Net, Final Judgment. A natural transition is observable running through all seven. They illustrate self conscious divinity of Christ: field is

strong man armed. If Christ by Satan was casting out devils, he must first have conquered Satan. 3. Warns them against the unpardonable sin. 4. Denounces them as generation of vipers, seed of serpent, i. e. children of Satan in their nature, opinions, actions.

§49. Mt. 12: 38-45; Lk. 11: 16, 24-36. *Pharisees seek a sign.* In face of all Christ's miracles they demand some evidence of Messiahship that will accord with their perverted Messianic notions. Mt.'s order is preferred to Lk.'s, because Ch. 12: 46 chronological sequence is given, "while he yet talked." Christ refused sign. He had already furnished ample miraculous proof of Messianic claims.

Parable of seven spirits, refers to present condition of people. Apparently changed in feeling toward Christ, they would shortly become more hostile toward him, than ever before. Shows that Christ was not misled by their seeming and probably sincere faith.

§50. Mt. 12: 46-50; Mk. 3: 31-35; Lk. 8: 19-21. *Mother and brethren desire to speak with him,* his increasing popularity and antagonism to the Pharisees giving them concern about him. He shows his earthly relations typify his spiritual relations to every true believer. Great advance in Pharisaic opposition; charge of blasphemy has been made and retorted.

§§54, 55. TEACHING. Mt. 13. Mk. 4. Lk. 8: 4-16. *Great day of Parables.* Syn. here mark decided change and advance in Christ's teaching. It was necessary Christ should still instruct the people, but in order to blind opposition, truth must be clothed in parabolic form, that his enemies may not employ his words against him.

Four general subjects twice repeated characterize the ministry in E. Gal. up to this point:

1. Organization, §29 and §40; 2. Miracles, §§30-33 and §§42-43; 3. Opposition, §§34-39 and §§44-50; 4. Teaching §41 and §§54-55.

Christ employs parables. 1. Symbolic method awakens imagination, excites interest, exercises memory and judgment. 2. "To him that hath shall be given." The recipients of God's grace, will be able to recognize his truth even when clothed in symbolic form. What is grace to believer, becomes judicial condemnation to unbeliever. Is. 6: 9 is thus fulfilled. (See Mt. 13: 11-15.)

the world, *he* sends *his* angels, *he* separates. He might naturally in Parable have referred to God, but avoids doing so. Christ's exposition of Sower and Tares is model of interpretation. Spiritual lesson should not be sought in every particular, some details serving merely to keep up connection. Fathers attempted to spiritualize all the minutiæ. Mt. 13: 36, Christ's going into the house makes apparent division in his discourse, parables spoken before being addressed to people in general, those afterward to his disciples only. Common opinion is that these parables were all delivered upon one day. Though this hypothesis is not necessary, there is certainly marked unity in these teachings.

Note. §§48–56—one day: §57 one day: §§58–60 one day. These three days though possibly not successive, are not widely separated.

§56. MIRACLES. Mt. 8: 18–27; Mk. 4: 35–41; Lk. 8: 22–25; 9: 57–62. *Crossed the Lake* on evening of same day, to escape crowds and avoid Pharisees. Certain man desires to follow Christ. He replies "Foxes have holes." Christ's poverty should not be exaggerated; it was voluntary, not forced. v. 60. Christ's service supersedes everything conflicting with it. New class of Miracles introduced, those over nature, teaching Christ's care and deliverance of his followers from danger. E. side urge Christ to depart, on W. beg him to remain.

§57. Mt. 8: 28–34; Mk. 5: 1–21; Lk. 8: 26–40. *Demoniacs at Gadara.* Text differs as to name of place. This case, palpable proof of individuality of devils. First recorded visit to E. of Lake; preparation for further sojourn. Tells demoniacs to publish cures, because here Christ was beyond the reach of Pharisees, and the report would prepare for his subsequent visit. Swine shows region outside Jewish influence. Their destruction no part of the miracle. Mt. mentions two demoniacs, others but one. Note contrast; dwellers on E. of Lake urge Christ to depart, on W. beg him to remain.

§58. Mt. 9: 10–17; Mk. 2: 15–22; Lk. 5: 29–39. *Levi's feast.* Not positively successive; most think so. Wieseler, Ellicott, Tischendorf, synchronize it with call of Mt. Mt. gives feast on account of Christ's intended de-

parture from Gal. Two new charges from Pharisees,
and disciples of John Bap.: *a.* Eating with publicans
and sinners. O. T. regulations insisted upon social
severance; no Jew was permitted to eat with those ceremonially unclean. *b.* Christ and his disciples neglect
fasting. Former charges were, Christ's making himself
equal to God, breaking Sabbath, casting out devils by
Beelzebub.

§59. Mt. 9: 18–26; Mk. 5: 22–43; Lk. 8: 41–56.
Jairus comes whilst Christ was conversing with disciples
of John, at Levi's feast. On way to Jairus' house, heals
woman with bloody issue. Peculiarity of cure, is mode
of approach. "Virtue (δύναμιν) had gone out of him"
does not signify emanation of unconscious power. Christ
voluntarily performed the cure. 'Trouble not the master' Lk. 8: 49, indicates respect of higher classes for
Jesus. Privacy of raising of Jairus' daughter was due
to Pharisaical opposition.

§60. Mt. 9: 27–34. *Two blind men and dumb demoniac.*
Organic disease symbolizing darkness of mind. v. 27
"Son of David," Messianic title used as argument to obtain cure, for *first* time. v. 28 "Yea, *Lord*"—Christ requires faith. v. 34. Blasphemous charge of Pharisees
reiterated.

§62. Mt. 9: 35–38; 10: 1, 5–42; 11: 1; Mk. 6: 6–13;
Lk. 9: 1–6. *Third circuit in Gal.* Christ now sends out
the Twelve. Opposition had become dangerous. The
crisis of his life was fast approaching. Whatever he
would do to impress the people of Gal. must be done
quickly. Design of mission of Twelve. *a.* To facilitate
making such impression. Their mission a practical comment on his own words, 'Harvest plenty, laborers few.'
b. To exercise apostles in independent action. Fourth
step in organization of his kingdom. They still held the
erroneous ideas common to the people, so Christ now
begins to separate them from the world. On their return, he retires with them to the desert for further instruction. *c.* To acquaint the people with apostles, as
those who had been with him from the first. Their
commission was temporary and national. Their circuit
ended, their miraculous power ceased. Into any
Samaritan village they were not to enter. Plenary apos-

tolic authority conferred at Pentecost. Subject of their teaching was, 'Kingdom of heaven at hand.' Their miracles were limited to acts of healing. Anointing with oil, oil being type of Holy Spirit, shewed that they were mere instruments, and made prominent in people's minds the Spirit's agency. Disciples were to be supported by those to whom they were sent. Mt. 10: 16 contains reference to future opposition Christ knew he was to encounter. First reference to coming trials.

Note prominent place given to his person and authority; whole work of disciples derives its authority from him, its trials are to be borne for his sake.

§63. Mt. 14: 1-2, 6-12; Mk. 6: 14-16; Lk. 9: 7-9. *Death of John Baptist.* Date of death rightly inferred to be just prior to third Pass., after feeding 5000.

Duration of his imprisonment depends on feast of John 5: 1. If Pass., then 16 months (Robinson), if not it varies from 5 months to 3 weeks. John Bap. dies before seeing the establishment of the kingdom he had heralded. His early ministry had been full of glory, its end is filled with gloom. His fate accords with his life. It was well that an ascetic, a preacher of repentance, a pioneer for righteousness sake, should die a martyr. His life had been long enough to disclose the unity of his work and Christ's; his death turned popular attention to Jesus. As his imprisonment had caused Christ to withdraw from Judea, his death led him to retire into the wilderness.

§64. Mt. 14: 13-21; Mk. 6, 30-34; Lk. 9: 10-17; John 6: 1-14. *Return of Twelve. Feeding of 5000.* John now parallel with Syn. Twelve begin to return from their mission, the disciples of John Bap. report their master's death, hence Christ withdraws to N. E. side of Lake, for rest and safety. Lk. 9: 10: Place belonged to a city called Bethsaida. Common opinion is there were two Bethsaidas, Bethsaida of Gal., Bethsaida Julias. Others think there was but one, built upon both sides of the Jordan: but this is improbable, no bridge being mentioned, and a ferry would have been very dangerous. Bethsaida was an easy resort from Cap. and crowds followed him, having seen him embark, going around the Lake, by land. Christ was moved with compassion for them, because they were as sheep having no shepherd,

their only teachers being Pharisees. He therefore spends the entire day in giving instruction.

The nearness of the Passover accounts for the concourse of such multitudes in that out-of-the-way place. Beside 5,000 men, there being women and children, there must have been congregated at least 10,000 souls. Their orderly arrangement in companies, prevented all confusion, and imposture. One of Christ's greatest miracles; a species of creation; extensive multiplication of created things.

Skeptics note following differences in the accounts: 1. As to place. Desert place, yet in vicinity of city. John says a mountain. 2. As to conversation. Syn., make the disciples the first to mention feeding the multitudes, John makes Jesus first to speak. 3. Repetition of feeding multitudes recorded by Syn. increases difficulty of accepting either as genuine. These difficulties, and the inconceivableness (to skeptics) of a miracle displaying such creative power, have led to unusual effort to explain it away.

1. *Mythical explanation.* No such actual event occurred. Christ's discourse concerning his body, John 6. furnished mythical basis for current tradition. Strauss finds its mythical origin, in manna of O. T. and in the analogous miracles of Elijah, (1 King 17,) and Elisha (2 Kings 4.) 2. *Naturalistic explanation.* Christ excited charity among those in the caravan journeying to feast, to supply from their store of provisions those fainting with hunger. Some say it was originally a parable of Christ's, relating to spiritual food, transformed into a narrative; others imagine that Mt. has unwittingly recorded two separate traditions of the same occurrence. Olshausen and Lange, note the compressing into a single instant of the many gradual processes of nature and of art; not only the growth of the grain, but also the preparation of the food. Effect of this miracle (John 6: 14.): People apply Messianic titles to Christ, and attempt to force him to adopt their views of the Messiahship, and to compel him to be their king. Lange remarks "the rabble think they have found their *Bread King.*" Disciples embark to cross the lake. The people are sent away. Christ goes apart into a mountain to pray. §65. Omitted.

§66. John 6 : 22—1 : 1. *Discourse in Synagogue at Capernaum.* Only extended passage in John's gospel, the scene of which is laid in Gal. John not only accords with the Syn. in giving the miracle, but also makes the same crises in Christ's life and same effect produced on his followers. Morning after the miracle, the multitudes missing Christ and his disciples, follow him to Capernaum. This is culmination of ministry in E. Gal. False Messianic excitement has been aroused by the miracle of the loaves. Christ therefore, in the synagogue at Cap. delivers a searching discourse calculated to separate the spiritual from the sensual among the crowds that followed him, thus drawing nearer to himself the true disciples and driving away the mere carnally minded. He unfolds the true character of his kingdom; its blessings spiritual, not material. Miracle furnishes theme of the discourse; earthly food is not to be sought, but himself, the bread which came down from heaven. v. 63. "The words that I speak unto you, they are spirit, and they are life," is the key-note of the entire discourse. Three divisions: 1. ch. 6 : 27-51. This the work of God, men should believe on Christ, and feed upon his flesh. Whosoever comes to Him shall not be cast out, but shall obtain eternal life. 2. Ch. 6 : 51-56: Comment on preceding statements. Christ's flesh, the true bread from heaven. 3. Ch. 6 : 59-71. Effect of discourse: multitudes are offended and desert him.

Never before, save to Nicodemus, had Christ declared that he came down from heaven. He claims the power to impart spiritual life. This discourse from a mere man would have been blasphemy and folly. This was a test event for his own apostles. v. 67 "Will ye also go away?" Peter answers v. 68 " To whom shall we go?" "Thy words are hard but it is a question of despair with us," (v. 69) " we believe and are sure that thou art that Christ." First time the title of Messiah passed between Christ and his most intimate friends.

Critics object to this discourse as unhistorical; could not have been delivered previous to institution of Lord's Supper, must have been wholly unintelligible both to Christ and apostles, until that event. Peter's confession of Christ's divinity is out of place before Pentecost.

Ans: The very mystery and difficulty of this discourse adapt it to the end for which it was intended, the sifting of believers from unbelievers. Christ shows (vv. 70, 71,) that this discriminating process must be applied even to the Twelve. " Have I not chosen you twelve, and one of you is a devil?"

John 7: 1 closes the ministry in E. Gal., and indicates the extent to which opposition had increased during this period, by the statement that Christ " would not walk in Jewry " and was unable to attend the approaching passover " because the Jews sought to kill Him."

THE MINISTRY IN NORTHERN GALILEE.

SECOND PERIOD.

Duration of the Period: From the third Passover (coincident with death of the Baptist) to the Feast of Tabernacles, six months later. The record is contained in Mt. 14: 13; 18: 35; Mk. 6: 30; 9: 50; Luke 9: 10–56. John gives all in one verse, 7: 1, which corresponds with the statement of the Synoptists. It is a period of great journeyings. The order of events in the Syn. is perfect. This is because the period is shorter, and there is less room for variations. Then the subjects of conversation are closely connected with the historic events.

Characteristics of the Period: 1. Dangerous opposition causing Christ's withdrawal from Capernaum. 2. This withdrawal widened the sphere of action. Instead of remaining in Capernaum he now goes into Phœnicia, then into Decapolis, passing up the Jordan to Cæsarea Philippi. He had two ends in view: *a.* To avoid danger; *b.* to extend his usefulness. Besides, his passing the borders of the Holy Land signified the calling of the Gentiles. 3. His teachings assumed a new character. For the first time he teaches publicly his death and resurrection.

Object of the Period: To strengthen the faith of his disciples. Hence he uses express terms to teach his Messiahship, in contrast with the preceding period. The disciples are now taught rather than the people. The main point was to prepare them for his approaching death. The central event of the preceding period was the Sermon on the Mount; of this period, the Transfiguration. The events on these Mountains mark the beginning and end of the Galilean ministry.

§67. *Christ justifies his disciples for eating with unwashed hands.* This charge of the Pharisees shows the strict watch they kept over Christ's actions. The previous charge was Sabbath-breaking. Now he is charged with disregarding the traditions of the Jews on which the Pharisees laid so much stress. Christ applies to them, Isa. 29: 13, and warns the multitude against this ritual burden. Vide Mt. 15: 1-20. Mk. 7: 1-23.

§68. *The daughter of a Syro-Phœnician woman healed.* Mt. 15: 21-28; Mk. 7: 24-30. The border between Galilee and Phœnicia is called, from its two larger cities, Tyre and Sidon. Did Christ go *to* the borders, or *beyond*, or *through?* (Mk. 7: 24.)

The last view is the best for three reasons: 1. It agrees best with the account in Mk. 2. It suits best the purport of the miracles. 3. It is put almost beyond doubt by the amended text—$διὰ$ $Σιδῶνος$ implying through Phœnicia.

Tyre and Sidon were opponents of the Theocracy. Therefore the miracle shows Christ's *intended mission* to the Gentiles. 1. Because the woman is called a Canaanite, which people belonged originally to the land. 2. She is called a *Greek*, which is the O. T. name for Gentile. 3. Christ's own words: "I am not sent but unto the lost sheep of the house of Israel."

§69. *Healing of the deaf and dumb man.* Mt. 15: 29-38; Mk. 7: 31-37, 8: 1-9. From Phœnicia Christ passes south through Decapolis, inhabited largely by Greeks. Some say he came around south of the sea; others that he traveled directly east from Phœnicia. It is more probable that he went north as far as Damascus, thus preparing for Paul. The same miracles are renewed because he is in a new country.

But the present miracle has some peculiarities. 1. It is the first case of combined deafness and dumbness. 2. Not an absolute but a partial dumbness—tongue-tied. 3. The mode of healing—takes the man apart and prays. Why? Because the Messianic question is not prominent, and the people are Polytheists. Therefore he wished to

teach them of the true God. Many other miracles were wrought, and the effect of them is stated in Mt. 15 : 31. Then follows the miracle of feeding the 4000, wrought from compassion for the people far from home, and especially to lead them to the true God.

§70. *The Pharisees and Sadducees again require a Sign.* Mt. 15 : 39; 16 : 1–4; Mk. 8 : 10–12. Our Lord comes back to Capernaum and again to Magdala, a little town south of Capernaum. For the first time, the Pharisees and Sadducees are united against him, which Lange thinks is proof that the Sanhedrim had passed official measures against him. For the fourth time the Pharisees seek a sign, and Christ's answer is recorded in Mt. 16 : 2–3.

§72. *Blind Man of Bethsaida healed.* This miracle is mentioned by Mark alone. It is private, and the cure is gradual, to illustrate, as some think, the gradual enlightenment of the regenerated soul.

§73. *Peter's Confession at Cæsarea Philippi.* Mt. 16 : 13–30; Mark 8 : 27–30; Luke 9 : 18–21. Luke mentions these events because so important. C. Philippi lay at the base of Mt. Hermon, which is about 8000 ft. high. The sources of the Jordan are here. (Vide Smith's Dict.)

Result of the Galilean Ministry. As a whole, the result has not been to lead any but the disciples to believe that he is the Messiah. This truth is not popularly proclaimed. He still enjoins them not to say that he is *the Christ.* But the truth is so clear that it brings out Peter's famous confession : " Thou art the Christ, the son of the living God." Christ's reply contains $\dot{\varepsilon}\varkappa\varkappa\lambda\eta\sigma\iota\alpha$ for the first time. It is used only once besides this in the Gospels. (Matt. 18 : 17.)

The Rationalists confess that the agreement of the Evangelists here denotes a crisis in the life of Christ, but they dispute as to its nature. Baur and Strauss say that " Son of Man " (Mt. 16 : 13) had not before been considered a Messianic expression. The change, therefore, was from an idea secretly and suddenly entertained by Christ to its open profession. Schenkel thinks the crisis to be that after this he offered himself for the first time as the Messiah.

But these theories require rejection of the Gospel by John, and they subvert the whole history. The only thing true is that the claim to be the Messiah had not been made prominent before. But the Disciples had recognized him as Son of God before this. Vide Mt. 14: 33. He now makes his claim public, and goes on to teach that his kingdom would be independent of the old Theocracy. "Upon this rock will I build my Church." That is, the doctrine contained in Peter's confession would be its corner-stone.

§74. *Prediction of his Death and Resurrection.* Mt. 16: 21-28; Mk. 8: 31-38; 9: 1; Lk. 9: 22-24. This is a new element in Christ's teaching. The Syn. recognized this transition. Our Lord shows them that he had not come to set up the material kingdom that they expected, but that he was to suffer death. This shocked them, and Peter says: "Be it far from thee, Lord." These predictions are important in three respects:

1. In correcting the mistaken ideas of his Apostles. These predictions prepared them for that suffering which they had not anticipated.

2. In preserving their faith. What would have become of them when Christ's death came, without these predictions?

3. Although they did not apprehend his words at the time, they did remember them during Passion Week (Luke 24: 7-8). The Divinity of the Savior gleams through these predictions in a striking manner. They are very minute. *a.* As to the *place*—Jerus., which he had avoided. *b.* His death was not to be a local but an official and national event. *c.* The mode of his suffering was predicted. He was to be "put to death"—but was to rise again on the third day.

The Rationalists make strong assaults upon these passages. 1. They claim *discrepancy in the accounts.* 1. John is enigmatical while the Syn. are plain. 2. John's references cover the whole life, while the Syn. refer only to the end. 3. In John the words are addressed to the multitude; in the Syn. to the Disciples. 4. Christ appeals to the O. T. and mistakes its meaning. He avails himself of certain Messianic passages which the Rationalists deny to be so.

Ans: *a.* Christ appeals to the O. T. as proof only to those who believe in the O. T. *b.* The objection is based

on the false assumption that only isolated passages refer to the Messiah, whereas the whole O. T., especially the whole ceremonial law, refers to Christ. He is the key to it all. *c.* The exegesis on which these discrepancies are based is accepted only by unbelieving Jews and Rationalists.

II. Again it is objected that if Christ predicted his death in this way, the surprise and vacillation and incredibility of the Disciples, when his trial and death did occur, are inexplicable.

Ans: *a.* Prophecies however explicit require fulfillment as the key to their significancy and inspiration. Although the second advent of Christ has been foretold, how much do we know about it?

b. Again this was a time of great excitement. The Disciples were struck dumb for the moment, and had not sufficient calmness to reason about these matters.

c. The true interpretation of these prophecies contradicted all their notions of the Messiah. Besides, O. T. prophecies were not all to be fulfilled in his present advent.

III. These predictions simply a shrewd forecast. His suffering would be at Jerus. because he could bring that about. But the question arises, How did Christ know he would not be arrested in Galilee, on this theory? To obviate this, Strauss says the whole matter was incorporated with the record and is without foundation.

Intermediate Position of Theistic critics: These predictions belong to Cæsarean period. Before this Christ had expected to convert the nation. But experience taught that death was necessary to victory.

Ans: 1. It is inconsistent with the record in Mt. 12: 40; 23: 38, 39.

2. This theory is inconsistent with itself. For if the Resurrection was not an actual fact, why did the Apostles suffer martyrdom for their belief in it?

3. Christ's knowledge of the O. T. renders it impossible (Isa. 49: 3.) The Sceptics themselves claim that he got his knowledge from O. T., and by a false exegesis applied it to himself. Hence on their own ground he had a definite conception of his sufferings and death.

Another objection attempts to relieve Christ from all participation in the theory of the Atonement. But see how one Sceptic devours another. For some of them say that all such passages are an interpolation, while others deny that they teach the Atonement.

Transition Period. Thus far Christ had addressed the Twelve. But he now turns to the multitude. He forewarns them of the cost of following him—great self denial required, yet with the rewards of eternal life. But those who do not follow him must suffer the loss of their souls. (This was the last N. T. passage commented on by Dr. Addison Alexander just before his death.)

§75. *The Transfiguration.* The events of this section occurred about a week after the preceding conversation. No difficulty in the fact that Mt. says *six* days, and Lk. *eight*, for both speak of one week, only one *includes*, and the other *excludes*, the first and last days. Besides Lk. says ὡσει="*about.*" Tradition makes Mt. Tabor in Gal. the Mt. of Transfig. But this goes back only to fourth cent., and then *not* to Palestine. Mt. and Mk. say "a high mountain," and Lk. "the mountain." Robinson and Stanley object to Tabor bec. at that time occupied by a fortified city. Last events occurred in the region of Caesarea Philippi. Lightfoot: "Evangelists intimate no change of place." Besides, Mk. 9:30 says: "And departing thence they passed through Galilee," implying that they were not then in Gal. Current opinion favors Mt. Hermon.

Taking with him Peter, James and John, he goes into the mountain to pray, and then took place the Transfiguration. What the Transfiguration was is a matter of much conjecture. It is sufficient to know that Christ's personal identity remained. (Farrar, chap. 36.) Peter proposed to make three Tabernacles, or tents, that they might dwell there. Then a cloud came, which is always a sign of Jehovah's presence, and on looking around they saw Jesus alone.

Three-fold design of the Transfiguration:

1. It afforded the Disciples a new proof from Heaven of Christ's divinity, thereby strengthening their faith for future conflict.

2. It was necessary for Christ's own spiritual support and comfort, before entering upon the agony and death which were near at hand—analogous to the baptism before the Temptation.

3. The design was symbolical—setting forth the nature of Christ's kingdom, and the glory that shall follow those that suffer for it. A specimen of the heavenly glory and of the resurrection. Also shows the essential oneness of Christ's kingdom with the O. T. dispensation. Moses and Elias representative. men—one the giver, the other the champion of the Law. These two last points set forth in II. Peter 1 : 16-18. Christ charged them to tell no man, because the multitudes had not faith to understand the scene, and the Disciples themselves could not understand "what the rising from the dead should mean."

In the next four sections, we have a. the healing of the demoniac child, b. the second prediction of Christ's death and resurrection, c. the miraculous provision of the tribute-money, and d. the contentions of the Disciples as to who should be greatest in Christ's kingdom.

LAST JOURNEYS TO JERUSALEM.

Our Lord now begins his last journey to Jerusalem, there to renew the evidence of his Messiahship. The time is from Tabernacles to the Passover, *six months* lacking one week.

Why is Luke so full? a. Because he is supplementary. b. It accords with his plan to bring out the personal relations and human sympathies of Christ.

The question of Harmony is very difficult, because John gives us five chapters which must go into the Synoptic narrative. Here is the problem: The Synoptists, after the Galilean Ministry, relate a journey to Jerusalem as if it were the last. But John records *three* journeys: (1) A journey to the feast of Tabernacles in October, (John 7, 10.) (2) A journey to the Feast of Dedication in December (John 10: 22-23.) On account of opposition Jesus retires to Bethany in Perea, but the death of Lazarus brings him to Bethany, near Jerusalem. Then on account of further opposition he retires to Ephraim, (John 11: 54.) (3) He sets out from Ephraim for Jerusalem "six days before the Passover" (John 12: 1.) Where was Jesus during the two months between the Tabernacles and Dedication?

How are these to be harmonized? It is best to confess that we have not enough material to settle the question satisfactorily. DeWette thinks the chapters in Luke are a collection of unhistorical material which the writer did not know where to place. Exegetical objections to this view: *a.* The unity of the discourses in Luke. *b.* All the material furnished belongs to this period. Hengstenberg thinks no order is discernible between Luke and John. Schleiermacher, Olshausen and Neander think that the accounts of the two journeys are blended, viz., the journeys to the Tabernacle and Passover. The narrative of the first two come in at Luke 18: 35. They record no conversations or incidents previous to their becoming parallel with Luke.

Greswell makes all the Synoptists connect with the last journey in John. Then Luke 9: 51 is parallel with John 11: 55. According to this view the Synoptists pass over the period and record only the last journey to Jerusalem just before the Passover. By this view the unity of Luke is preserved, and the Synoptists appear to record only one journey. But the difficulty is that early in Luke's narration Christ is brought into the house of Mary and Martha at Bethany, (chap. 10) and then in chap. 17: 11 he is passing through Galilee and Samaria. Greswell thinks Luke refers to another village near Jerusalem. But this would make the journey protracted and irregular. Again John says our Lord passed some time in Ephraim, after raising Lazarus.

Wieseler fixes on three points in Luke where it is said Jesus was going to Jerus. and makes them correspond with John's journeys:
1. To Tabernacles, Luke 9: 51 compares with John 7: 10.
2. To Bethany,   "   13: 22   "   "   " 11: 1.
3. To Passover,   "   17: 11   "   "   " 11: 55.

Arguments for Wieseler's view: It is claimed that the narrative in John *fits in* to the break in Luke, e. g., we are told that the journey to the Tabernacles was made secretly. This agrees with Luke's statement that he went through Samaria. The common way was through Perea. The Samaritans reject him because his "face was set towards Jerus." Here comes in the parable of the good Samaritan. Such striking coincidences all through have won over many supporters. Ellicott follows it in full. Tischendorf qualifies it by saying that it is not so certain as it seems to be.

Objections. 1. Lack of positive evidence. But in such a case we look only for *probabilities.* 2. Luke purports to give only one journey. Ans.: Luke does not say there was but *one* journey. 3. Luke 9:51 seems to refer to a period just before his death. Ans.: Could as well refer to the whole period of six months. 4. Luke 13:22 must mean, it is said, *into* or *up to* Jerus. But this interpretation denies that εἰς ever has the sense of direction. 5. The plan implies a sojourn in Jerusalem from the Tabernacles to Dedication. This is said to be contrary to John 12:1. Tischendorf takes an exception to Wieseler and makes the Dedication occur in John 10:22. Andrews agrees as to the last two journeys, but makes this difference: He considers Luke 9:51 the journey to Dedication, and makes it parallel with John 7:10, which passage he makes refer to a final departure. Objections to Andrews: 1. It assumes a new return to Galilee after Dedication. 2. It is unnatural to put John 7, 8, 9 at the close of the Galilean ministry. They belong to this period of journeyings.

Robinson makes Luke 13:22—19:28 the last journey; Luke 10:17—11:33 the journey between Tabernacles and Dedication, and Luke 11:33—13:10 he puts in the ministry in Eastern Galilee. Objections: 1. It is arbitrary. 2. It breaks up the connection just where commentators find a striking unity. 3. Robinson himself says, "I suggest." The sceptics say that this diversity proves the record unhistorical.

Coincidences of John and Luke: 1. Both represent Jesus, after the Galilean Ministry, as entering upon an extended period of journeyings. 2. Both agree that the region was Judea and Perea. 3. Both agree that it was toward Jerus. 4. Both agree as to the character of the works and teaching, for both refer to a period of hostility which brings out declaration of his Divinity.

Design of the Period: A more open avowal of Messiahship—at the feast and while journeying. He offers himself again at Jerus. and is rejected. Notice the advance in the doctrine of his person. He speaks of coming forth from God; of his pre-existence; of his oneness with the Father; of his being the source of life. But he still withholds the titles, Messiah and Christ.

The sphere of labor is now changed from Galilee to Judea. In the Synoptists this is brought out in the journeyings through Perea. The opposition increases. The Pharisees seek to break down his popularity by putting difficult questions so worded that a direct answer would offend one party or another. For example, the question about divorce. On the other hand, our Lord delivers a series of discourses against the Pharisees, warning the people against them. John gives evidence of the covert purpose of the Pharisees to put Christ to death, John 7: 25.

Christ now proceeds to give private instruction to his disciples, in reference to the change so soon to occur. He gives new charges, prophecies and parables. (The numbering of the sections, from this point, is irregular, but Tischendorf's plan is preferred.)

§81. *Final Departure from Galilee.* Luke's expression is remarkable: "He steadfastly set his face to go to Jerusalem." The journey was not compulsory but voluntary.

Objections: 1. He said to his brethren that he would not go, and afterwards went up secretly (John 7: 8-11.) It is claimed that this is either vacillation or deception. Ans: Our Lord's words refer to the time and manner of his going. Did not say he was not going, but " I go up *not yet.*" He refused to go in the public procession.

2. Again, it is said that the rejection of his messengers at the Samaritan village (Lk. 9: 53) does not agree with the favorable reception in John 4th.

Ans: The latter was at the beginning, the former at the close of his Galilean ministry. The rejection by the Samaritans is now caused by their prejudices. Christ's face now toward Jerus. He was therefore regarded as favoring the Jews.

3. Again it is said Lk. 9: 52 represents Christ's last journey to be through Samaria. But Mt. and Mk. make it through Perea. Andrews (p. 361) answers this by the reasonable supposition that he started to go through Samaria, but after his rejection changed his plan and went through Perea.

§83. *Feast of Tabernacles.* This was one of the great annual feasts of the Jews, (Lev. 23: 34) to commemorate

the Divine goodness in the Wilderness, and also to show gratitude for the rich fruits of the season. It was the most joyous of all the Jewish festivals,—so joyous that Plutarch mistook its character and called it a festival in honor of Bacchus.

There was a division of sentiment concerning Christ among those at Jerus. Some said, " He is a good man : others said, Nay but he deceiveth the people " (John 7 : 12.) Another expression of John is noticeable : " Howbeit no man spake openly of him for fear of the Jews." This refers to the Jews who opposed Christ. The people did not know which side to take, because it was uncertain what the Sanhedrim would do.

Historic Points : 1. Christ takes up his discourse with the Pharisees where he had left off (John 7 : 23) eighteen months before. The miracle to which he refers in v. 21, is the healing of the impotent man at Bethesda, which was followed by the charge of Sabbath-breaking. He here openly charges them with their purpose to kill him.

2. The emphatic statements in verses 28–31 of his Divinity. This gave great offense to some, but no man laid hands on him, and many believed in him, asking " When Christ cometh will he do more miracles than these which this man hath done ?"

3. The official act of the Sanhedrim to arrest him, because of his influence over the people. All this on the first day. Now we come to the second day—" that great day of the feast" which was the last. Jesus stood and cried : " If any man thirst, let him come unto me and drink." The water which suggested this invitation is supposed to have been that which was taken from the pool of Siloam on each of the seven days and poured upon the ground in commemoration of the miraculous provision of water in the Wilderness. In it Christ saw a type of that Spirit which the world was to receive through him. The officers report to the Sanhedrim that they were unable to arrest him. The reason they give is remarkable : " Never man spake like this man"—showing the strong impression Christ's personal bearing had made upon them. The answer is received with ridicule : " Are ye also deceived ?"

Except for the remonstrance of Nicodemus (v. 51), the Sanhedrim would have condemned Christ, immediately. To him they sneeringly replied: "Art thou also of Galilee? Search and look, for out of Galilee ariseth no prophet." But in the last statement they were mistaken.

§84. *Woman taken in Adultery.* Most critics reject the first eleven verses of the 8th of John. The external and grammatical evidence against it is very strong. Tregelles claims that it is not original with John, but is an ancient extra-canonical record of an actual fact. The passage is not in the Sinaitic, Peshito, A., B., or C., uncial MSS. It is found only in the Vatican MS. and some of the early Fathers. But it seems to accord too well with the character of Christ, to be an invention.

§85. *Discourses in the Temple.* The effect of striking out John 8: 2-11 would be to bring all these discourses on the last day of the feast. But it is more natural to consider the references in John 7: 37 and 8: 14 to relate to two different days. If this be correct, there are two prominent periods of teaching: (1) 8: 12-21; (2) 8: 21-59.

In the first, Christ proclaims himself the Light of the world. The Pharisees object to his bearing witness of himself, and say his record is not true. Our Lord proves its truth, *a.* by saying that the Father bears testimony of him; and *b.* by declaring his oneness with the Father.

In the second, he discourses of his origin, of his going away, and of their dying in their sins. He charges them with the design of killing him, and alludes to the manner of his death in verse 28th: "When ye have lifted up the son of man."

The pre-existence of Christ is asserted by him in express terms. The Jews regard the declaration as blasphemy and give way to rage. They tear up the stones from the Temple pavement to put him to death as a blasphemer. But Jesus hid himself, and so got out of their way.

§90. *Healing of a man blind from birth*, on the Sabbath. Robinson postpones this till just before the Dedication. But the prevailing opinion is that it comes in immediately after stoning referred to in John 8: 59. In proof of Messiahship, Jesus opens eyes of blind man. The Phari-

sees after conversing with the latter, are enraged because he adheres to Jesus, and cast him out of the Synagogue. (Farrar, chap. 41, Vol. II.) The effect of this miracle was to produce a division among the people. Many of them claimed that he had a devil. Others, that a devil could not open the eyes of the blind. (John 10 : 19–21.)

§89. *The Seventy sent out.* Tisch. places this section in the interval between Dedication and Tabernacles; Wies. while Jesus is on the way to Tabernacles. Place: Majority say Perea, some Gal. *Best*, Perea, Judea and Samaria. The design has a clear reference to Christ's coming once more to offer himself as the Messiah. Meyer: This whole journey intended to present to the people opportunity for final decision. Andrews: Their mission was not only to preach the kingdom, but to proclaim the King. In addition, probably a desire to accustom the disciples to their work, and familiarize the people with them as witnesses of the truth. Some say that the second order of church officers, viz.; Presbyters, is here established. Wies.: The Seventy represent the calling of the Gentiles. Their mission was the counterpart of that of the Twelve. The latter chosen in reference to the twelve tribes; the seventy with reference to the seventy nations of the Gentiles for which prayers were offered, or the number may have reference to the seventy elders of Israel, or to the Sanhedrim. But the leading idea seems to be a visitation of the whole country. (Vide Ebrard, pp. 322–3; Andrews, pp. 352–355; Farrar, Vol. II., ch. 42. Also comp. Gen. 10 and Gen. 46 : 27 with Deut. 32 : 8.)

Objections: I. Silence of the other Evangelists, Lk. being the only one that mentions the Seventy. Ans: *a.* The objection would be valid if the Seventy had been set up as a permanent order in the church. Other Evangelists silent concerning a great portion of this period, but say nothing contrary to Lk's account.

II. Instructions to Seventy and Twelve so similar that the Evangelists give different accounts of same occurrence. Ans: *a.* The instructions were similar because the duties were similar. *b.* But there is an important difference in the fact that a permanent commission was given to the Twelve but not to the Seventy. Ebrard:

Address to Twelve has the character of induction into a *permanent* office, whereas that to Seventy has reference to a *single task*.

III. Symbolical use of number Seventy is proof of a later date, and of artifice. Ans: Some number of messengers must have been chosen, and whatever it might be the Sceptics would be sure to find fault with it.

§89. *The Seventy return.* Difficult to assign this section with any certainty. The Seventy probably returned, *two* by *two*, bringing a glorious report (Lk. 10: 17–21.)

§86. *The Good Samaritan.* Lk. 10: 25–37. In the parable Christ teaches that God may make distinctions among men, but men may not. *All* men are our neighbors. Hence, we must do good to all men.

Second Group of Parables: There are seventeen in all, closely connected and illustrating personal duties—fourteen of them peculiar to Lk. Three things worthy of notice: 1. Their appropriateness to the plan of Luke's gospel. They set forth God's mercy to sinners, and the duties consequent therefrom. Mt.'s group of seven all addressed to the people and the Disciples; Lk.'s intended for publicans and sinners. Mt.'s relate to the kingdom of God; Lk.'s point out the way of salvation. 2. Their appropriateness to the period of Christ's life, in which he fina'ly offered himself to the nation. 3. They are directed against prominent errors of the Pharisees.

Classification of these Parables. They may be reduced to a four-fold division:

I. Those showing the love of God in Christ as the source of all blessing. *a.* To the poor and lowly—parable of Marriage Supper. *b.* As preventing grace—Lost Sheep, Lost Piece of Money, Prodigal Son.

II. Those showing the means of obtaining God's mercy, and the resulting duties. *a.* Importunity in prayer—Friend at Midnight, Importunate Widow. *b.* Repentance and humility—parable of Pharisee and Publican. *c.* Watchful preparation—the Waiting Servants (Lk. 12: 27.) *d.* Counting the cost—Building a Tower. *e.* Universal love to our neighbor—the Good Samaritan. *f.* Using this world's goods without abusing them—Unjust Steward.

III. Those showing the judgments which follow neglect or abuse of God's mercy. *a.* Abuse of God's grace—Barren Fig-tree. *b.* Abuse of God's providence—Rich Man that built Larger Barns. *c.* Abuse of Wealth—Dives and Lazarus. *d.* Danger of partial moral reformation. Leads to worse state than the first—Return of Unclean Spirit. (Lk. 11: 24.)

IV. Those showing that rewards and punishments are to be proportioned to fidelity of stewardship—Parable of Ten Talents—Mustard Seed—Leaven.

Sections 48, 49 and 51 are parallel with Mt. 12, and for this reason Robinson treats them together. Vide small syllabus, p. 12.

§91. *Feast of Dedication.* Previous to this feast, (John 10: 22.) Jesus had retired to Bethany in Perea. Why return to Jerus.? Not merely to keep the Feast, since the whole land kept it, but to confront the Pharisees. Not a feast of the Law, but instituted by Judas Maccabaeus, 164 B. C., in honor of the cleansing of the Temple, and the rebuilding of the Altar, after the Expulsion of the Syrians. *Season*: The only feast in the wintertime, which, according to Wieseler, fell this year on Dec. 20. (Vide Farrar, chap. 45.) Christ was walking in this place because it was winter, the porch being part of the original temple which escaped destruction by Nebuchadnezzar.

Scene interesting because it discloses the struggle in the minds of the Pharisees. "How long dost thou make us to doubt? If thou be the Christ tell us plainly." (John 10: 24.) Request not unreasonable for Christ had all along claimed the office, and *dis*claimed the title. Two views in regard to the spirit of the question:

I. That it was insidious and dishonest, intended to draw out a definite claim of Messiahship so that they could have something definite on which to base their charges.

II. That it was honest and fair. Christ had never told them positively that he was the Messiah, and now when challenged he still does not answer directly, because of their misconceptions. According to their understanding of the term he was not the Messiah. But he affirms his Messiahship to them in three ways: 1. He had told them before, and they did not believe him. 2. By referring to the works he had wrought. 3 His gift to his sheep is eternal life, and he is the Son of God, one with the Father. This enraged the Jews and they took up stones to stone him. "But," says Farrar, "his undisturbed majesty disarmed them with a word." "Many good deeds did I show you from my Father; for which of these do you mean to stone me?" He then quoted the 82nd Psalm, where judges are called gods. But *he* executes a higher office. This seems to ascribe his Sonship not to his nature, but to his being *sent* by the Father.

Ans.: 1. The terms used imply his *pre*-existence. 2. Even if he does here advance only the lowest claim to the title, "Son of God," it is no proof that he does not elsewhere use it in highest sense. No one besides Christ ever says, "I and my Father are one."

Then they attempt to seize him, but Farrar says "they could not. His presence overawed them. They could only make a passage for him, and glare their hatred upon him as he passed from among them."

Because of the opposition Christ goes to Bethany in Perea, where John had been baptizing. The latter is mentioned because a witness for Christ. How long he staid there is not known, but St. John tells us that many resorted to him and believed on him, being convinced of the truth of John Bap.'s testimony. (John 10: 41-42.) (The sections from 95 to 101 were passed over.)

§§92, 93. *Raising of Lazarus. Counsel of Caiaphas.* A message comes to Christ in Perea from the sisters of Lazarus, stating that their brother is sick. After two days Christ came to Bethany and found that Lazarus had been buried four days (John 11.)

Theories explaining the time: *a.* Lazarus died on the day when the message was sent. Christ delayed two days, and then went to Bethany occupying one day with the journey.

b. Christ received the message that Lazarus was sick, waited two days for his death, and occupied four days with the journey. Farrar takes the former view, mainly on the ground that Bethany in Perea, where Christ was, is only about 20 miles from the Bethany near Jerus., where Lazarus lived. He also infers that the family of

Lazarus was one of wealth and position from its proximity to Jerus. and from the concourse of Jews who had come to sympathize with the bereaved sisters. (Farrar, chap. 47.)

Opposition among the Jews: This is again referred to in the remonstrance of the Disciples against Christ's going up to Jerus. lest he should be killed. Thomas says: "Let us also go that we may die with him." (John 11: 16.) Christ goes up voluntarily to sacrifice himself.

Design of the Miracle: To understand it aright, recall design of period—to give the people final opportunity of accepting him as Messiah. On the other hand, the people hesitated to come to a decision because the action of the rulers was uncertain. Christ's object was to secure a decision of the people, for or against him. Hence the prayer at the grave of Lazarus,—" because of the people which stood by." (John 11: 42.) This culminating event is, therefore, reserved until near the close of Christ's ministry, and for the neighborhood of Jerusalem. The proof that the Father had sent him is thus given in the presence of the rulers. Still, there is a contrast between the openness of his private teaching, e. g., to Martha when he says, " I am the resurrection and the life," and his public teaching when he says, " that they may believe that thou has sent me."

Effect of the Miracle: Very profound. Many believed, and others ran with excitement to tell the rulers. (John 11: 45-46.) This was the last link in the chain of events which led to the malicious decision of the Sanhedrim. Farrar: " They *could* not deny the miracle; they *would* not believe on him who had performed it; they could only dread his growing influence, and conjecture that it would be used to make himself a king, and so end in Roman intervention and the annihilation of their political existence."

Why should the people's faith in Christ produce such a result? Two ans: 1. Some say this was a mere pretense by the Pharisees. 2. True view is that Pharisees recognized real result of Christ's claims. If the spiritual view of Christ's kingdom were now to prevail with the people all hope of political deliverance and independence would be lost, as well as their present sources of livelihood. Being engaged in a bitter struggle for national independence, they were convinced by the address of the High Priest that it was better for one man to perish rather than that the whole nation should perish (John 11 : 50-51.) They would not even stop to inquire whether this one person were innocent or guilty, says Farrar. Still, though selfish and Pharisaic, their reasons contained elements of power. " Then from that day forth they took counsel together for to put him to death," although this was not the first time the Pharisees, as a party, had so determined. Vide John 5 : 16-18. At Tabernacles Jesus accused them of this design. John 7: 19.

Advice of Caiaphas: John remarks that the words of Caiaphas were not his own, but a prophecy of the Atonement, he " being the High Priest that same year." (Vide suggestive note by Farrar on the expression "that same year." Vol. II., p. 174.) Common view is that the prophecy was involuntary on part of Caiaphas. But what *he* meant in a low sense, God meant in a high sense.

Objections to the Miracle: Sceptics flourish here. Spinoza says if he could have believed that miracle he would have become a Christian and broken in pieces his own philosophical system.

1. It is said the Disciples misunderstood Jesus when he said, " Our friend Lazarus sleepeth," and that Martha misunderstood him when he said, " Thy brother shall rise again," which would not have been the case if he had been in the habit of working miracles.

2. It is alleged that the Jews would not have referred to an inferior miracle—opening the eyes of the blind—if Christ had power to raise the dead.

Ans: The Jews refer to the blind man's case because it was of recent occurrence, and had made a deep impression. The other cases of resurrection had taken place in Gal., and could have been known to the Jews near Jerus., only by report.

3. It is alleged that we cannot consistently believe that Christ would wait two days after receiving the message that Lazarus was sick. If Lazarus was not dead, it was *cruel* in him to tarry; if he was dead, it was mere ostentation to delay.

Ans: If there was any delay, which some deny, its object was to exercise the faith of the sisters and the Disciples. Besides, it is possible that he had an important work to finish in Perea.

4. The prayer at the grave is objected to. It is said to be out of analogy with his other miracles. Strauss does not hesitate to call it a "sham prayer," offered for the sake of appearance, in reference to those that stood by.

Ans: Christ did not not pray on other occasions, because he desired to give evidence of his own power and divinity. Here he prays to show his relation to the Father, appealing to God in the sight of the Jews.

5. Another objection is found in the silence of the Synoptists concerning a family made so prominent by John. Luke mentions Martha and Mary, but neither Lazarus nor Bethany.

6. The Synoptists silent about the miracle, which was the most important of all.

Answer: *a*, Lazarus and his family were specially obnoxious to the Jews because of their intimacy with Jesus, and especially because Lazarus was a living witness of his power to raise the dead. Hence there is a convincing argument in the fact that the Syn., writing first, forbore to make this family prominent lest they should suffer persecution. This obstacle, however, no longer existed when John wrote. But it may be added danger to themselves seems never to have influenced the Evangelists to hide any of the facts of Christ's life.

b. But a better answer is found in the settled plan of the Syn. not to relate any events occurring at Jerus. until the closing week of Christ's life. They confine themselves mainly to Gal. Min. Each tells the things most directly within his own scope. Hence, Farrar: "Now since raising of Lazarus was no greater evidence, to them, of miraculous power than those which they recorded, and since it fell within the Judean cycle, the omission of the miracle is no more inexplicable than the omission of the miracle of Bethesda (John 5,) or the healing of the man born blind, (John 9.") Farrar, chap. 47.

It is further objected that we cannot accept the Syn.'s account of the sudden burst of applause with which Jesus was received in Judea after the Gal. Min: Mt. 19:

1, 2. But notice that it is Feast-time when he reaches Jerus., and multitudes from Gal. are already there.

Naturalistic Theory of the Miracle: 1. Not actual natural death. Only a case of trance. "He is not dead but sleepeth" is to be taken literally. Renan claims there was actual collusion between Christ and the sisters. 2. The miracle grows out of a misunderstanding of the conversation with Martha about the resurrection.

Mythical Theory: Strauss held this theory at first, but he at last adopted the Tubingen view mainly. He says raising of Lazarus is a fiction based on one of Luke's parables. Baur and others say it is a creation of the 2nd century, and its germ was the expression, "I am the resurrection." But all these theories illustrate the credulity of unbelief, since any one of these views is harder to support than the plain Gospel narrative. (Vide Ebrard, pp. 351-358.)

Christ retires to Ephraim. On account of the action of the Sanhedrim, (John 11: 47-54) Christ retires to the city of Ephraim, to delay the execution of the decree until his time should come. Where is Ephraim? Some say east of the Jordan. More likely near Jerusalem. Some identify it with the Ephraim in 2 Chron. 13: 19, near to Bethel, or twenty miles north of Jerusalem. Josephus speaks of a cavalry expedition of Vespasian by way of Ephraim to Bethel. (Vide Robinson's Greek Har. pp. 203-4; Farrar, Vol. II., p. 176.) Intervening sections not touched upon. Vide small syllabus, p. 14.

§107. *Third Prediction of Christ's Death.* This prediction more specific than in 74th or 77th section. Judicial death now predicted, to be accomplished by the help of the Gentiles, (Mt. 20; Mk. 10; Lk. 18.) He foretells the *manner* of his death, viz., by crucifixion, and predicts that he shall rise on the third day. He tells this to the Twelve alone. Mark notes the fear of the Disciples, chap. 10: 32, from which it may be inferred there was something supernatural in Christ's appearance.

PASSION WEEK.

Natural Divisions: 1. From the arrival in Bethany to the Passover Supper—six days. 2. From the Supper to the Crucifixion. 3. From the Resurrection to the Ascen-

sion. Recorded in Mt. 21-28 chaps.; Mk. 11-16; Lk. 19-24; John 12-21. Space given by each Evangelist; Mt. little more than one-third; Mk. little less than one-third; Luke one-fourth; John nearly one half. In many cases three, in some four, parallel accounts.

Characteristics of the Period: I. A period of voluntary sacrifice. Christ's hour is now at hand, and he submits voluntarily to be condemned and executed by his enemies. Seeks the most public places. Takes possession of the Temple, and for three days holds his foes at bay. All their former plots to take him had failed. But now, by an event, accidental on their part, but designed on his, they are enabled to seize him, and he without resistance gives himself up to them. His death, therefore, voluntary, and hence sacrificial—a sacrifice for sin. No other theory can explain the facts.

II. It is a period in which Christ prominently asserts his claims to the title of Messiah. This he does in three ways: *a.* Typically by securing the Hosannas of the multitude as he enters Jerus. *b.* Publicly during his trial. *c.* By his teaching.

III. The Teaching is supplemental and appropriate to the period. In all Christ's teaching there is a marked advance. We have here three kinds of teaching: *a.* The last of the three groups of Parables: 1. Concerning "Kingdom of Heaven;" 2. The way of salvation; 3. The Judgment. *b.* Final discourses against Pharisees. *c.* Consolatory instruction to Disciples. In Mt. these instructions largely prophetic; in John both prophetic and consolatory. Explains to them that he must go away in order that the Comforter may come.

Order of Events. The Evangelists governed by same plan. The order is alike in all four except in two instances: *a.* John makes the Supper at Bethany the first event of the week, while Syn. place it on the eve of the third day. *b.* They differ as to the time of cursing the barren fig-tree. In their plan, Mt. refers to prophecy, Mk. to details, by days, and Lk. is supplementary. Ruling idea is contrast between Christ's personal dignity and gentleness and his cruel treatment by the priests, rulers and people.

Succession of days. This is obtained from Mk. by counting back from the Passover Supper five days; and also from John 12 : 1. " Then Jesus six days before the Passover came to Bethany." John's peculiar idiom means, literally, six days. Notice we have in John a *week* both at the beginning and end of Christ's ministry. Mode of counting days involves two questions : *a.* Shall we count in both extremes? *b.* Was 14th Nisan, Thursday or Friday? Did the Supper come on the day of the feast, or on the evening before? The day of Crucifixion, we have seen in the opening lectures on Chronology, was Friday, 15th Nisan. The Supper was the regular Paschal meal eaten on Thursday the 14th.

Theories: 1. Wies., Lich., Andrews count back six days from Thursday the 14th, excluding the latter, which brings us to Friday, the 8th as the day of arrival in Bethany. 2. Lange includes Thursday which gives the 9th, or the Jewish Sabbath as the day of Christ's arrival. Lange supposes that Christ halted on Friday a Sabbath-day's journey from Jerus. 3. Those who follow Bleek's arrangement, as Tisch., Ell., Alford and Schaff, make Friday the 14th Nisan. But as they count backward six days excluding Friday the days of the week remain unaltered. 4. Robinson holds Friday to have been the first day of the feast. Six days before would make the arrival in Bethany on Sunday, and he supposes the Jewish Sabbath to have been spent in Jericho.

Objections to Robinson: *a.* He begins a day later than any other Harmonist and compresses the 4th and 5th days into one. (Mk. 14: 1.) *b.* The feast did not begin on the 15th. (Levit. 23 : 5.) *c.* It is contrary to tradition which makes Palm Sunday the commemorative day of Christ's entrance into Jerus. Robinson makes the entrance on Monday. *d.* His own earlier editions take the other view. Farrar : " Thither (the loved home at Bethany) he arrived on the evening of Friday, Nisan 8, A. U. C. 780 (March 31, A. D. 30,) six days before the Passover, and before the sunset had commenced the Sabbath hours." Vol. II. p. 188. Vide Andrews, pp. 396-7-8.

§§111, 131. *Supper at Bethany.* John places this on the evening before the public entrance into Jerus. The Synoptists place it on the eve of Tuesday, or two days

before the Passover (Mt. 26 : 2.) This difference alleged to be irreconcilable.

Ans: Neither John nor the Syn. date the Supper positively. The six days of John do not date the Supper but the arrival in Bethany; and the two days of Mt. and Mk. do not date the Supper but the betrayal of Judas. Farrar: "It is only in appearance that the Syn. seem to place this feast two days before the Passover. They narrate it there to account for the treachery of Judas, which was consummated by his *final* arrangements with the Sanhedrim on the *Wednesday* of Holy week; but we see from St. John that this latter must have been his second interview with them—at the first interview all details had been left indefinite." (Farrar, Vol. II., p. 188, Note.)

Robinson follows order of Syn. These are his reasons: 1. The offence taken by Judas at this feast was the occasion of his treason. Rulers had resolved to delay arrest. But Judas' proposal on Tuesday, (Supper on Tuesday eve.) gave them an unexpected opportunity. Ans: It does not appear that Judas went immediately to the priests.

2. The τότε of Mt.—" then Judas went out." Ans: But τότε is not always used by Mt. in reference to time. He often makes it connect passages which are not successive.

3. John transposes events in order to complete account of occurrences at Bethany.

Arguments in favor of John's order : 1. John more complete. 2. Τῇ ἐπαύριον (John 12 : 12)—" the next day "—was the day of public entrance. Best exegesis favors John's order. 3. Whole passage in Mt. and Mk. seems to be parenthetical. Balance of probability in favor of John's order. According to latter Christ arrived in Bethany on Friday. His friends make him a feast, as had been done when he left Capernaum and Perea. He did not decline this mode of being honored. Sisters of Lazarus improve the occasion to display their gratitude, and Jesus makes reference to his approaching death.

Popular Excitement. In John 11 : 55–57, we read that many went from the country to Jerus. to the Passover. The great theme of conversation among the rulers was

Christ. "What think ye, that he will not come to the feast?" They expected negative answer. He had not come to previous feast. From John 11: 57 we learn that the Sanhedrim had made public charges against Christ, and were waiting to take him. But their doubts are soon solved by the public arrival of Jesus, which increased the excitement. Multitudes flocked out of the city to meet him.

Place of the Supper: It is urged that it must have been in the house of Martha and Mary because they were present and " Martha served," which is supposed to contradict Mt. and Mk. who say it was in the house of Simon the leper. But, as Ebrard suggests, why could not Martha insist upon "serving" in the house of the host with whom her family were intimate? Some say that Simon was the father of Lazarus; others that he was the husband of Martha. Or he may have been the owner of the house in which Martha and Mary lived.

Mode of Anointing: John says the *feet;* Mt. and Mk. the *head.* Ebrard, in reply to objectors, inquires, Why not both? Then according to John, it was Judas who objected to the *waste;* according to Mt. it was "his disciples." Ans: Where is it denied by John that none of the disciples but Judas objected? John mentions Judas in order to give the motive for his objection.

Another objection is founded upon the resemblance between this anointing and the one in Lk. 7: 36. Lightfoot: Three anointings: one in John, one in Mt. and Mk., and one in Lk. He denies any contradiction. Strauss claims that the whole record has to do with only one case of anointing. Ebrard answers Strauss by saying that the only resemblance between present anointing and that in Lk. 7: 36 is that the name in both cases is *Simon* and *the feet of Jesus are wiped with the hair.* But one Simon was a Pharisee, the other a quiet follower of Jesus. Ebrard also suggests that there was quite probably more than one Simon in Palestine, and that it was not impossible that the circumstance of wiping the feet should be repeated. (Ebrard, pp. 366–369.)

Lessons taught. 1. The offering was valuable in itself— "very precious." This may apply both to the box and

the contents. 2. The quantity was large—worth about fifty dollars. Farrar from this infers that the family was rich. Judas is indignant at the waste, but Jesus defends Mary's act, and declares that it shall be a memorial of her throughout the world. The inference is that the expression of a lofty religious sentiment justifies great expenditure, provided it is subordinate to deeds of charity to our neighbor.

Other suggestions: *a.* Character of the sisters always the same. Martha "serves;" Mary sits at Jesus' feet. *b.* Meaning of "this Gospel." Meyer says the reference is to his death of which he had first spoken. The wide preaching of the Gospel is also referred to. Alford says it is the prediction of a future written Gospel. Notice how literally the prediction concerning Mary has been fulfilled. The rebuke stimulated the malice of Judas until he became a traitor.

§112. *Public Entrance into Jerus.* 1. *Time:* It was on Sunday, 10th Nisan. Bleek says Sunday, and Robinson, Monday. That it was a day after a night in Bethany appears from John 12: 12. *Meaning of the event:* He rode upon a carpet of branches and garments. It was a public acknowledgment of his kingly claims as the Messiah. His hour had come. Hence the contrast with his previous conduct is very noticeable. Important that the people should be impressed as well as the Disciples. Appropriate that his last public act should be the clearest proof of his Messiahship.

Significance of date. His entrance on the 10th of the month is directly associated with the Law in Exodus 12: 3. It was the day when the Paschal lamb was set apart. So the Lamb of God sets his willing seal to his own consecration as the sacrifice for sin. *Symbolical acts:* a. Riding on an ass's colt. This was fulfillment of the prophecy in Zech. 9: 9. *b.* It was specially significant of his kingship. Not on a war-horse, but on an ass significant of peace in Oriental countries. The animal, too, was a colt "whereon never man sat." Like the alabaster box unprofaned by other use. *c.* Strewing branches and garments also significant of royalty. *d.* The people also bore palm-branches in their hands, as emblems of victory.

Sudden Enthusiasm of the People. This was occasioned by his acceptance of their homage. Always ready to support him when the result seemed likely to be their restoration to temporal and political superiority. The multitudes quoted Ps. 118. This originally composed at the restoration of the Temple, and now applied to the Messiah by the people, showing that they regarded Jesus as one whom they had looked for. "Hosanna to the Son of David." Jesus had never before allowed the public ascription of Messiahship, because it would rouse opposition before his work was completed. But now his work was done. The Pharisees, feeling scandalized, said unto him: "Master rebuke thy Disciples." Jesus answered that "if these should hold their peace, the stones would immediately cry out," i. e., to silence the people would be to suppress eternal truth. Robinson introduces the Hosannas of the children, the day after the feast at Bethany, in this place. But most Harmonists follow Mt's order, and introduce this after cursing of fig-tree. Prophecies fulfilled: Isa. 62: 11 with Zech. 9: 9; also Gen. 49: 10, 11.

Lamentation over Jerus. This scene is preserved by Lk. and connected directly with public entrance. While they are hailing him as king, he foresees the sad fate of the city. Judicial blindness had seized the rulers and the people. He sees that the majority will rebel against him and aid in putting him to death; that the enemies of the Jews will dig a trench about Jerus., and not leave one stone upon another. (Lk. 19: 43, 44.) This prophecy was literally fulfilled, for the Roman army was encamped on the very spot where this prediction was uttered.

The Pharisees were ready to give up in despair when they saw Christ's popularity. Effect on the people: The whole city was moved—$\dot{\varepsilon}\sigma\varepsilon\iota\sigma\vartheta\eta$, i. e., *shaken*. Christ thus had an opportunity to finish his work, for his enemies no less than his friends were involved in the excitement. *Road by which he entered:* Mount of Olives not a single hill, but a ridge with three summits. Three roads cross it. The northern one is steep; the second is half way down the mountain; and the third, which Christ probably took, and "which sweeps round the southern shoulder of the central mass," is the main road for all kinds of travel. On this road there is a projecting mass

of rock around which the road suddenly turns to the north, and then the whole city bursts suddenly upon the vision. This angle has been fixed upon as the place where Jesus stood as he wept over the city.

Location, of places: Bethany signifying House of Dates, is from 1½ to 2 miles S. E. of Jerus. Its modern name is Lazarieh, which thus continues to bear witness to the great miracle wrought there. Now a small village of some twenty houses, occupied by Bedouin Arabs. Bethphage, House of Unripe Figs, according to Lightfoot was a suburb of Jerus., though hardly any two opinions agree. (Andrews, pp. 404–5.)

Objections: 1. The Syn. introduce the narrative as though the last journey were continuous. John says that Jesus passed the night at Bethany, and the " next day " went to Jerus. Ans: John gives the natural order of events while the Syn. record simply the connection of events. Ebrard denies that it is anywhere stated that Jesus went to Jerus. the *same day* he left Jericho, as Strauss assumes in order to prove an alleged contradiction. 2. If Jesus started from Bethany as John says, then he could not have sent there for the animals. Ans: Who says he did send there for the animals? The "village" referred to by Mt. and Mk. refers not to one of those named, but to another on the way to Jerus. And, as Ebrard suggests, why could he not send forward for the colt after he had gone some distance from Bethany? (Vide Ebrard, pp. 371–2 on the expression "drew nigh.")

3. Mode of obtaining the animals supposes a mythical origin for the narrative. Ans: The objection is trifling. The method chosen is in fulfillment of prophecy. Some suppose the owner of the animals believed in the Lord: others, that a pre-arrangement had been made with him.

4. It is said that Mt. (21 : 7) represents Jesus as riding on both animals. Ans: A similar expression is used in Acts 23 : 24. But nobody infers that Paul rode several animals at once. (Ebrard, p. 372.) Christ's entrance is alleged to have been an attempt to excite revolution. This is an old charge. It is refuted by the fact that after the triumphal entrance he immediately withdraws to Bethany, thereby, as some suppose, signifying that he left Jerus. to its fate.

§113. *Cursing the Fig-tree; Cleansing the Temple.* Bleek puts these events on Sunday, 10th Nisan; Wies. on the 11th and Rob. on the 12th. Difference between Mt. and Mk. very slight. Mt. puts the events in their natural connection, without noticing the division of time. Puts cleansing of Temple immediately after entrance, and cursing of Fig-tree next morning. (Mt. 21: 17-18.) This tree often planted by the way-side for its shade and because " the dust was thought to facilitate its growth." Its fruit was common property. Being hungry he approached this tree whose rich foliage promised fruit. Finding nothing but leaves, Jesus said, " Let no fruit grow on thee henceforward forever."

Objections: 1. It is said if he had known there were no figs he would not have sought them. If he did not know then he is not omniscient. Ans.: The objection assumes that he was bound to tell all he knew. 2. Why did he expect fruit at this season? Mk. says, " for the time of figs was not yet." Ans.: *a.* " It was not the *time of year,* but the striking *quantity of leaves* for the time of year, which led to the expectation that there would certainly be figs upon the tree," says Ebrard. *b.* Although not the general season for figs as Mk. states, " there is to this day, in Palestine, a kind of white or early fig which ripens in spring, and much before the ordinary or black fig." Furthermore, the autumn figs often remained on the trees through the winter, until the new spring leaves had come. (Farrar, Vol. II., pp. 213-4.)

3. It is charged that this act was not only the destruction of a shade tree but also an expression of unworthy anger. Ans.: The lesson taught is of far more importance than the tree. Farrar asks, " Is it a crime under *any* circumstances to destroy a *useless* tree? If not, is it *more* a crime to do so by miracle?" This is the only instance of a miracle of Judgment. The act was a symbolic one. The tree with its luxurious leaves was a type of the Jewish Church, outwardly flourishing, but inwardly barren. It was therefore destroyed. The act is related on the one hand to the lamentation over Jerus., on the other, to the parable following, (Farrar Vol. II., pp. 215-16.) Ebrard says Strauss's conjecture that Christ was

moved only by anger at not finding any figs, "is too worthless and wicked to have sprung from anything but utter insanity."

Cleansing the Temple. Symbolically, this act is the counterpart of the preceding. Christ here assumes possession of the Temple in anticipation of the future reign over the church, and his final success. It was also the manifestation of his Messiahship, as the Pharisees plainly understood. For they said, "By what authority doest thou these things?" The whole Temple services were fulfilled in Christ, who is God with us. Temple was the place where God then met with his people. Now, in Christ God meets with them. In John 2: 16, it is written "make not my Father's house a house of merchandise." In Mk. 11: 17, "My house shall be called of all nations the house of prayer." These two passages generally considered to form a climax. Emphasis in latter passage is on "all nations," making the final universality of Christianity prominent. The second point is the spiritual relation of the people of God. John 2: 13 points to reformation; Mk. 11: 17 to judicial judgment. Jews must be driven out to make room for others. The rulers are again enraged and seek to destroy him, but fail in their purpose. This Monday was a day of great triumph, for, despite the Pharisees, he taught all day in the Temple and at night went out of the city.

§114. *The barren Fig-tree withers away.* On the way to the city, in the morning, the Disciples saw that the fig-tree had withered away. "The quick eye of Peter was the first to notice it." Instead of explaining its meaning, Jesus gives them a suggestive lesson on Faith, and the encouragement to prayer.

§115. *Authority of Christ questioned.* Having arrived at the Temple Christ walked about and taught as if he had sole authority. The second step in events of the week is found in events of this day. Christ does not yield possession of the Temple to force. When he goes it is voluntarily. Here we meet with efforts of the priests to destroy his influence. It was necessary that his power should be thus tested, so that the subsequent surrender of himself should be clearly voluntary. The moral triumph of this day is the preface of his trial. Notice 1.

The assault of the Sanhedrim upon his authority. It is followed by three parables—the two sons, the wicked husbandmen, and the marriage of the king's son. All set forth the judgment to come. 2. Crafty questions intended to involve him in difficulty with civil authorities, and break down his influence. Attempts by Pharisees, Sadducees and lawyers. 3. Long judicial discourses against the Pharisees. 4. The prophetic discourses concerning destruction of Jerusalem and the final judgment pronounced upon his departure from the temple. (Mt. 25.) This discourse is the last of his public teaching, except the one on occasion of the visit of the Greeks. Jno. 12 : 20–50. This day has been called the great prophetic day. Disproportionate length of narrative accounted for by fact that it is the day of final teaching.

Result of the consultation of the Sanhedrim : They question him concerning his authority. It was official: put to him as soon as he reached the temple, and involved 1. The fact that the rulers were divinely appointed, and that Christ was acting in opposition to them. 2. Showed an appreciation of his true Messianic claims. Hence it was a well chosen question, for the people were unwilling for any other than a temporal Messiah. The Pharisees had thought to receive the answer, " I am the Christ." But if question was subtle, the answer shows Divine wisdom. " The baptism of John, was it from heaven or of men?" Alleged that this answer, like their question, a *trap*, and unworthy of Christ. But it is no evasion ; for 1. The Pharisees put the issue between them on the ground of authority. 2. If John had divine authority then his record of Jesus was a sufficient answer to their question. The answer is at same time an exposure of the hypocritical pretence of the rulers of their zeal for authority. They are obliged to confess their ignorance. Three parables concerning judgment follow closely on this defeat. Lesson taught by them all is : rejection of Christ by the nation transferred its privileges and blessings to the Gentiles. Association of the three kept up in the figure. Parable of two sons. Makes his enemies judge themselves. He sets forth their sins, hypocrisy, unbelief, and disobedience. Primary application was either to Jews and Gentiles, or to Pharisees and Publicans. Same principles involved.

§116. *The Wicked Husbandmen.* The disobedience was national, and not negative but active persecution and consequent judgment. The figure of vineyard is sustained—there conduct was personal, here national. Sin was not only in refusing the Lord his vineyard, but in killing his son. The vineyard was therefore taken from them and given to the Gentiles. Shows the love of God to his church; the exaltation of Christ, Ps. 118. "The stone which the builders rejected is become the head of the corner." By striking transition Christ depicts a *negative* judgment. "Whosoever shall fall, &c.," and then a positive judgment "on whomsoever it shall fall, &c." The verb here means to *winnow*, but in our version figure of stone is retained and is probably correct. Personal application of parable to Pharisees is made in Mt. 21: 43, and results in an attempt by them to assault him.

§117. *Marriage of the King's Son.* Figure retained; successive missions, ill-treatment and refusal. The previous parables dwelt on failure of duty, this teaches forfeiture of privileges only alluded to at close of last. The grace of God more prominent in this. Main reference is to the calling of the Gentiles. Should be carefully studied with, and distinguished from, parable of the Great Supper in Lk. 14. Point of view different in Mt. Calling of Gentiles here checking of Pharisaic pride. Climactic relation of two. Mt. closes with entrance of man without wedding garment. Showing that personal, not national qualifications are required. Publicans and harlots might otherwise be led to think they were heirs of the kingdom. Baptism, Charity, Faith, Christian life—a new heart indispensable. Element of mercy in all this severity of Christ—warning men of danger common to all and into which the Jews had especially fallen.

§118. *Question of Pharisees concerning Tribute.* The Pharisees thus baffled retire and take counsel. Renew attack, intending this time to embroil Christ with Pilate—send spies, literally perjurers with instructions to be respectful in manner. Dilemma—he must offend either people or the government. They expected a negative answer which would justify a charge of rebellion. Lk. 5: 20. Notice hypocrisy of rulers—this decision expected of them by Christ as basis of a charge, was to them a matter of conscience—independence being a part of their religion. Question also touched point of contrast between his and their doctrine of the Messianic kingdom. These two questions involved whole case of Pharisees—containing the two charges against him at his trial of blasphemy and sedition - they wanted him to avow his Divinity and also to oppose the Government; the second, a natural sequel of first, if you have such authority, how reconcile it with Cæsar's. But he replies by calling for coin—the coinage of money is prerogative of the ruler in all countries. He recognizes distinction between two spheres of duty and that they are not inconsistent. Precise relation not here stated. His answer surprises questioners, silences them, yet without offence.

§119. *Question of the Sadducees.* Probably they came at the instigation of Sanhedrim. Reply to previous question was on their side and they try now to evoke a reply against the Pharisees. This question differs in spirit from previous one which tho' hypocritical was serious and important—this *frivolous*. Sadducees at first denied tradition simply; then certain portions of SS., and finally denied the resurrection and future punishment—because of their sceptical views. Their question, based on Deut. 25: 5 which as law now obsolete on account of loss of land boundaries, was not a real one. Impossible case of woman married to seven brothers. Treats question as unworthy of notice, proves resurrection from Ex. 3: 6, "I am the God of thy father &c." He is not God of dead but of living. No marriage relation after resurrection.

Strauss charges Christ with rabbinical finesse. 1. The words in Ex. simply meant continuance of covenant relations with Abraham's posterity. 2. Admitting words refer to future state, they prove not resurrection but immortality of the soul. Hence proof is irrelevant. Ans. to first objection. *a.* Christ, some say, not arguing, but simply stating the meaning of passage. *b.* More commonly held that he does argue. The relation between God and the Patriarchs was a covenant relation and therefore an enduring relation of force in both worlds. Ans. to second objection. It *is a complete* answer to Sadducees, because their denial of resurrection was based

upon denial of immortality of soul and greater includes the less. Effect on multitude great, scribes even exclaim, "Master, well said." Parties divided. Comp. with Acts 20.

§120. *Lawyer's question as to greatest commandment.* Naturally follows previous one, which had to do with the law. The dilemma? Two views. 1. The question was much discussed among various parties of the Jews, and any commandment specified by Christ would offend the advocates of all the others. *Stier* quotes from one of the Rabbins, that Moses enjoined 365 prohibitions and 248 commands—in all 613.

2. A profound explanation is that attributed by Schaff and Lange, (really as old as Chrysostom). The temptation lay in the opportunity given our Lord to assert his own Divinity. They expected him to fix on the unity of God as the most important O. T. truth, and the command to love him, the greatest. Had he done so he would have given them an opening by which to lead him to assert his equality with God. That this is true view appears from Christ's counter question, "How could David call him Lord who is his Son." Christ's answer asserts the unity of the law as opposed to the divisions of the Jews, and the true principle of obedience as love to God, whence flows love to man. The lawyer is struck with conviction—"Master thou hast well said."

§121. *Christ's question to the Pharisees.* "How does David call him Lord?" This is not as some assert a mere evasion. It is really the climax of the whole disputation. To perceive this we must bear in mind the two charges made at his trial, blasphemy and treason. Both had been implied in the question concerning his authority and the paying of tribute, and both are best answered here. Christ calls his enemies to the main point in dispute, "What think ye of Christ." Quotes Ps. 110—admitted by Jews to be Messianic—they do not deny his Davidic descent. Christ shows that O. T. declares him to be very God and very man. He is David's son and yet David's Lord. By introduction of this element, the greatest commandment of the Law is fully stated. The effect was —the common people heard him gladly. His opponents cease their questioning. *Notice:* the statement, "No man durst ask him any more questions," is made by each of the Evangelists, but at different points: Mt. 22: 46,—after Christ's counter questions; Mk. 12: 34—after Lawyer's question; Lk. 20: 40—after Sadducees' question. This difference not contradictory; for connection is really the same. Account of woman taken in adultery, John 8: 1–11, inserted here by Lange. But external authority is against the genuineness of the record.

§122. *Judicial discourse against the Pharisees.* The appropriate close of the struggle appears in the denunciatory discourse. Christ sums up all that he has said against the Pharisees during his ministry. A considerable part of the discourse appears in Lk. 11. How is the resemblance to be explained? *Two theories.* 1. The same language could have been twice uttered. It is likely therefore that one Evangelist borrowed from the other—or supplemented by memory from other discourses. 2. Both passages are historical. No warrant for any other view—appropriateness of passage here is evident. *Divisions* of the *discourse* in Mt. vs. 1–13 are occupied with a statement of the true character of the Pharisees—desire of praise, uppermost rooms, greeting in the market, &c.

§123. *Discourse continued. Woes upon the Pharisees.* Series of 7 or 8. These are the severest words ever uttered by Christ. All previous blood shed from Abel to present required of this generation. Jews guilty of same sins as their fathers and were to suffer for sins of fathers. The sins of Pharisees were national and brought national disaster. Yet Christ shows his mercy and love in his lamentation over Jerusalem vs. 37, 38. "Blessed is he that cometh" refers to second advent or resurrection of Christ.

Counterpart of Sermon on Mount, often noticed. In that, we have delineation of character of those who receive the kingdom and statement of consequent blessings. In this, a description of those who reject the kingdom and a recital of consequent woes.

§124. *The Widow's Mite.* From connection in Mt. it is inferred that departure from the Temple was immediately after close of the judicial discourse. In departing our Lord has one warm glance at piety of O. T. Incident here recorded is in contrast with preceding dis-

course. Sitting down to watch the worshippers casting gifts into the treasury, he sees a widow cast in two *lepta*, less than one-fifth of a cent. Bengel remarks that light is thrown upon her act by her throwing in *two* lepta, for she might have kept one. Christ commends her sacrificing spirit.

§125. *Visit of certain Greeks.* John 12: 20–26 is pertinent illustration of supplementary character of John's gospels. *Notice:* 1. Connection in John—he records nothing of long discourses against the Pharisees. But a knowledge of it is essential to the understanding of this event. John therefore puts it in contrast with the bitterness of the Pharisees as recorded in the Synoptists. 2. Connection in harmony suggests similar idea. At the close of the day of conflict with Pharisees, the Greeks appear as the representatives of the Gentiles and accept that kingdom which the Jews reject. Many harmonists refuse to separate this event from connection in which it stands in John, making it take place on the day of Christ's public entrance. Lange arbitrarily places it on same day the Temple was cleansed. But it comes in most naturally when he leaves the Temple finally. Were the Greeks allowed to see Jesus? Some think that the interview was deferred until after the Resurrection, but there would be no force in Christ's reply to the disciples, if the Greeks were not present. The incident an appropriate close of the day of conflict.

§126. *John's reflections upon the unbelief of the Jews:* John 12: 37–50. Verses 44–50 are last words of Jesus or a summing up of the Evangelists, because 1. They are introduced after Christ went away and hid himself, as if they were something remembered. 2. Jesus stood and cried, which implies a great audience.

§§127–130. *Great Prophetic Discourse on the destruction of Jerusalem,* the end of the world and the second advent. Having kept possession of the Temple for three days and having been rejected by the Jews, Christ now leaves it finally. Seated upon the Mt. of Olives his disciples come to him and speak concerning the Temple. His public teaching had ended, but there were two important instructions to disciples. 1. The outward progress of the kingdom of Messiah until the second advent. 2.

John 14—17 chaps. give the inward and spiritual conditions by which the outward triumph was to be secured. Such instructions naturally private, and necessary for completion of his church's preparation. In the O. T. prophecy, the advent, the outpouring of the spirit, the foundation of the church and the final triumph of the Messiah's kingdom are as a whole connected together. To the O. T. prophecies concerning himself, he had, at different times, added his suffering, death and resurrection, the persecution of his disciples and the necessity of patient self-denying labor. The great prophecy belongs therefore to the transition stage in the development of prophecy. It stands related both to the O. T. prophecies and those of Paul and the Apocalypse. Two things must be always remembered: 1. The main design of the discourse was practical, to induce patient watchfulness. Hence a large part of Mt's 25 ch. is in form of parables enforcing this duty. Signs of the advent given are all negative. The disciples are to be on their guard against misunderstanding them. 2. The indefinite conceptions of disciples connecting the advent and the end of the world largely condition the form of our Lord's discourse. The combination of these events is the great difficulty of the prophecy. Christ says " this generation shall not pass away before all be fulfilled." The disciples, questions contain three periods according to the pre-millenial theory: 1. When shall these things be? 2. What shall be the sign of thy coming? 3. And of the end of the world.

It is best to find only two periods with two corresponding questions. 1. When shall the destruction of Jerusalem be? and, 2. When shall be the time of thy coming? with which the disciples naturally associated the end of the world.

Relates other Parables—the stewards, the virgins and the talents. Parable of virgins teaches not only duty of watchfulness but of watchful preparation. Bridegroom delaying his coming shows that the time of advent is distant. A current pre-millenial theory encounters in this parable a serious difficulty. Strauss, Alford and others make it refer to Christ's coming at the first Resurrection. Bride is restored Jewish Church; the virgins

are the Gentiles who will accompany him. Some hold that the exclusion of virgins is not final.

Parable of the Talents. This adds fruitfulness to watchful preparation. A close relation between parable of King's Son and the Great Supper. So this resembles that of the *Pounds* given in Lk. The differences are in the sums given and the returns obtained. In Lk. equal sums produce different results. In Mt. the sums are different, the increase is proportionate and the rewards are equal. Taken together they teach that the gifts of Heaven are all of grace, but that men are to be rewarded according to their fidelity. In verses 31-46 we have the last words concerning the judgment day, where we find ground upon which rewards and punishments are to be based — the treatment of his people.

Is the discourse parabolic or prophetic? Arguments for the former: 1. Its position, following so many parables. 2. Its figures — the goats and sheep, and their separation, the colloquy between the good and the evil and the Judge. For its prophetic character and literal interpretation: 1. The language is didactic and not figurative and the form is changed from the parabolic to the prophetic. 2. The king of the previous parables is not mentioned — prominent figure is the Son of Man. But if this be a prophecy which judgment is meant? of the elect or of the non-elect? or is it the General Judgment? The Millenarians as Stier, Alford, &c., say it is judgment of the $ε\theta νη$ as distinguished from that of the $εκλητοι$, and give these reasons: 1. Test of judgment is not faith but charity. Christians are however to be judged by their faith. Ans: The works mentioned are expressions of faith — the outward duty is taken for the inward state. 2. The parties judged are self-righteous "Lord when saw we, &c.," Ans.: The language used is in reality an expression of humility. Is it the final judgment? The majority of authorities take this view. The prophecy is the fitting climax of his teaching concerning his kingdom.

§131. *Conspiracy of Rulers and Treason of Judas.* The perplexity of the priests stands in contrast with Christ's foreknowledge. They had concluded they could not take him at the feast, but Jesus knew that he was to die.

Mt. 26 : 1, 2 contain a distinct prediction of the crucifixion. The baffled rulers hold council and seek how they may accomplish his death by craft. Opportunity for them—Judas appears. They are rejoiced and offer him a bribe. The traitor sets himself to watch an opportunity to betray his master without inciting resistance. Opportunity is offered sooner than he expected. The Synoptists go back to the Supper at Bethany to account for his appearance. His hypocrisy was there exposed and by his malice the purpose of God was accomplished. *When did Judas go to the Priests?* If he went to them on Saturday night after the Supper he was in collusion with them during the prophetic day; or he may have formed the design in his mind during the feast, and have held an interview with the priests on Tuesday night when they were enraged by Christ's discourses, and ready to make a bargain with him. Or if Robinson's arrangement be correct, placing the Supper on Tuesday night, then Judas was with the priests on Wednesday. The choice is between the two first views. When did consultation of priests occur, Tuesday or Wednesday? It depends upon the method of counting the "two days" spoken of by Christ. Some, as Alford and Ellicott, count inclusively, making it Wednesday night. The more common way is to count exclusively. Two days before Thursday brings it then to Tuesday evening. The plotting was at same time as the discourses. This leaves Wednesday as a day of rest in Bethany, a feature of the history which Robinson's scheme leaves out. *The Consultation of the Pharisees* was informal, and held in the court of Caiaphas—tradition says at his country house at the top of the Hill of Evil Counsel, where monument of Annas the father-in-law of Caiaphas is found. *The price of betrayal*, recorded by Mt. only, was 30 pieces of silver, about $18, the price of a slave, Ex. 21 : 32. Zech. 11 : 12, 13. Smallness of price shows contempt of rulers for Christ. *Character and motives of Judas*. His name Iscariot is variously explained. Some make it mean, man with a bag; others, strangling, alluding to his death. But most commonly, *ish Kerioth*, a man of Kerioth, a place in South of Judea. His office among the Twelve was steward or almoner,

(Lk. 8 : 1–3.) The money entrusted to him was not only for the support of Christ and his disciples but for charity.

Difficulties: 1. Strauss and Meyer say that Synoptists and John do not harmonize—former say Judas went to the Priests immediately after the feast in Bethany, the latter, after Satan had entered into him at the Supper. Ans: According to the accounts Satan entered into him at different times. The objection takes for granted that Judas could not have dallied with an evil thought for several days. All that John says is that his sin was in consequence of the entrance of Satan. 2. It is alleged that the Gospels do not furnish an adequate motive for Judas' treachery—the amount paid is too small even for the priests to *offer*, much less for Judas to *accept*. Ans: The objection does not properly estimate either the power or the extent of covetousness. The smallest sum is sufficient incentive for the greatest crime when it is once admitted as a motive power.

Contrast with Mary: At the Supper, the disciples complained of the waste occasioned by the anointing of Christ. In succeeding verses Synoptists go on to show that Judas sold Christ for 30 pieces of silver, one-third the cost of anointing. Contrast not fortuitous. John says Judas did not care for the poor, but complained of the waste because he was a thief and had the bag. John therefore puts character of Judas on a still lower level,—not only covetous but dishonest. 3. It is said that the rebuke of Jesus was too mild to cause resentment; i. e. Judas was too bad a man to be offended at a mild rebuke. Ans: To be exposed for meanness before a company is not pleasant however mild the language of rebuke. *Dilemma:* Did Jesus know the character of Judas when he chose him for a disciple? John says he knew his true character a year before. If so how then explain Mt. 26 : 24? If Jesus knew him, why did he appoint him treasurer and place him in way of temptation? Why did he choose him as a disciple at all, and why did he bear so long with his hypocrisy? Yet on other hand if Christ did not know him, he was not omniscient. Ans: Judas was necessary to the bringing about of the crucifixion. Strauss declares he was not. We answer, the divine plan was that Jesus should suffer at the feast, and to this end was Judas foreordained. Christ's death was to be accomplished by the lowest form of human depravity—dying for the sins of men, he must die through the most heinous phase of sin. His humiliation is the deeper on account of Judas's treachery. *Neander's* idea: Christ thought he could reform Judas, who was a *political adventurer*. This view is held by some. Judas expected to hold a high position in Messiah's kingdom, but Christ's public entrance and the discourses following assured him his hopes could not be realized, and filled with rage and disappointment he betrays Jesus. *Alford* and others think Judas may have been uncertain as to the result. His betrayal of Jesus was intended only to result in his trial. Even on this theory, notice Judas took care to get the money. Whately and Hanna aver that Judas thought Jesus would rescue himself by some great miracle, expecting thus to have establishment of Christ's external kingdom hastened. His motive thus made out to be a good one. Ans: 1. It is inconceivable that Judas could have had such an idea—he must then have been insane. 2. In the Gospels the motive made prominent is covetousness, which was sufficient to produce the result. To this is joined resentment for rebuke received from Christ at the Supper.

3. A fair inference is that he was disappointed in his expectations as to the nature of the kingdom. This however does not alleviate the bad character of the man. "By their fruits ye shall know them." Lange says that when Judas received the money he put himself outside the pale of honorable motives.

§132. *Preparation for the Passover.* Wieseler and Robinson say Nisan 14th. Bleek and Tischendorf say Thursday, Nisan 15th. Wednesday had been spent as a day of quiet at Bethany. The common arrangement adds to this rest a portion of Thursday. The Passover Supper was eaten on the first ($\tau\tilde{\eta}$ $\pi\rho\omega\tau\eta$) day of the feast of Unleavened Bread—in the evening. During the day close search was made for leaven which was the symbol of that which must be put away. That this Supper was the regular Passover Supper is proved, 1. By $\tau\tilde{\eta}$ $\pi\rho\omega\tau\eta$. This expression implies that it must be so. 2. From the definite expression that follows, "When the Passover

must be killed." 3. Agrees with fact that priests had to kill the lamb in the Temple. 4. The remark of the disciples, "where shall we prepare," &c., shows that the time had come. Sends two disciples who find the place by a miraculous method. *Objection* that Mt. makes no mention of this. But there is no contradiction, and the miraculous is implied. *Objection*: Difficulty of obtaining a place after preparations had been so long delayed. Jerusalem crowded, even surrounding hills being occupied with tents. *Answer*: Enough for the man to be told, "the master needs a room." Secrecy the reason of delay; state of feeling in the city concerning Christ and bargain of Judas on previous evening made it necessary. Finding room as directed, Peter and John prepare for the Supper, unleavened bread, bitter herbs, and a lamb. Lamb, previously purchased and set apart, was carried to temple between three and six o'clock; slain by the priests and its blood sprinkled.

Passover Supper. Order of Events. Difference of opinion—on several points certainty is impossible. But best harmonists are substantially agreed. Mt. and Mk. agree in simple narrative. Lk. gives Christ's words at opening of the meal. John gives incident of washing disciples' feet. Commonly agreed that contention for precedency and the washing of feet are to be placed together; because (*a*) Former would naturally occur upon taking places at the table; (*b*) Latter, in beginning or during the meal. Our version (John 13:2) implies it was after the meal—$\gamma\epsilon\nu o\mu\acute{\epsilon}\nu o\upsilon$ should be $\gamma\iota\nu o\mu\acute{\epsilon}\nu o\upsilon$, supper " being come"; (*c*) connection in Lk. (v. 24) $\dot{\epsilon}\gamma\acute{\epsilon}\nu\epsilon\tau o$ $\delta\dot{\epsilon}$, an aorist, better rendered "there was," not " had been "; (*d*) Design of Lk. for narrating events out of natural order, was to contrast solemnity of scene and Christ's authority and dignity with laxity of disciples. Lk.'s order is: Christ's words—question of precedency —Peter's denial, and desertion of all; (*e*) Find natural order in John; (*f*) The internal agreement of Luke's account with John's reads like one narrative.

Was Judas present at the Eucharist? Lk. puts institution before pointing out of traitor; Mt. and Mk. after. Most reformed writers deny presence of Judas, because *a*. Inherent probability that he was sent out before the sacrament. *b.* John says, (13: 30,) Judas went out immediately after receiving the sop, and Eucharist not before that. *c.* Pointing out was while eating, but sacrament was after supper. Judas took wine as well as bread before he left. *d.* Lk. changes order. 1. To contrast spirit of Supper and spirit of disciples. 2. Mention of cup in v. 17 naturally leads him to describe the Supper.

Exact time of instituting Sacrament. See Lightfoot for description of Rabbinical customs. Possible that Christ followed all the customs and observances, but still evident that Lord's Supper was grafted on the Paschal Supper. Cannot identify exact time. Christ may have chosen to contrast the Supper.

§133. *Opening words and contention of the Twelve.* They were seated—original rule to stand, reminding of haste in leaving Egypt. Christ in sanctioning this departure from the rule, teaches that we are not bound in unessentials. *Prominence of Suffering.* "With desire I have desired to eat this Passover with you before I suffer"—hinting that his suffering was near at hand. Reason for the desire—"For I will not eat again until it be fulfilled in the kingdom of God"—makes last supper emphatic. He takes "cup of blessing"—not cup of sacrament, which is mentioned in 20 v. Inference is unfounded, that Christ did not partake. Main idea of passage is in $\pi\lambda\eta\rho\omega\vartheta\eta$. Central point of economy of Redemption is reached—type fulfilled in presence of Antetype. Notice allusion to the formulas of feast in $\varepsilon\nu\chi\alpha\rho\iota\sigma\tau\eta\sigma\alpha\varsigma$.

Contention for pre-eminence. *Objections* to its occurrence. 1. Strauss and DeWette. Mentioned only in Lk. and the promise of exaltation is out of place. 2. Unnatural that such dispute should occur among disciples at such a time. Ans: It had occurred before, and clearly shows strong impression existing among them even now of external nature of Christ's kingdom. Jesus rebukes their worldly spirit—teaching that only humility can exalt; commends fidelity and promises exaltation to thrones of judgment of twelve tribes.

§134. *Washing Disciples feet.* It may have been done on entering, John 13: 1–20; hinted at in Lk. 22: 27. John puts it after receiving of wine. *Three lessons:* *a.* Proof of continued love of Christ. *b.* Example of

humility. *c.* Implied sanctification—washing of grace, a part of Christ's service. John only refers to Judas's treachery 13: 11. Ps. 41: 9 fulfilled.

§135. *Pointing out the Traitor.* Separation of Judas preceded the sacrament. Christ's distress very great at horror of the crime and sorrow for Judas. Announcement withheld till now that Judas may be kept near. Made *now:* 1. To show Christ's foreknowledge, and make disciples believe after it occurred. 2. To be rid of Judas' presence. 3. To carry out Christ's design of being crucified at the Feast. 4. As a warning to disciples and all his followers.

Effect on Disciples: At intimation of Christ that one of them should betray him—natural they should not suspect Judas. Ask each other "Is it I?" Translation does not give force of Gk.; better read, "Lord it is not I, is it?" More simple and negative. Synoptists make each disciple ask it of Christ. John omits this; says Peter beckoned to John to ask. Mt. and Mark give Christ's reply, "He that dippeth," &c.; John, "To whom I give the sop."

Objections: 1. John's account does not imply private communication of Peter, and act of dipping together could not be distinctive. Ans: The act of simultaneous dipping could be so marked as to call attention to Judas. 2. If public sign given, it could not afterwards be said they did not understand his treason. Ans: Objection based on wrong conception of amount of their knowledge. They did not know that betrayal would lead to crucifixion. Andrews, &c., put questions of Syn. prior to that of John, and point to iniquity of deed. Again Mt. and Mk's description more general than John's. "Son of Man goeth . . . . . but woe, &c.," often quoted in proof of eternal punishment on ground that hope of salvation after period of disappointment would always render life desirable rather than never to have been born.

Judas's perplexity: Feeling that the words were directed to him and seeing attention of disciples directed to him, he asks also, "Is it I?"—consummate hypocrisy. Night when he went out, implies quickness of his plan—time was God's, deed was Judas's. Also significant of darkness he was soon to enter. Christ's glorying is come. Departure of Judas was sign of his victory—and the beginning of his death and glory. "*A new Commandment;*" *new* not in principle or in measure, but in degree and mode. Brotherly love among christians made test of discipleship—love flowing from faith in Christ.

§136. *Prediction of Peter's denial and dispersion of the Twelve.* John relates *denial* in close connection with Christ's prophecy about going away. Lk. in connection with strife for precedence; Mt. and Mk. after the sacrament, as if spoken on way to Gethsemane. *Two alternatives:* Robinson combines these—prediction uttered once and before sacrament. Mt. and Mk. therefore relate them retrospectively. Meyer, &c., say, prediction was uttered twice to include twelve with Peter; at the Supper, John and Lk.; and on way to Gethsemane, (Mt. and Mk.)

Design of prediction to fortify disciples and prepare them for trial of their faith—their conception of Christ's kingdom was so mistaken, they needed to be humbled. This design shown also in Christ's appointment to go before into Galilee after his resurrection. What they did does not indicate utter apostasy—still sheep, though scattered. He will deliver them by interceding—"I have prayed for you that your faith fail not." The *Cock's Crowing.* Mt., Lk. and John—"cock not crow;" Mk., "not crow *twice* till thou hast denied me thrice."

§137. *The Eucharist.* The last passover culminated in the institution of the Sacrament. It now becomes a commemorative and not a typical ordinance. Changed by Christ in person, its celebration by his people in future will signify to them; *a.* A memorial expressive of his dying love. *b.* A pledge or seal of his covenant. *c.* To be partaken of by all on his authority and thus unite them to him. Shows man's inability to live a spiritual life. Needs an outward sign to strengthen weak faith. This rite is distinctive mark of Christians in all ages; sets forth Christ's death, and spiritual presence—"the life of the crucified Savior." *Precise time* not certain. Paragraph in John so close that it is impossible to break it. Lange and Tisch. place it in 32 v. A more prevalent view is that sacrament came between 13 and 14 chaps. of John—confirmed by hymn being sung after-

wards. Some associate the bread with the supper, and cup after—but more probable that the elements were not separated. Variations in words of record: Lk. and Paul (1 Cor. 11: 24) are alike; Mt. and Mk. are alike; but add, after distribution of bread the blessing of the cup. *Explanation:* Some think prayer was repeated—yet this was not essential to celebration or Paul would not have omitted it. But the *blessing* or *thanksgiving* should be made for both elements. Sceptics magnify these discrepancies. But these words are repeated conversationally and taken from Aramaic where "*is*" is not expressed: "this my body." Note also that 1. These variations give fuller idea to the meaning. 2. They allow freedom in celebration of the sacrament. 3. How are we to distinguish between binding acts in the ordinance and those not binding? Ans: *a.* Nothing actually binding which does not appear in each account. *b.* Nothing binding which is not intended to be such by Christ. 4. Is there distinction between breaking bread and pouring out of wine? The two acts are really one. Paul makes no distinction—neither without the other. *Bread* signifies nourishment of life. *Wine* shows more clearly *atonement:* by blood of new covenant we are united to Christ. 5. Did Jesus commune? Lk. 22: 17. "Took cup and gave thanks," &c. Meyer and others think our Lord only gave to disciples and did not partake himself. Alford, that he took of Supper, but not of Sacrament. Most think there is no distinction. He partakes with his people—as their head. "I will no more drink of it," &c., implies that he drank.

Sceptical Objections: Strauss admits a degree of probability in the occurrence of the Supper. Jesus may have instituted it as a rallying point for his disciples. Others deny any evidence that it was to be repeated as a binding ordinance. It was only for disciples—had no reference to the future. The celebration is due to and rests upon Paul's words (I Cor. 11 ch.,) written long after its adoption by the church and therefore must have grown up at a later period. Ans: 1. Perpetual observance *is* alluded to by the Syn. Mention of the Passover itself is enough. "My blood of the new covenant shed for many," has no meaning if confined to disciples.

"I will not drink it until I drink it new in the kingdom," &c., referred by best exegesis to union and communion of Christ with his disciples. 2. Institution does not rest on divine communication to church alone, but on authority of the Twelve as inspired witnesses. It is thus one of the most important and authoritative monumental records. It was universal in the church from earliest times, must therefore have been established by the apostles. *Second Objection:* John's Gospel leaves out the Supper, but gives washing of disciples' feet. Ans: John is supplementary.

Strauss asks why then did he not leave out the feeding of the 5000, which is in all other Gospels? John would naturally be disposed to mention supper, especially on opportunity to correct a false representation. Ans: Supper already in church when John wrote and therefore needed no mention. Strauss says too important to be left out. Ans: It was not adapted to John's purpose. Strauss denies this.

Others say John was ignorant of the institution. This supposition would accord with John's context but not with his practice. His purpose to record Christ's long discourses requires mention of feeding 5000. Omission of Lord's Supper only shows characteristic difference between John and other evangelists.

§§138—141. *Final Discourse and Prayer.* John's account, 14-17 chs., to be inserted in Mt. 26 between 29 and 30 vs.; in Mk. 14 between 25 and 26 vs. *Different opinions:* *a.* He went into a safe room unknown to Judas. *b.* Lange, &c., infer that John 14 was spoken at table, and remainder of discourse on way to Gethsemane. *c.* Difficulty then of separating discourse. When was hymn sung? Whether last thing before they went out, or after John 14: 31, or after the whole is uncertain.

Historical position and design of Discourse: A summing up of Christ's teaching as a system—complete—connected with his going away. It is our Lord's fullest exposition of the consequences of his resurrection and gift of Holy Spirit—properly a transitional discourse. Personal position of disciples a type of the church—they were in sorrow and fear. He teaches necessity of his going away and promises to send Holy Spirit to build up

the spiritual kingdom he had established. Compare previous discourse in Mt. 24 and 25 on great prophetic day. Interval of vicissitudes and judgments between his death and second Advent, but inward life and knowledge of church were also to be extended. It combines the general elements with personal elements of tenderness and love. Every distress of the believer finds relief in these chapters—germ of the Gospel. Meyer says no need to descend to proof of divine origin.

Common misconception in regard to the disciples thinking too much of what they *ought* to have been. Narrative guards against this: Christ said so much in order that the spirit might bring to their *remembrance* what had been said. They were in trouble and in sympathy with their Lord, but did not understand their condition. The whole prophecy was addressed to their misconception.

Analysis: Ch. 14, Christ goes to the Father, and promises the Spirit—vs. 1–14; going to the Father, he would answer prayer—vs. 15–17; give Holy Spirit—vs. 18–24; does not imply separation from his disciples.

Conditions, vs. 25–26: Inspiration; vs. 21–30. Benediction. Ch. 15, *Christ the Vine:* Fundamental work of the spirit, union with Christ. Those holding that he set out for Gethsemane after record in 14th ch., say figure was suggested to him by a vine on the roadside and by burning of pruned branches: others, that he took figure from gold vine around the pillars of the Temple; others, with more probability, that association of the cup was sufficient. Vs. 1–11: Union, condition of fruitfulness and of God's love; vs. 12–19; Union with each other; vs. 20–25: Relation to the world; vs. 26, 27: Personal and official gift of Holy Spirit. Chp. 16, *Work of Holy Spirit;* vs. 1–4, belong to last ch.; persecution predicted; vs. 5–15: Work of Holy Spirit in the world to convince and guide the church to truth; vs. 15–22: Departure immediate; vs. 23, 24: Hearer of prayer; vs. 25–33, Father's love and warning.

Ch. 17, *Sacerdotal Prayer:* Vs. 1–5, for himself, that he may be glorified; vs. 6–11, for disciples that they might be one; vs. 12–19, that they may be sanctified; vs. 20–23 prays for all believers; vs. 24–26, that they might be brought to his glory.

§142. *Gethsemane.* The Syn. record the agony in the Garden. After singing the Hallel., Christ descends to the streets to go to Olivet. A cold night—Peter warmed himself; and it was moonlight, for the Passover was at full-moon. Preparation completed, he went according to his custom to Olivet to spend the interval in prayer. Passing out of the eastern gate, he descends to the brook Kedron (fr. $\kappa\varepsilon\delta\rho o\varsigma$, cedar, or to be dark) now red with blood of sacrifice; a stream dry in Summer, but swollen in Winter from rain; its bed 60 to 80 feet below the present surface. Crossing this they reach $\chi\omega\rho\varepsilon o\nu$, a cultivated spot—Gethsemane—surrounded by a stone wall 150 or 160 feet high, situated half a mile from the city wall. *Objection:* Too near the city for retirement. Ans: It may have been concealed by trees. Traditional site contains eight olive trees said to have been growing in time of Christ, and the tax-levy on which can be traced up to occupation of Jerusalem by Arabs in seventh century.

Leaving the rest to pray, he takes Peter, James and John to witness his sorrow: prays alone, returns, finds them asleep; remonstrates " Could ye not watch with me one hour?" "The spirit is willing but the flesh is weak." Some say this is an apology for their weakness; others that spiritual or regenerated nature was willing but corrupt nature weak; others, sleep due to force or depth of personal feeling. But Jesus evidently treats it as a weakness. *The prayer:* Mt. and Mk. say it was thrice repeated " falling on his face." Lk. says " kneeling down " and intimates no repetition—an angel appeared and he prayed more intensely. Lk. adds also, " his sweat was as it were great drops of blood." Some say, like blood, i. e. in large drops. More commonly understood as *blood-colored*—showing sympathy of his physical with spiritual nature; agony caused palpitation of heart, weakening the frame so that blood oozed from the pores and colored the sweat. Prayer for relief not to be explained away; it was real and sincere. " Thy will be done;" same words he taught his disciples. These words play conspicuous part in discussions of Person of Christ—being exhibition of weakness of his humanity. No authority to restrict the " *cup* " to suffer-

ings in Gethsemane—refers also to his death. Mk. says this hour, i. e. appointed season of the passion. That suffering was natural anguish upon approaching death, is lowest view and unsatisfactory, giving ground to infidels who say others not having as lofty notions as Christ died more nobly. Strauss makes it derogatory to character of Jesus and considers accounts given only as opinions. Renan suggests a moral ground for his suffering—his disappointed expectations, and sorrow for his people. None of these theories sufficient to account for fact. Suffering therefore must have been for *sin*. His anticipations, though great, were exceeded by reality. This excess of anticipated distress not superfluous. Some suggest its important relation to agony on the cross; showing suffering as moral in nature, not merely physical. But suffering in garden was greater than at crucifixion—throws light also on mind of Jesus and gives important examples. *Notice:* First trial—in blood-like sweat—was private. His inevitable anguish hidden from profane eyes of men; at cross he was as a lamb led to slaughter.

Objections: 1. Discrepancies between Mk. and Lk. 2. Lack of sympathy in the discourse. John passes over agony entirely. 4. *Main objection:* Synoptists' account inconsistent with John 14–17 chaps. especially in prayer; not only an impossible change of mood but a falling from state of strength and majesty to one of doubt and conflict; hence either one or both accounts not historical. 5. Unnatural for Christ to deliver a long discourse at such a time and impossible for John to remember it. Strauss, more consistent than the rest, considers it a *myth*, and makes these its stages: *a*, After the Passover, reverence of believers led them to think Christ's sufferings were foreknown to him. *b*, He not only foreknew, but had actually experienced them. *c*, Had also intended them beforehand. *Ans:* No real difficulty; John says he *speaks;* Syn., *agonizes.* No change of purpose but of feeling. Perfection of human nature would tend to change state of mind, while steadfast purpose under all suffering proves his divine nature.

Reasoning of Rationalists Suicidal. They say natural anguish at approaching death not sufficient to account for his intense suffering. They therefore admit the historical fact of the suffering. But this suffering is unaccountable except on ground of union of divine and human in Christ, and his suffering for sin. As long as history stands, sceptics are condemned.

§143. *Betrayal and Arrest.* Jesus, returning from prayer the third time, and finding the disciples asleep, says, "Sleep on," and yet adds, "Arise." Sudden transition explained: *a*, As only a question: "Sleep ye on still?" (Greswell and Robinson): *b*. As ironical (Calvin, Meyer); *c*. Better to suppose interval of time elapsed between the sentences. From his elevated position he sees the approaching procession after he spoke first. He then adds, "Rise, let us be going." *Mode of Betrayal:* As Christ pointed out traitor by "a sop," Judas points Him out by "a kiss." Judas was at work while previous discourse was going on. Priests still afraid of people, who would likely be about the streets on Passover night. Judas directs the priests. Mk. and Mt. say a crowd; Jno. a band and leader. Was it a Temple watch of Levites, or a Roman troop? More likely the latter, as priests would get these on the plea of keeping peace. John says they came with torches; yet it was moonlight. No inconsistency because they expected to search in secret places. John says Jesus went forth and said, "Whom seek ye?" They *fell to the ground.* Some regard this as effect of personal power of Jesus on their feelings. But words show it was miraculous—his answer to their display of force. Some charge that it was a theatrical display of power which he did not intend to use. *Ans:* A miraculous evidence of divinity appropriate to the occasion, and served also to shield the disciples. *Question of harmony:* John says Jesus immediately surrendered; Syn. say Judas gave a sign. Some think he surrendered, and then Judas, to keep his word, gave the kiss. Judas may have advanced too far beyond his companions, who could not notice the kiss, and therefore waited till Jesus came forward and addressed them. Robinson, Alford, &c., put incidents in John 18:4-9 before Judas' kiss. More probable that kiss was first. *Peter's Sword:* Christ rebukes him and heals the servant. John gives names. Syn. make Christ refer to cup of Gethsemane

which John had not related. Lk. adds another class of persons—priests, elders and captains of Temple. These may have been present from first and taken no part, or have arrived subsequently. *Flight of Disciples* needs explanation. They could not understand all the predictions. Until now they had always seen Christ victorious, and seeing him make no resistance are thrown upon their faith, which fails them. To understand their action, must look from their standpoint. *The young man with linen garment*—mentioned only by Mark. Why insert this when so much else of importance? *Ans:* a, Incident is a stroke of reality. When the mind is aroused the smallest thing will strike it. Minute things confirm the account. b, A familiar incident in court of justice. Garment a common night dress, conspicuous. It attracted the men and they seized it, when he fled naked. c, The young man was John Mark himself (Lichtenstein). Omits name from modesty. This removes all difficulty. Likely, for his mother was living in the city. Lange thinks he owned the vineyard and had been asleep in the watch tower.

§144. *Jesus led to Annas.* Difficulties in harmony are here presented. Jesus is led before Annas and examined before Caiaphas. Jews are under necessity for haste. The arrest is contrary to law, and they are afraid to hold him prisoner on account of the people and his own miraculous power. While one part engaged with Judas, another notifies the Sanhedrim. Their plan—to secure sentence of death before an ecclesiastical court, then as matter of form receive permission to execute it from the civil court. If Sanhedrim sentenced him on charge of blasphemy, the people would be gained to their side. Plan almost succeeded, but was made subservient to foreordained plan of God. *Difference in accounts:* Each gospel has its own plan; Mt. contrasts Christ as Messiah and King with his rejection by the people; Mk. gives vivid descriptions of particular events, e. g., of Peter's denials; Lk., human maltreatment of Jesus contrasted with his dignity and love. So much is recorded in the different accounts, and each having a different design necessitates differences; but a knowledge of all removes all difficulties. *Three stages in the ecclesiastical trial:* 1.

Preliminary questioning by High Priest. 2. Trial before Sanhedrim. 3. The sentence and resolution to take Him to Pilate. Mt. and Mk. thus give the order: Before Caiaphas, Peter's denials, Sanhedrim in morning. Lk. gives: Peter's denials, the mocking, the morning trial. Jno. gives: Meeting with Annas as the first High Priest, Peter's first denial, examination, Peter's denials. Mt. and Mk. alike, except Mk. omits name of High Priest. Jesus is charged and condemned by His own confession. Lk. differs, giving Peter's denial, then the morning trial, account of which is almost same as that given by Mt. and Mk. of council and trial held at night. 1. Question of Harmony is between Syns. and Jno. Jno. represents Jesus before Annas; Syn. before Caiaphas. Is Jno. 18: 13–24 a preliminary examination before Annas, or only before him to be sent by him to Caiaphas? Wieseler, Tisch. Ell., Lange, &c. consider it one examination. But this difficulty arises: Syn. say Peter's denials occurred in house of Caiaphas, and examination and denials were at same place at same time. Hence Meyer and Blackie consider this an irreconcilable contradiction. One supposition, however, removes all difficulty: Annas and Caiaphas occupied same house. No improbability in this. Annas was old man and father-in-law to Caiaphas (Stier, Ebrard, Alford, &c.) *Solution:* John's examination was also in house of Caiaphas. *a*, John's form of expression—gives long description of Caiaphas, only naming Annas. They led him to Annas first, as father-in-law to Caiaphas. Again, John and Peter follow Jesus; John knowing the High Priest entered his palace, and throughout describes the questioning as before High Priest, who was Caiaphas. Passage therefore is easy if we admit that Annas sent Jesus to Caiaphas at once. *b*, The denials of Peter are thus explained: Syn. and John represent them in hall of Caiaphas. *c*, Objections to this view an argument in its favor; v. 24, "Now Annas had sent him bound to Caiaphas, the High Priest." In beginning they took him to Annas. Natural then to conclude that whatever occurred before v. 24 happened before Annas. On the other view the aorist $\alpha\pi\varepsilon\sigma\tau\varepsilon\iota\lambda\varepsilon\nu$ must be translated as a pluperfect, "had sent;" but no need for forcing tense thus. Statement (vs. 24–28) must be taken parenthetic-

ally in connection with the blow of the hand. He was bound and therefore defenseless. Most harmonists take this view.

Preliminary Examination, probably during interval before Sanhedrim could assemble. Robinson's plan adopted, though he obscures plan by grouping Peter's denials by themselves. Why should Jesus be taken before Annas at all? Because he was father-in-law to Caiaphas and a man of influence and ability. In questioning, Jesus might show ground for accusing him. The examination was *informal*. John shows it to be such, evidently, whatever view is taken. The High Priest's questions are concerning his doctrine and disciples; $διδαχής$ includes substance and mode of teaching. Christ's answer, as in the garden, shields the disciples. His teaching had always been open. "Ask them which heard me." He disappointed the purpose of the High Priest and he was struck by an attendant, and only returned a mild rebuke. Violence having commenced, steadily increased. *Objection to John's account:* He omits examination of witnesses and forms of trial as given by Syn. as well as Christ's avowal of Messiahship. Hence gives no issue to the trial. *Ans:* a, John adheres to his supplementary plan. b, Conclusion is involved in 19 ch., 7 v.: "We have a law, and by oūr law he ought to die." c, Charge of blasphemy was not real ground on which Caiaphas consented to crucifixion—but consent of Pilate.

Peter's Denials: In John, during first examination; Mt. and Mk. postpone them till the formal trial. All agree it was at night, before cock crew. Lk. therefore puts denials first, because failure of the disciples' faith in him was no small element of his suffering. John tells how they gained admission to the palace—one of them being known to the High Priest. They were soon separated. Peter warms by the fire in the court. *First Denial:* No special difficulty. Addressed by damsel or portress, whose attention was probably attracted at his entrance. No one joined her in her accusation. *Second Denial:* Went to the porch afterwards when the cock crew. Mk. same girl; Mt. another; Lk. a man. John, "they." Probable that portress addressed him again in presence of another maid who joined in—others repeat it. *Third Denial:* An interval perhaps of an hour had elapsed. Peter, to allay suspicion, joins in conversation and betrays his Galilean language. Kinsman of Malchus (John) begins to accuse him, and is joined by bystanders. Charge now made by so many, and on good grounds, threatens immediate danger, and Peter therefore denies with oaths. Cock crew about 3 A. M. Sceptics say eight or nine denials; but the charges may have been many, with only three denials. "Looked upon Peter." Jesus was in the large hall, Peter in the court in sight. Or it may have occurred as Jesus was passing from Annas to Caiaphas. See Andrews, p. 491, seq.

§145. *Jesus before Sanhedrim.* Mt. and Mk. put meeting of Sanhedrim and condemnation *before* Peter's denials, as if at night, and distinguish a reassembling in the morning. Lk. speaks of no night meeting but records all as happening in the morning. Is examination in Lk. 22: 66–71 different from Mt. 26: 57, 58, or is Luke's simply a fuller report of a second morning examination recorded in Mt. 27: 1? Or is the last the same meeting, and therefore Mt. and Mk.'s accounts are to be transferred to the morning? Sceptics say they are irreconcilable. Most orthodox interpreters resort to the harmony, 1. The simplest method is to consider that Mt. and Mk. describe a different meeting from Lk. (Lange and Andrews). The order then is: Christ taken from Annas and sent immediately to Caiaphas, who, while Sanhedrim is convening, questions Christ — then Peter's denials begin. Sanhedrim opens — trial goes on — mockery &c. — in the morning a formal session of Sanhedrim whose same questions are repeated and a charge of blasphemy brought. Christ sent to Pilate. This order has its plausibilities: *a.* It keeps each account in its own order, Mt. 27: 1, Mk. 15: 1 agree with Lk. 22: 66 as to time. *b.* The order of time favors it, "When it was day." Mk. is still stronger — $ευθεως$; Mt. and Lk. say early dawn. Lk.'s examination in the morning is parallel with what Mt. and Mk. say was early in the morning; natural impression from Mt. and Mk. is that trial was at night. *c.* Certain differences in the accounts imply two different meetings. In Lk. no formalities, no witness given. "Art thou the Christ," as if question was repeated, and designed to leave no

doubt in any mind that Christ really claimed to be such. This was the more necessary if morning meeting was fuller and more formal. *d.* Jewish authorities affirm that it was illegal to try any case at night or pass sentence on same day as trial. *e.* The buffeting and mocking which Lk. records before morning session is likely same as Mt. and Mk. record at night. Robinson thinks they were repeated—difficult to suppose however. *f.* Andrews &c., argue that morning session was in a different place from the informal one at night. Lk. says they brought him to their own Council Chamber; the trial therefore in the house of High Priest is different from that in the Council Chamber. *The Council Chamber of Sanhedrim*—connected with the Temple enclosure. They were driven out of the place a year before the crucifixion, and held their session in shops. Argument for plan is doubtful. 2. Robinson, Ellicott, Alford, Meyer, Lichtenstein maintain that Mt. and Mk. are parallel with Lk.—only one trial, and that in morning. *Main Reason* for this view: the question in Lk. is so much like that in Mt. and Mk., it is not necessary to suppose it was repeated. The *order* then is: From Annas to Caiaphas—preliminary questions before Caiaphas when morning comes. *Objections* to this view: *a.* Mt. and Mk. speak of presence of Sanhedrim in house of Caiaphas, when Jesus first arrives there. Robinson assumes that they mention this by anticipation. *b.* Mt. and Mk. transpose the denials of Peter, putting them *after* the trial, whereas they happened during the night and *during* the trial. *c.* Mt. 27 : 1 and Mk. 15 : 1 seem to imply a night and morning meeting. Some say not mean a new meeting but only a resumption of the narrative interrupted by mention of denial. Others suppose Matt. 27 : 1 was simply a private caucus of members. This method yields a perfectly good and historically true narrative. The only historical difference between the two views is: Adoption of a trial by night would prove an unseemly haste on part of priests to carry out their design so early in morning.

The Trial. Was the court legally constituted and the trial fair? Salvador (Institt. de Moïse) views the trial from a Jewish standpoint. Answered by Dupin. Philipson, that all was done by the Romans. Comp. Friedlieb.

Jews claim Christ was an imposter, and that the trial should be judged from their point of view. False claim. Peter at Pentecost puts it in proper light—done by "lawless hands," (Acts 2 : 23), "through ignorance" (Acts 3 : 17). Even granting Jewish claim, the trial of Christ was neither fair nor legal.

1. It was prejudged. Since previous Passover, Jews "sought to kill him" (John 7 : 1). After raising of Lazarus a formal council and plot to put him to death (John 11 : 47–53). Did not now design to give him fair trial.

2. The charge before Pilate not the real ground of their persecution. His gathering men for a spiritual kingdom would distract attention from resisting the Romans, yet they represent to Pilate that he is plotting against Cæsar (Lk. 23 : 2). Their charge of blasphemy (John 19 : 7) founded on an admission forced by High Priest during the trial. Real ground is political jealousy. They fear the influence of his doctrines.

3. It was conducted in haste and in cruelty, (thus against their own law). "They spat in his face; they smote him with rods; they struck him with closed fists and with their open palms." (Farrar.) At same time, it was a representative, national act; jurisdiction belonged to Sanhedrim. The legal form of obtaining witnesses was obeyed. This necessary because of Romans (John 18 : 31) and because people were in his favor. The chief priests and Sanhedrim "sought false witness." When before High Priest, there were no witnesses. Christ then appealed to publicity of his ministry and demanded witnesses (John 18 : 19–23). They must, therefore, obtain true testimony, yet apply it against Christ. This is difficult. At last, two bear witness: "This fellow said, 'I am able to destroy the temple of God and to build it in three days.'" Falsity lay in their application—wresting his meaning. Yet not even so was their witness ἴση (Mk. 14 : 59). Difficult to prove Christ claimed to be Messiah. Some say, strange, since Christ had publicly claimed Messiahship and divinity. *Ans:* His mode of teaching was nevertheless enigmatical. Most take ἴση to mean witnesses *not agree* (so E. V.) Law required at least two (Deut. 17 : 6). Sanhedrim in a dilemma: will not acquit, cannot condemn. This

equivalent to a confession of his innocence. Even this semblance of a trial writes their own accusation. Notice the facts of his life, miracles, doing good, etc., not denied. In charge concerning temple, possibly they thought a claim to divinity or threat against temple involved. So high priest: "Answerest thou nothing?" "But he held his peace." Farrar contrasts with trial of Herod before Sanhedrim (Jos. Antt. Bk. 14: 9: 4).

Why Christ makes no reply? Before High Priest, in private, and before Pilate, a heathen, Christ answers. To false witness now, he answers not a word. Strauss finds in this silence a *myth* founded on Is. 53: 7, "As a sheep before her shearers is dumb, etc." Reasons for silence:

1. Their testimony proved nothing, and was confuted by their disagreement.
2. They would not believe, had he answered.
3. Not his design to be acquitted. A voluntary sacrifice.
4. Silence thwarts them and brings out his dignity and resignation. "They felt before that silence as if they were the culprits—he the judge."

Priests now change plan: would make Christ condemn himself—illegal. Excited High Priest stands: "Answerest thou nothing?" Adjures him, "Art thou the Christ, the Son of God? (Mt. 26: 63) the Son of the Blessed?" (Mk. 14: 61). Does "Son of God" here imply idea of divinity—or is it simply a Messianic title?

In favor of latter view: 1. "Son of God" one of current titles of the Messiah, based on Ps. 2: 7, not implying divinity. Idea of divine nature of Messiah lost among Jews.

2. In his answer Christ puts another Messianic title over against this—"Son of man," based on Dan. 7: 13. Held by Meyer and Gess.

In favor of former: 1. Christ had used it as implying divinity, and they so understood him. (John 5: 18; 10: 36.)

2. This accounts for their rage. Mere claim of Messiahship does not account for it. Rage because, *a*, privileges to be taken away, and *b*, Jesus claimed to be the "Son of God." Form of question makes the distinction —adjures him " by the living God."

3. This accounts for charge of blasphemy—not so other views. Mt. 26:65, 27:40, John 19:7 show their ground of accusation was in this title.

Christ answers, in this decisive, tragic moment, the only time when silence might have saved him: "I am, and hereafter ye shall see the Son of Man, etc." (Matt. 26:64, *Σὺ εἶπας*). Comp. Dan. 7:13. Some refer words to last judgment. Yet *ἀπάρτι* (from now on) would appear to refer to spiritual kingdom. Whatever the exegesis, Christ's design appears two-fold: 1. To assert his divinity. 2. To warn his enemies. "Jesus simply intends to indicate the point of his deepest humiliation as the *turning point* between his redeeming work and that of judgment, and to declare that at the very period when they thought to destroy him, his true glory would begin." (Ebrard.) Note, this the *first public assumption of title, Messiah*. Had before revealed it to woman of Samaria (John 4:26); to disciples at Cæsarea Philippi (Matt. 16:20); cautions disciples to tell no man. His claim to be "Son of God" always aroused violence, e. g. at the feast of the Jews (John 5:17, 18); in Galilee (John 6:40, 41); at Dedication (John 10:30, 31); Jews not sure he is the Christ (John 10:24). Now first asserted before his enemies, when he intends to abide consequences. Culminates in a long conflict between him and the priests who would have accepted him had he accommodated himself to their views of Messiah. *Effect:* 1. High Priest rent his clothes, forbidden by Lev. 10:6 and 21:10. Farrar says: "But Jewish *Halacha* considered it lawful in case of blasphemy (1 Macc. 11:71; Jos. B. J. 2:15:4)." 2. All vote him "worthy of death." From Lk. 23:51 some except Joseph of Arimathea from Council. Say he was not called. Probably both he and Nicodemus present. Even small minorities may be right. 3. Buffet and mock him. They "struck him in the face," "spit in his face," "smote him with the palms of their hands, saying Prophesy, etc." Does this occur twice, or is Lk. parallel with Mt. and Mk.? Ebrard says twice. Robinson, Greswell, say once. Probably parallel: 1. Improbable Luke would represent violence occurring in regular court. 2. Position in narrative explained by contrast of men mocking, with Peter weeping bitterly. By whom? Mt.

says indefinitely, "they ;" Mk. says "some;" Lk., " the men that held Jesus." Inference that Sanhedrim did it first, and Roman officers or soldiers followed their example. Jews reject this interpretation. Where occur? Some say, in prison ; Lange, in guard-room of priest's house. These are only guesses. Strauss says mockery a myth founded on Is. 53, "bruised for our iniquities, etc."

§146. *Morning Meeting of Sanhedrim.* (Lk. 22 : 66–71.) On Friday 15th Nisan, Wieseler, Lange, Robinson ; 14th Nisan, Bleek. Was this an informal consultation, or a continuation of night session ? Or was all by daylight, or a new meeting very early? In our view a new meeting for threefold purpose: 1. To convince by-standers. 2. The Oral Law ordained trial by daylight, Zohar, 56. Farrar: "And they who could trample on all justice and all mercy were yet scrupulous about the infinitely little."

3. To consult how to put him to death. Farrar: " His 3d actual but His first formal and legal trial," and in a note:—" It is only by courtesy that this body can be regarded as a Sanhedrim at all. Jost observes that there is in the Romish period no traces of any genuine legal Sanhedrim, apart from mere special incompetent gatherings. (See Jos. Ant. XX. 9. §1 ; B. J. IV. 5, §4)." The question " Art thou the Christ?" and his answers read as though referring to a former trial. Then they "bound him " and led him Pilate, a transfer from ecclesiastical to civil court. Their evidence of his Messianic claim established. Strauss retains trial, on charge of overthrow of existing institutions, and condemnation for claim to be Messiah. Some Jews maintain that as they had not power of life and death, responsibility rests on Romans.

§151. *Judas hangs himself* (Mt. 27: 3–10, Acts 1 : 18, 19). Robinson transposes suicide till Christ was given up to be crucified. "Till then he had hoped, perhaps, to enjoy the reward of his treachery, without involving himself in the guilt of his master's blood. Mt. places it here. Better to follow order of Evang. till proof to contrary. Introduced as showing by striking example the effect of ill-treating Christ ; also brought by Mt. in contrast with repentance of Peter. Another testimony to innocence of Christ (Mt. 27:4.) Lange, as symbolical of the suicide of the nation. Theory that condemnation of Christ took Judas by surprise inconsistent with spirit of his own confession (v. 4) and every fact of case.

Casts money in the Holy Place, where he had no right to enter—intent to return it to them. Significant that blood-money returns to Temple, Christ's body. Differences: 1. Mt. says "hanged himself"—Peter (Acts 1:18) "falling headlong, he burst asunder"—not inconsistent if he hanged himself and rope or branch broke.

2. Mt. says "priests bought." Peter: "Now *this man* purchased a field." Farrar: "There is in a great crime an awful illuminating power. In Judas as in so many thousands before and since this opening of the eyes which followed the consummation of an awful sin to which many other sins have led, drove him from remorse to despair, from despair to murder, from murder to suicide." Robinson "In Acts 1:18 $\dot{\varepsilon}\kappa\tau\dot{\eta}\sigma\alpha\tau o$ is to be rendered: *he gave occasion to purchase*. Analogous to Mt. 27:60; John 3:22; 4:2, etc."

§146. (resumed.) *Jesus before Pilate.* Had Sanhedrim the power of life and death? No.

1. Distinctly stated in John 18:31 and confirmed by Talmud (Berachôth f. 58; 1—see Buxtorf Lex. Tal. p. 514.)

2. Impossible that the Romans would leave them such power.

3. Accounts best for anxiety to procure Pilate's consent.

Döllinger thinks they had this power but could not put to death at feast time. Objection: Sanhedrim stoned Stephen. This, however, was the tumultuous act of a mob. Paul after being tried by Sanhedrim was sent to Rome. Two results accomplished by Providence: 1. Christ's death by crucifixion (John 18:32.) 2. Participation by Gentiles.

Pilate was fifth Procurator of Judea which was a hard country to govern. Not under Questor, nor was it a proconsular or imperial province. Pilate insulted the Jews, *a*. by removing army and images from Cæsarea to Jerusalem (Jos. Antt. 18:3, §1.) *b*. By expending sacred

money—Corban—on aqueducts (Jos. B. J. 2: 9, §4). c. By setting up in Jerusalem shields dedicated to Tiberius (Philo. Legat. ad Caium §38). d. By mingling the blood of Galileans with their sacrifices (Lk. 13: 1). Removed A. D. 36 (Same year as Caiaphas), by Vitellius, Legate of Syria, on accusation of Samaritans for having slain many while assembled on Mt. Gerizim (Jos. Antt. 18: 4, §§1, 2). Eusebius says, wearied with misfortunes, he killed himself. Traditions: 1. Banished to Vienna Allobrognm, where there is a pyramid called Pontius Pilate's tomb. 2. At Mt. Pilatus by the lake of Lucerne, plunged into dismal lake at the summit. (See Smith's Dict.)

Has strong conviction of innocence of Jesus and endeavors to free him. He is impressed by Christ's claim to be the Son of God, and by his wife's dream. Pilate is perplexed by the Priests accusing, while the people are favoring Christ. His great fault is cowardice. He acted from policy and not from principle (Chrysos). Collateral evidence in Tacitus Ann. 15: 44; "*Per procuratorem Pontium Pilatum supplicio affectus erat.*" Also know from Justin, Tert., Euseb., that Pilate made report to Tiberius (of Christ's trial and condemnation), which is lost. "Acta Pilati" now extant, spurious.

Accusation of Sanhedrim. Still early when they lead Christ to the Prætorium, which is generally understood to be the white marble palace of Herod; by some (Ewald, Meyer, Lange), the tower of Antonia. In John 19: 13, "the Pavement," outside of the Prætorium. Bears on direction of Via Dolorosa. Jews did not enter Prætorium lest they should be polluted for Passover. John 18: 28, not proof it was Nisan 14th. So Pilate goes out to them. Synoptists give general description. John gives conversation between Pilate and the Priests, also between Pilate and Jesus. Farrar: "The last trial is full of passion and movement: it involves a threefold change of scene, a threefold accusation, a threefold acquittal by the Romans, a threefold rejection by the Jews, a threefold warning to Pilate and a threefold effort on his part, made with ever increasing energy and ever deepening agitation, to baffle the accusers and to set the victim free."

Pilate and the Priests. First attempt is to obtain as a favor crucifixion of Christ. Charge of blasphemy against God not sufficient before heathen Pilate, and they had no other. "What accusation bring ye?" If he were not a malefactor etc., implies guilty of no ordinary crime. Pilate is sarcastic; "take ye him and judge him." If you condemn, you must bear the responsibility. I execute, when I judge. Jews say "not lawful for us." Then began they to accuse him (Lk. 23: 2 between John 18: 32 and v. 33) of perverting the nation, forbidding tribute, and claiming to be king. *Notice:* 1. Not same charge as before Sanhedrim. 2. Charge false in fact. They knew Christ taught submission to the government. 3. Ignominious, as Priests advocate that for which they condemned Christ.

Pilate and Jesus go within the Prætorium. Pilate did not trust the Jews; knew they would not condemn Christ for treason against the Romans,—endeavors, according to Roman law, to obtain confession of accused. Synoptists give affirmation. John fuller: "Art thou a king then?" Could not say "no." Pilate might not understand "yes." Reply: "Sayest thou this of thyself?" Design: Hengst., Stier, to arouse Pilate's conscience. Meyer, Christ demands who is his accuser. Olsh., Lange, to bring out sense in which Christ put the question. Jesus makes clear that his kingdom is not of this world. Pilate, "thou art a king then?" deprecating accent on *then*. Ans: "Thou sayest it . . . every one that is of the truth heareth my voice." Pilate's famous question, "What is truth?" Whether in earnest (Chrysos.), impatient (Farrar), contemptuous (Meyer), skeptical, or indifferent, Pilate gives additional testimony to the innocence of Christ: "I find in him no fault at all."

Priests enraged make new charges. He stirreth up the people, beginning from Galilee (Lk. 23: 5). Pilate hearing the word Galilee, eagerly dismisses him to Herod. Second effort to release Jesus.

Objections: 1. Synoptists give Pilate's question to Jesus, *as if* outside; John says in the Prætorium. Ans: Synoptists give general account, do not say it *was outside*. No contradiction. 2. How did John know private interview? Ans: He was present, or Pilate reported, or Jesus stood at the door and all heard, or some prosecutor

was voluntarily within. Strauss, all an invention of John. Baur finds a *tendency* of Evangelist to throw guilt on Jews. 3. The narratives separately unintelligible. Acc. to John, Pilate's questions to Jesus before accusation. Ans: John assumes possession of Synoptists—also, Pilate knew much of Jesus. Whole city in excitement. In Synoptists, Jews accuse, Jesus admits and without investigation (mentioned by John), Pilate pronounces him innocent. John supplements not contradicts.

§147. *Jesus before Herod.* (Lk. 23 : 6–12). Priests disappointed. Pilate sends Christ to Herod : 1. To get rid of a troublesome case. 2. To keep from offending the priests. Other motives subordinate. Herod Antipas, tetrarch of Galilee, was in Jerusalem to keep the Passover. Receives Jesus with curiosity. A frivolous, unscrupulous, dissolute monarch, sensuous and mercurial in character, susceptible of religious impressions, unwilling to renounce sins. Shows no appreciation of the case ; hoped to see a miracle. Had Christ worked one miracle here or before Pilate he might have caused his release. Reserve of Christ sublime. Herod is disappointed and sends Jesus back with *scorn*. Judas, Priests, Pilate and Herod all testify to his innocence. He is mocked and arrayed in cloak. Color? $\lambda\alpha\mu\pi\rho\dot{\alpha}\nu$—bright. If white, means innocence or a candidate for office : if red, royalty. Probably red military robe. Shows mockery. Fulfillment of Ps. 2. (See Acts 4 : 25–27). Herod and Pilate made friends. Enmity probably because of Galileans slain (Lk. 13 : 1). Where Herod lodged doubtful ; probably in old Herod Palace, Pilate in the new. Objections : 1. Why was Jesus sent back ? Ans : Olsh., because birth in Bethlehem was ascertained. More likely, could not find ground to condemn him, would not oppose Priests by acquitting, so preferred to return Pilate's compliment. 2. Why mentioned by Luke only ? Strauss, because it never happened. Ans : Not essential to history. No effect except additional humiliation and new testimony to innocence.

§148. *Pilate's third effort to release Jesus.* (Mt. 27 : 15–26 ; Mk. 15 : 6–15 ; Lk. 23 : 13–25 ; John 18 : 39, 40). Synoptists full. John two verses. Mt. and Mk. contrast *Jesus and Barabbas*. Pilate proposes to chastise and release him; a compromise between sense of justice and fear of insurrection. Not succeeding, proposes to release a criminal, according to custom at Passover. People, influenced by Priests (Mt. 27: 20), demand Barabbas. Pilate had been warned by misgivings of conscience. Now a second solemn warning in the dream of his wife. Again urges release; failing, he yields him to be crucified. Notice, Pilate comes out and takes a seat on the bench (Mt. 27: 19) in a place called "Pavement," *Gabbatha* (John 19: 13). Probably, portable, mosaic pavement (Cæsar carried one) in definite locality *Gabbatha*. Where? Lightfoot, outer court of Temple, i. e. of Gentiles. Common opinion—open space before Prætorium. Not secret, examined in their presence; acquits him fully. If innocent why punish? May have thought him worthy of some punishment, and wished to please the Priests. Now proposes to treat him as guilty -- fatal step. Expects support of the people to release him but is disappointed. No custom known of releasing at feast. Originated probably with Pilate. Ewald, to commemorate deliverance from Egypt; others, an allusion to scape-goat. Not so; scape-goat referred to Christ. Was Barabbas mentioned first by Pilate (Mt. 27: 17), or by people (Lk. 23: 18)? Ans: By Pilate, as Mt. is most specific. People choose. Note 1. Barabbas guilty of crime charged against Christ. 2. Hypocrisy of Priests confessed in choice of Barabbas, a murderer, political and social disturber. 3. Christ's purity in strong contrast.

Barabbas probably a zealot, making insurrection against the government. Name—Son of the father. Olsh. supposes he was a false Messiah. Syriac version reads Jesus—Barabbas, which reading is adopted by Tisch., Meyer and Schaff. Accounted for by supposition that he was pseudo Messiah: rejected by Lachm. Treg. Popular mind changed; now demands Barabbas. Meanwhile comes message from Pilate's wife (Claudia canonized by Greek Church). A disturbing morning dream ($σήμερον$). Some say suggested by God's spirit; others, by Devil to avert crucifixion because of consequences. Bible does not attribute foreknowledge to Satan. Proves Pilate not unimpressible. Pilate remonstrates,

but is overborne by the tumult. The voice of the people and the chief priests prevailed. Choice of people renders rejection of Christ national. How account for change of popular mind towards Jesus? *a.* People at entrance to Jerusalem mostly Galileans, now Jerusalemites. Inadequate reason as from narrative we infer that people as a whole do both. *b.* Hatred of Romans, and unpopularity of Pilate. People side with thier own priests. *c.* Christ now convicted of blasphemy. *d.* Fundamental reason, disappointment of Messianic hopes. At Christ's entrance, looked for external kingdom. Now humiliated, condemned, mocked. Might defend himself by miracles but refuses. His own disciples forsook him and fled. While this explains, it is no excuse for their conduct. Nothing can wipe away the stigma, the great sin of the world by *vox populi.*

Why did they cry "crucify," when this was not a Jewish mode? J. A. A.: Jesus was substituted for Barabbas, who was to be crucified. It was simply because they expected the Romans to perform it. They thus denationalized themselves. Handwashing by Pilate, given only in Mt. 27 : 24. Andrews transposes to John 19 : 15 (§150). Tisch. and Rob. follow Mt's order. Objected to as Jewish practice (Deut. 21 : 6-9). Ans: Also heathen (vid. Livy 37 : 3, Ov. *Fast.* II. 45); a natural symbolic act, evidence of Pilate's inner convictions.

Compare words of Judas and Pilate. Judas: "I have betrayed the innocent blood." Priests. "See thou to that." Pilate: "I am innocent of the blood of this just person : see ye to it." Then the terrible imprecation by all the people, " His blood be on us and on our children." This curse fulfilled in history of Jews to this day. Strauss says imprecation invented later to account for destruction of Jerusalem. Ans: There is no real argument against its historical character, for it arises naturally in the struggle between Pilate and Priests ; it is not needed to account for the destruction of Jerusalem (this long ago foretold) ; it explains Pilate's readiness in giving up Christ and releasing Barabbas.

Pilate proves false to traditionary Roman tolerance in religion, and yields Christ on the ground the Jews first urge, as a favor. The Hierarchy, Political power and the people here combine to condemn the Lord of Glory. (Comp. Ps. 2: 1, 2). Some say scape-goat typified Barabbas. But Barabbas bears away no sin. Both goats typify Christ. Skeptics throw away historical accuracy of trial.

§149. *Jesus delivered up, scourged and mocked.* (Mt. 27: 26–30; Mk. 15: 15–19; John 19: 1–3.) Lk. alone mentions abuse from Herod. Mt. and Mk. allude to scourging as part of usual process before crucifixion; John as though Pilate wished to excite compassion or contempt and procure his release. That this was purpose of Pilate, see Lk. 23: 16–23. Many hold Christ was twice scourged. Improbable that Pilate would allow to be repeated this cruelty so dangerous to life. Soldiers were employed, and not lictors, as Pilate was a sub-governor, and not Proconsul. The word used ($\varphi\rho\alpha\gamma\varepsilon\lambda\lambda\omega\sigma\alpha\varsigma$) implies that it was done not with rods but with the *flagellum*. Farrar: "It was a punishment so hideous that, under its lacerating agony, the victim generally fainted, often went away to perish under the mortification and nervous exhaustion which ensued." Why such malignity of Roman troops? Sharing the hatred against the Jews, inflamed by popular clamor and by contrast of claims and humble appearance of Christ, they are rude enough to enjoy this brutal sport as a break in the dull monotony of their life. The publicity is noticed; $\sigma\pi\varepsilon\tilde{\iota}\rho\alpha\nu$, technically, cohort, is the whole band (armed by Pilate for fear of tumult). Scourged in the Prætorium, enclosed court of the Palace. Then mock him as king, putting on him a scarlet (Mt.), or purple (Mk.) soldier's cloak; on his head the painful crown of thorns; in his hand a reed. Did Christ grasp the reed with his hand? Slight importance. Probably hands bound. They soon "took the reed and smote him on the head," and then paid mock homage. Why all this indignity allowed? 1. Exhibits the evil of sin; human cruelty exhausting itself against a Savior. Nevertheless "by his stripes we are healed." 2. Shows Gentiles voluntarily participated in rejecting Christ. Brings out character of Jesus—his sublime forbearance, his superhuman dignity. A mere man could not have borne it. All this quietly wiped out by skeptics. Strauss concedes the scourging may have been performed.

§150. *Pilate still seeks to release Jesus. Ecce Homo.* Jno. 19: 4-16.) Given by John alone. Some take this section with §148. Confusing, and forbidden by fact that this is after scourging. Pilate tries to excite pity or contempt by leading Christ out in humiliated appearance, and says " Behold the Man !" An arch on Via Dolorosa marks the scene. Doubtful. Effect is only to call out new rage—" Crucify him, crucify him." Meyer insists that the populace is not mentioned in whole section. Some say, because priests were afraid of vacillating populace. Most, priests mentioned as being leaders. Jews fear Pilate will insist on releasing Christ, when he says ironically, " take ye him and crucify him, etc." So they now introduce the charge of blasphemy : "We have a law, and by our law he ought to die, because he made himself the Son of God." Effect on Pilate extraordinary —hears it for first time. Superstitious and afraid before, he now associates this claim of divinity with his notions of demigods, and is more afraid. Leads Christ back to Prætorium, and in tones of deepest agitation asks: " Whence art thou ?" Contrast spirit of question with that in previous chapter. Jesus now silent. Pilate threatens. Jesus answers: " Thou couldest have no power, etc., . . . therefore he that delivered, etc." John 19: 11-12. Why *therefore ?* Not because lesser guilt rests on weakness and timidity of Pilate (Luther), but because Jews illegal and willing persecutors, while Pilate with less knowledge is the unwilling though rightful judge. Farrar: " Thus with infinite dignity, and yet with infinite tenderness, did Jesus judge his judge." Pilate felt it, and on that (E. V. "from thenceforth,") determined to release him. If ever a prisoner had a chance to be released by his judge, Christ had now. This is the crisis of the trial. Jews threaten, "If thou let this man go, thou art not Cæsar's friend." Pilate knows the jealous severity of Tiberias towards subordinates, and remembering his own former cruelties, now yields to the threat. He brought Jesus forth and sat down on the judgment seat, and said in scorn, " Behold your king !" They cry, " Crucify." Pilate: " Shall I crucify your king ?" They answer: "We have no king but Cæsar." This is the lowest point in their hypocrisy. They claim loyalty to Cæsar and thus renounce all expectation of the Messiah. This ends the trial. Notice Pilate has made six efforts to release Christ. 1. Told priests and people, "I find no fault in this man." 2. Sends him to Herod. 3. On return from Herod, "I will therefore chastise him and release him." 4. Appealed to the people to release Christ rather than Barabbas. 5. After scourging, said, "Behold the man!" 6. After claim of "Son of God" made known.

§151. See §146.

§152. *Jesus led away to be crucified.* (Mt. 27 : 31–34; Mk. 15 : 20–23 ; Lk. 23 : 26–33 ; John 19 : 16, 17.)

I. *Time of Crucifixion:* Important discrepancy between John and Syn. Alexander: Impossible there should be a mistake in so public a transaction. Mk. 15 : 25 says, "it was the *third* hour (9 A. M.), and they crucified him." This agrees with M.M.L. that there was darkness from sixth to ninth hour, and with time required for trials. John 19 : 14, "And it was the preparation of the Passover and about the *sixth* hour (noon); and he saith unto the Jews, Behold your king!" Various attempts to remove the difficulty (see Andrews). 1. John's reading an error of transcription. $\tau\rho\iota\tau\eta$ instead of $\xi\kappa\tau\eta$ supported by D. L. X., Euseb., Theophyl., Robinson, Farrar. But best text is $\xi\kappa\tau\eta$. So A. B. E. X. etc. 2. That John uses Roman reckoning from midnight. Therefore 6 A. M. So Tholuck, Olsh., Ewald, Wieseler. But John does not reckon in this way elsewhere, and 6 A. M. would be too early. Too short time for trial, too long between condemnation and crucifixion. 3. That preparation denotes not whole day but part immediately preceding Sabbath from 3—6 P. M. Thus 6th hour before preparation would be 9 A. M. 4. That $\omega\rho\alpha$ is division of day —3 hours. "Thus 1st hour of day was from 6—9 ; the 3d from 9—12 ; the 6th from 12—3, the 9th from 6—9 (Andrews). The 3d hour of Mk. was from 9—12. During this period Jesus was crucified. John refers to end of period as 6th hour. So Grotius, Calvin, Wetstein, but unsupported by usage. 5. Hofmann and Lichtenstein put comma after $\pi\alpha\rho\alpha\sigma\kappa\epsilon\upsilon\eta$, and read 6th hour of the Passover; counting from midnight, which brings us to 6 A. M. But feast began at 6 A. M. not at midnight.

6. That "about the sixth hour" taken in loose sense, would be after 9 and before 12. So Andrews and Ellicot. Norton translates, " towards noon." 7. Lange (best) that the two writers date according to different idea. Mark may date from before scourging because of significant antithesis he wishes to institute between 3d and 6th hour. John says " towards noon," because the second, more Sabbatic half of παρασκευή was approaching. (See Lange on John 19: 14.) Any one of these solutions is more probable than to say none possible.

II. *Place of Crucifixion:* Mt., Mk. and John give the name Golgotha (Aramaic), translated χρανίου τόπος: Calvariae locus (Vulg.), " place of a skull " (E. V.). Lk. 23: 36. Lk. gives χρανίου, only place translated " Calvary." Supposed by Jerome to be so called from uncovered or unburied skulls; others, that it was a place of execution. But " Skull " is in the singular not plural, and Joseph, a rich man, would not have a tomb in such a place. Common explanation is that the name arose from *conical shape* of the hillock or rock. *Mount* Calvary is a modern expression. 1. Place was outside city walls. (Heb. 13: 12, Mt. 28: 11, (John 19: 16, 17.) 2. It was near the city. (John 19: 20). 3. It was near the sepulchre, which was in a garden and hewn in a rock. John 19: 41. Fisher Howe adds *a.* it was near one of the leading thoroughfares (Mt. 27: 39); *b.* it was eminently conspicuous (Mk. 15: 40; Lk. 23: 49). Andrews; " If the trial of our Lord was at the palace of Herod on Mt. Sion, he could not have passed along the Via Dolorosa." Church of Holy Sepulchre is the traditional site, supported by Williams, Tisch., Lange, etc., and opposed by Robinson, Wilson and others. The main difficulty lies in settling the course of the second wall—a question of time and money. Eusebius says Helena (mother of Constantine) built a church over the site. Fergusson, on architectural and other grounds, says that Mosque of Omar marks the true site of the sepulchre. (See Smith's Dict. art. Jerusalem.) Answered conclusively in *Ed. Review and Bib. Sacra.* Yet architectural argument against traditional site, is strong.

III. *Significance of Crucifixion:* Why this mode of death? Crucifixion known to Grecians, Romans, Egypttians, Parthians, Phœnicians, Indians; not used by Jews. Significant that his death was in a mode familiar to whole heathen world for lowest criminals. Josephus says: "Titus could not find wood enough to make crosses or places to put them when he took Jerusalem." Cicero (Verr. 5: 64) speaks of it as a cruel and terrible punishment, such as was not inflicted on Roman citizens. Before Christ, *to bear the cross* was a classic phrase expressing dishonor. This mode of punishment was abolished by Constantine, through reverence for the cross. Unknown to Jews, except after death the body was sometimes hanged (Deut. 21: 22, 23), as special curse (Num. 25: 4; 2 Sam. 21: 6). Controversial Jews do not use the phrase *crucify*: these say they *hanged* him. Yet crucifixion was predicted: Christ to be *pierced* (Ps. 22: 16; Zech. 12: 10). Also the scourging, the drink, and the parting of the garments belong to this mode. The same dishonor associated with Jewish hanging (Deut. 21: 23) inflicted on Christ (Gal. 3: 13).

From the Crucifixion we learn: 1. Judicial nature of his death. He paid the supreme penalty to rescue us from the curse of the law. 2. He died for the whole world. Jewish Messiah died by Roman punishment, that "the blessing of Abraham might come on the Gentiles," (Gal. 3: 14). So he declared; "And I, if I be lifted up, etc.," (John 12: 33). 3. His death was conspicuous. Lifted up as brazen serpent, an object for faith of all. 4. It was ignominious and painful. This shows the nature of sin. See Plato's portrait of the just man (Republic, II. 362), "He shall be scourged ... and crucified." Clem. Alex. says Plato speaks like a prophet; Lightfoot, that only chronological impossibility saves him from imputation of plagiarism. 5. It was a lingering death. We have three years with the living Christ; this gives three hours intercourse with the dying Christ. 6. It was fully attested: not done in a corner. No rationalist can deny the fact.

No wonder death of Christ transformed the cross to symbol of highest glory. Chrysostom says: "Symbol seen everywhere, for we are not ashamed of the cross." In decline of the church it became an object of worship.

IV. *The Form of the Cross, etc.* There were three ancient forms in use: *a.* the *crux decussata* in shape of

letter X (St. Andrew's); *b.* the *crux commissa*, in shape of letter T; *c.* the *crux immissa*, with upright one-third of its length above the transverse † (Roman). Origen says like T. So Tertullian, who argued from the mark like a cross placed on forehead (Ez. 9:4). Same form on coins of Constantine, commonly supposed to be Roman *crux immissa*. So gathered from comparisons of Justin, Jerome, etc., to man praying with outstretched arms, to four quarters of heavens. So in catacombs and early paintings. So writing nailed above his head.

The cross (not a tree) was probably made of sycamore or olive. Artists make it too high or too heavy. The feet would come quite near the ground. The hyssop was only an herb, and the sponge on a hyssop branch reached his mouth. The thrust from a spear was therefore nearly horizontal. Cross was light enough to be carried by one man.

"And when they had mocked him, they took off the purple from him and led him out to crucify him," (Mk. 15:20). Crown of thorns not mentioned; probably removed. Roman law that condemned should be immediately executed; important to priests as well as against their law that body should remain out all night (Deut. 21:23). They proceed immediately to crucify. A quaternion of soldiers, and not lictors, as Pilate was only sub-governor. The centurion was usually mounted. Not told how far customs were observed. Roman custom, a tablet hung around neck or carried before criminal. Jewish custom, a herald crying his name and crime. Roman usage made condemned bear his cross. John 19:17 says Jesus bore his cross; Syns., they compelled Simon, a Cyrenian. This probably when Jesus became faint. Perhaps both together (see Lange on Lk. 23:26). Meyer supposes him a slave; some say he was seized because a disciple; probably because he was near. Cyrene is in Libya. There a colony of Jews; many in Jerusalem (Acts 2:10). Simon Niger and Lucius, prophets or teachers, were from Cyrene (Acts 13:1). From fact that he was "coming from the country," no inference that this was a working and not a great feast day. Multitudes of people and women followed lamenting. Not the usual lamentation for dead, which, at least according to later traditions, was forbidden for criminals. Some say, they were his Galilean friends. This does not agree with " Daughters of Jerusalem." Some say, from mere pity. Yet Christ deems them worthy of a particular address. Christ's reply, like his lamentation over Jerusalem, alludes to prophecies fulfilled. (Is. 54 : 1 ; Hos. 10 : 8 ; Ez. 20 : 47, comp. 21 : 3 seq.) These his last words of any length. Josephus gives a dire comment when he tells of women eating their children during the siege. No instance in gospels of women doing or saying anything against Christ. Arrived at Golgotha, they proceed to crucify. Wine mingled with myrrh offered to deaden pain. Farrar : " It had been the custom of wealthy ladies in Jerusalem to provide this stupefying potion at their own expense, and they did so quite irrespectively of their sympathy for any individual criminal." No analogous custom at Rome. Mt. says "vinegar mingled with gall." Mk., "wine mingled with myrrh." No contradiction. Soldiers carried a light acid wine (Mt. 27 : 34). This was mingled with $\chi o \lambda \dot{\eta}$, i. e., anything *bitter*. Our Lord refuses ; an act of sublimest heroism. Not his purpose to avoid suffering.

§153. *The Crucifixion.* (Mt. 27 : 35-38 ; Mk. 15 : 24-28 ; Lk. 23 : 33, 34, 38 ; John. 19 : 18-24). Mt. and Mk. speak of dividing garments too soon. Was he condemned and affixed to cross before or after its elevation ? Commonly after ; so early fathers. About centre of cross a *sedile* to support weight of body. Binding to cross essential to prevent tearing. Disputed whether the feet were nailed separately or together. Most fathers say nailed separately. Because Christ walked afterwards, Rationalists say feet simply bound, hence Christ did not die, only swooned. Justin and Fathers say Ps. 22 : 16 fulfilled, and cite Lk. 24 : 39 : " Behold my hands and my feet." Two malefactors, robbers, were crucified with Christ. Was this caused by the Jews to degrade Christ, or by Pilate to insult the Jews ? Probably the latter. Is. 53 : 12 fulfilled. Mk. 15 : 28 omitted by A, B, C, D, X, Tisch., Alf., etc.

The Seven Utterances. Luke only (23 : 34) gives first utterance, " Father forgive them." No limitation in

truth implied. Universal, hence appropriate in Luke. Conjectured that these words were uttered during nailing. They signify: 1. Intercession of Christ as Priest, a sacrificial act. 2. The state of mind of Christ in midst of suffering. 3. The spirit of his teaching, "Love your enemies." Fruits of this prayer at Pentecost. Comp. Stephen's last words.

Parting of garments. Custom to divide garments among executioners. Condemned was stripped naked, not even cloth about the loins. Divided upper garment into four parts. Cast lots for his coat. Priest's tunic seamless. Must not infer Christ's coat a priest's. Prophecy fulfilled (Is. 53:12). Mt. 25: end of v. 35 an interpolation.

Title over Cross. Mt., "This is Jesus the king of the Jews." Mk., "The king of the Jews." Lk., "This is the king of the Jews." John, "Jesus of Nazareth, the king of the Jews." Notice differences: 1. John full, others compress. 2. Three languages used. This might account for differences. Farrar: "Title written in the official Latin, in the current Greek, in the vernacular Aramaic."

Why did Pilate write this superscription? *Ans:* a. To make a show of legality. b. To ridicule the Jews. This last strongest, and proved by remonstrance of the priests, "Write not, The king of the Jews; but that he said, I am king of the Jews." What Pilate had written in scorn was in reality a profound truth. Pilate had vacillated in serious matters, now obstinate in small. Lange insists (from Mt. 27:38) that the thieves were brought on by a different guard of troops, after the title was set up. Mt.'s use of τότε not strongly temporal.

§154. *Jews mock at Jesus on the cross. He commends his mother to John.* (Mt. 27:39-44; Mk. 15:29-32; Lk. 23:35-37, 39-43; John 19:25-27.) Four classes participate in mocking:

I. The passers by. (Mt. and Mk.) Not only the casual passers, but the crowd railed at him, wagging their heads. Fulfillment of Ps. 22:7. Words of mockery: "Thou that destroyest the temple, etc.," significant as now being fulfilled.

II. Chief Priests, Scribes and Elders (Sanhedrim) mock his official character. (MML.) They sneer (literally turn up the nose) at meaning of *Jesus.* "He saved others, himself he cannot save." They mock also his trust in God. Ps. 22: 8. They unconsciously express the profound truth that the salvation of others implies sacrifice of self.

III. The soldiers mock, saying, "If thou be the *King of the Jews,* save thyself." It was near noon, their dinner hour. They offer him vinegar (Lk.) i. e. their light acid wine. Some identify this with previous offering; others with offering just before his death. Ebrard: "A distinction is very properly made between (1) the *myrrh* offered in order to stupefy; (2) the tantalizing offer of the *posca* in Lk. 24: 36; and (3) the offer of the *posca* immediately before the death of Jesus."

IV. The two thieves railed on him, saying "If thou be the Christ, save *thyself and us."* Notice, each class of scoffers brings out specific difference between Christ and themselves. All involve the false idea of the Messiah and his kingdom. Strauss objects to the differences in the accounts, and that priests could not quote Ps. 22:8, 9 without acknowledging themselves enemies of the Messiah. *Ans:* Proves too much. Strauss admits many facts which were clearly predicted; this Psalm was Messianic, and so naturally used.

Conversion of thief. Word implies violence rather than theft. Substitution represented—"He was numbered with the transgressors." Cross of Christ discriminates among men—election represented. Christ shown as Prophet in words to penitent thief; as Priest, in offering up himself; as King, in pardoning. True repentance at eleventh hour represented. Abuse of the example removed by example of the other thief.

Second Utterance: "To-day thou shalt be with me in Paradise." Paradise used three times in N. T. Decisive against Purgatory, not necessarily against an intermediate state of the dead. Still a question where Christ was during three days. This utterance predicts Christ's death *on this day.* Speedy death unusual. Objections: 1. Mt. and Mk. say both reviled; Lk. says one. *Ans:* M.M. speak generically, or (better) both mocked, then one repented.

Third Utterance: "Woman, behold thy son!" "Behold thy mother!" Women at the cross, his mother and his mother's sister, Mary the wife of Cleophas, and Mary Magdalene. This utterance shows Christ's human love for his mother and confidence in his friends. Shows his grasp of the future of his people, and that he makes provision for them. Objected that M.M. speak only of women, Lk. of his acquaintance, and only John of himself and Mary. No contradiction. Objected that John says they stood by the cross, while Synoptists say afar off. The Synoptists refer to later period. This utterance Andrews supposes before, Krafft after, the darkness and final mocking—unimportant. Gospels show that Mary laid up these things and pondered them in her heart. It may be her influence is seen in John's gospel.

§155. *Darkness. Death of Jesus.* (Mt. 27:45-50; Mk. 15:33-37; Lk. 23:44-46; John 19:28-30.) A new element in supernatural accompaniments, darkness, earthquake, rending of veil, and opening of graves. These are divine attestations to Christ, and symbols of the effect of his death. Would have been unnatural and out of analogy had no signs been given now. Darkness from sixth to ninth hour. How long Jesus had hung upon the cross depends on harmony of Mt. 15:25 with John 19:14. It was high noon, when light and heat greatest, that sun was darkened. Meyer says that Luke implies sun partially obscured till noon, then darkened. Substantiated by Cod. Sin., which supplies in v. 44, τοῦ ἡλίου ἐκλιπόντος.

Extent of Darkness: Was it confined to Palestine, or more extended? If the former, explains lack of mention by contemporaries. Cause of darkness. Many fathers say eclipse. Phlegon of Tralles says in 202 Olympiad occurred greatest eclipse ever known. But this eclipse was a year or two too late, and could not occur during full moon. Seyffarth holds to eclipse, and supposes the Passover two weeks after regular time. Some connect darkness with earthquake. Majority say it was entirely miraculous.

Objections: 1. John omits all supernatural additions. 2. No adequate cause for them. 3. Not mentioned in history. 4. Not appealed to by Apostles. 5. Motive for mythical origin obvious. *Ans:* 1. Friedlieb quotes Tertullian and Lucian as saying that the fact was recorded in heathen accounts now lost. 2. Apostles refer to Resurrection as proof of supernatural, and greater includes the less. If no other proof, authority of the three Evangelists sufficient. The darkness symbolizes sympathy of nature. The earth cursed because of man's sin now participates in redemption. Corresponds also with darkness in soul of Jesus. At his birth a new star came forth; at his death the sun was darkened.

Fourth Utterance: "My God, my God, why hast thou forsaken me?" Some say after darkness, because drink offered; others, just before. This the only one of the seven utterances preserved by M.M. Mt. gives Hebrew, Mk. the Aramaic. Meaning of this utterance: It expresses a reality. God had really forsaken him. His human soul is left destitute. Expresses the extremity of what he came to bear. Lange, sympathy of soul with body; Meyer, physical pain. Naturalistic interpreters deny importance of the words. Others, little stress on mere words, as they are simply the opening words of a Psalm of triumph (Ps. 22). Others, an ordinary ejaculation of distress. Others, failure of his plan. Others, mythical. Bystanders say, "Behold he calleth Elias." Olshausen, Lange, that terrified and confused, they think judgment and Elijah truly coming. Most say, it was a wilful misunderstanding.

Fifth Utterance: "I thirst." Was this to fulfil prophecy (Ps. 69: 21), or a real want? When he used the language "I thirst," he meant it. Meyer: 1. John never puts telic clause first. 2. Ps. 69: 21 refers to previous offer of vinegar. 3. Christ would not now say "I thirst," if not true. (See Meyer on John 19: 28.) This the only word from the cross expressing physical suffering. Gethsemane shows spiritual suffering not to be lost sight of; this shows the same in regard to the physical. One ran and filled a sponge with vinegar and gave him to drink. Having satisfied this compassionate impulse, he joins the rest in mockery: "Let alone; let us see whether Elias will come to take him down." Last words somewhat differently reported. Mt. and Mk. say he cried with a loud *voice*, and gave up the ghost. But word for voice ($\varphi\omega\nu\acute{\eta}$) means articulate utterance.

Sixth Utterance: "It is finished," given by John. To be taken before utterance given by Luke, because more appropriate and intelligible here. Evident reference to v. 28. Perfect tense; it has been and continues finished. All O. T. prophecies and types fulfilled. He does not mean simply the *scripture* has been fulfilled. The words go back to the counsels of eternity. Redemption, and Revelation of God to man are finished. Comp. John 17: 4. Hengst. finds reference to Ps. 22:31. Finished is his farewell greeting to earth; the next utterance marks his entrance to heaven.

Seventh Utterance: "Father, into thy hands I commend my spirit." (Lk. 23:46.) Tisch. reads παρατίθεμαι. This more natural. His last words not an assertion of divinity but trust. He resigns himself to his Father. Taken from Ps. 31:5.

These seven utterances have a literature of their own. Notice, 1. how many come from O. T.; 2. how wonderful their comprehensiveness; 3. how natural their sequence. He who exhausts them has little to know about either covenant.

The first is a prayer for pardon of his enemies.
Second, Shows judgment and saving power.
Third, Christ's tender care for his people.
Fourth, Depth of punishment for sin.
Fifth, His humanity and physical suffering.
Sixth, His triumphant victory.
Seventh, His trust in God.

It is remarkable that the four Evangelists avoid the expression, "he died." They say, "He gave up the ghost." It was a voluntary act.

§156. *Supernatural accompaniments continued. Impression on different classes of witnesses.* (Mt. 27:51–56; Mk. 15:38–41; Lk. 23:45, 47–49.) The veil of temple rent, earthquake, graves opened and dead raised. Luke puts rending of veil before statement of Christ's death. The same word used in LXX. for both inner and outer veil. Means here, inner veil. Denied, because 1. known only to priests, who would not tell, and 2. not referred to later in N. T. Naturalistic interpreters describe it as effect of earthquake upon veil old or tender or fastened at four corners. Tradition in Gospel of the Hebrews says a beam fell against it. Its meaning is plain. The typical system is ended. All believers are now priests and may enter through the Veil to the Holiest of Holies (Heb. 10 : 19). Earthquake and grave-opening mentioned by Mt. alone. Objected 1. That this resurrection of saints was never appealed to later. 2. What became of them? 3. What was the use of it? Some try to destroy the text. Some say earthquake opened graves, which were found empty, hence the report. (Farrar.) Others, it was all visionary. Strauss, all mythical; they had not yet separated second advent from first. Do the words "after his resurrection" qualify their leaving the graves or their going into the city? Most place all after his resurrection, because 1. Christ is called the first-fruits, and 2. His resurrection necessary to new life of the saints. How did they rise? Was it in physical bodies to die again? Most likely in resurrection bodies — recognizable — not to live with men, but to ascend with Christ. Who were they? Some say those recently dead, or they would not have been recognized. Others say O. T. Patriarchs and prophets. Tradition gives their names. Meaning clear: The sacrifice now made is victory over death. Schaff: "So much only appears certain to us that it was a supernatural and symbolic event which proclaimed the truth that the death and resurrection of Christ was a victory over death and Hades, and opened the door to everlasting life." The centurion and soldiers, after Christ's last cry (Mk.), and the supernatural accompaniments (Mt.) say "Truly this was the Son of God." Luke gives, "certainly this was a righteous man." Some say the words must be taken in heathen sense, i. e. a demi-god (So Meyer). More common opinion is that the centurion had some knowledge and this is incipient faith. At all events he is convinced that Christ is true. He is the precursor of Cornelius, the first fruits of Gentiles acknowledging the Savior. We have important witness to truth of these details. The mass of the people are impressed. Stricken with terror and remorse, they smote their breasts and returned (Lk. 23 : 48). Representatives of Israel and the Centurion of the Gentiles are witnesses to the fact and power of his death. The friends of Christ are also present. Lk. says "all his acquaintance." Mt. and Mk.

the walk to Emmaus are fatal to the visionary theory. Notice the peculiar inconsistence of *Strauss*. He says "A myth originating in Gal. some time after Christ's death. It grew out of a growing reverence for Christ and a study of Messianic prophecies." But how does it suit *Dr. Strauss* to account for Mary's seeing Christ here? Her idea cannot be accounted for on this theory, for she had no thought of the resurrection and *Strauss* says Christ had never predicted it!

"Touch me not." The rebuke is to Mary's mistake. She supposed that ordinary intercourse was to be renewed. Jesus warns her that it is not to be so. He virtually says, "No longer is sense, but faith, to be the mode of communion." So when he said to the eleven and Thomas, "Handle me," there is no inconsistency, as then he wished to convince them of his bodily identity. Mary is here already convinced of that.

§162. *Jesus meets the women.* Mt. says Jesus met the women and gave them the message; how can we reconcile that with this? Some argue that they are the same occurrence. But it is better to regard them as different. Three Evangelists distinctly state that the Apostles did not believe the report of the women. This is natural. It doubtless sounded strange to them that the women alone saw what Peter and John did not see. They were in a state of fear and excitement.

§165. *The Report of the Watch.* Reported by Mt. only as he alone gave the account of its being set. The offer of bribes to the soldiers. The story is incredible on the face of it. It was impossible for the disciples to steal the body. Grotius collects evidence of its currency among the Jews in the 2nd and 3rd centuries, and says it was still believed by them! Strauss objects: "Is it likely that the whole Sanhedrim at a regular meeting would unite in giving official sanction to a lie?" Ebrard replies: "Is it likely that the whole Sanhedrim at a regular meeting would unite in a judicial murder?—The marvel is what pious, conscientious men the San. become in the hands of Dr. Strauss. The whole of Christendom, a multitude of humble, quiet men, may have devised and adhered tenaciously to a bare-faced lie; but the murderers of Jesus were incapable of persuading these soldiers to propagate a trifling untruth, which their own conduct had rendered necessary!" The priests believed the resurrection, as they knew of the empty tomb, not with a full faith, but as they had already witnessed many miracles. Their consciences were uneasy. The Apostles do not refer to this because they had better proofs, and this lie was not current in the places to which they were sent. Why not mentioned in Acts 4? Because the Sanhedrim did not deny the resurrection in their earlier persecutions.

§166. *Jesus seen of Peter. The two go to Emmaus.* The third appearance, and first to an Apostle, was to Peter after the two went to Emmaus: Lk. 24:34; I. Cor. 15:5. An honor to Peter considering his denial, and intended as a help to his repentance. The walk to Emmaus shows the feeling of the disciples. The mistake of these men and their non-recognition are incompatible with the visionary theory. Who were the two? Wies., &c. understand Cleopas to be Alphaeus (Mt. 10:3), and the other, the Apostle James his son. This is not probable. Lightfoot thinks the second person was Peter. Some, that he was Luke. Discrepancy: Mk. says their report is not believed; Lk. that the eleven anticipated them with "The Lord is risen indeed and hath appeared unto Simon." Therefore they did believe. The question of Harmony is interesting, as on it turns the point, whether the Apostles believed at all on testimony, or remained unbelieving till they saw for themselves. The margin of the E. V. makes Mk.'s statement a question, which has little foundation. Some say they believed Peter, but could not believe the two from Emmaus, as it was a seeming contradiction that Christ should be seen by both. If this is a true solution it remains that all but Peter (and Thomas) believed upon testimony. The two going to Emmaus betray a dim idea that the third day should bring some change and yet it was almost ended. The breaking of bread probably not Lord's Supper. The instructions of Jesus to the two agree with Lk's report of the words of the angels.

§167. *Jesus appears to the Apostles. Thomas absent. Sunday evening.* Most important and perhaps most decisive for then were their doubts finally overcome, and they are appointed witnesses for the future. Given by Mk., Lk., John, Paul. Mk. and Lk. close their narrative here, as the last essential thing. Mk. introduces a third appearance; Lk. shows his bodily presence,—the nature of his resurrection body and the scars of his crucifixion. The question now was not the fact of his resurrection but the reality and identity of his body. They were at their evening meal, perhaps in the room where they kept the passover. Coming through closed doors—Lutherans say it shows the ubiquity of Christ's person. The point of the visit was to show that he was not a spirit. He declares his body to be " flesh and bones." Handling him was an important evidence. (1 John 1: 1). Lk. adds a crowning evidence in Christ's eating. It is commonly accepted that it was not for nourishment, but as evidence of his material body. The identity of his body could not be better proved.

The Apostolic Commission is now given, which shows the spiritual import of the resurrection. It was because they were personally convinced that they are made witnesses. Paul (1 Cor. 15: 5) speaks of Twelve. Syn. give eleven. Clear and important that other Christians were present as μαθηται. The two from Emmaus were plainly present. Thus the powers here conferred were not confined to apostles alone. Was the commission given to-night? Mk. and Lk. add it here as the last thing. Van Oos. puts it after v. 44. John leaves no doubt that the commission was given here. So it was twice given. The commission to witness, preach and administer discipline was based on the gift of the Holy Ghost as authority. John says he breathed on them, and saith " Receive ye the Holy Ghost." This was in consequence of the resurrection. It was not however plenary, but partial and preparatory, corresponding to their wants till Pentecost. There was need of it; they were passing through a critical period. A transition from doubt to faith. They had still to gather and guide the body of disciples till Pentecost. (N. B. The distinction between πνευμα άγιον here and το πνεῦμα άγιον in Acts is untenable). *Strauss* says the command to tarry at Jerus. (in Lk.) contradicts the command to go to Gal. Van Oos. and Alf. say this command was not given till after the return from

Gal. But there is no inconsistency. One qualifies the other. The "tarry" qualifies the Commission. Make Jerus. your headquarters, and do not go to preach till after Pentecost.

§168. *Jesus appears to the Twelve. Thomas present.* Time 2d Sabbath. John alone records it. 1. How came the apostles still in Jerusalem? *a.* They would not travel during the feast, which lasted till Friday. *b.* Some think unbelief kept them. Thomas and others still doubted. *c.* Others suppose the command to go was accompanied by an intimation as to when and how. 2. Why together on the first day of the week? To commemorate the resurrection? Certainly it is the beginning of the Christian Sabbath. They meet Christ on these days only. The force of their example is sanctioned by Christ. What was Thomas's reception? Jesus commends Thomas for faith, but shows there is a higher faith based on spiritual evidences and shows the danger of subjecting faith to sense or reason. Thomas is convinced before putting his test to practice, and joyfully believes.

An important point: that the claim of Divinity is variously made elsewhere, but here only in the Gospels is θεος applied to Christ by the disciples or accepted by him. The Gospel of John begins: "The word was God" and closes with "My Lord and My God!"

§169. *Jesus appears to seven Apostles on the sea of Tiberias.* By most harmonists put before Mt.'s narrative because of Jno. 21:14. The charge of Meyer that Paul's statement (I. Cor. 15: 5–7), cannot be reconciled is not sustained. One explanation is that Paul includes under the expression "seen of the twelve," the three of John; or it may be that Paul summarizes. The first appearance would be at the grave, then at Jerus. in vicinity of the tomb. But it must not be confined to Jerus. as the witness is to extend to hundreds of believers in Gal. It is also to show the bodily relations of Jesus; he was superhuman as to extension. Again, by this he corrects the mistaken idea of the disciples, that the new Dispensation should be also a Theocracy in Jerus. Comp. Acts 1. Disciples had gone to Gal. and returned to their daily occupation. Early in the morning Christ appears on the shore and repeats the miracle that had called them at first—thus reinstating them. A promise of great success in their work is seen in the number of fishes taken. There is no evidence that the fire and the bread were miraculous. They were significant of rest after toil. The results of toil give joy. Peter is especially reinstated. The three-fold question refers to the denials: "Simon, Son of Jonas!" alludes to his original nature, reminding him of his unrenewed state. Notice the comparison "more than these" based on "though all should forsake thee, yet will not I." Peter's humility appears in his not using the comparison. Peter asserts but the humbler personal love, φιλεω; Jesus used the higher, αγαπαω. but at last descends to use even φιλεω. Notice also (a) lambs, (b) sheep, (c) little sheep. Also ποιμαινειν and βοσκειν. The martyrdom of Peter is added to show his confidence in Peter's constancy. When this book was written Peter had been long dead and there is a reference to John's life and exemption from martyrdom. Upon Jno. 21:24 is based a strong argument for the authorship of the book.

§170. *Jesus meets the Apostles and 500 on a mount in Gal.* Paul, I. Cor. 15:6. This is the same as Mt.'s eleven. It involves the question whether the commission was given to the whole church or not. Not so, unless others besides the eleven were present. The chief evidence is from Mt. himself: 1. Why appoint a meeting on a mount in Gal. for eleven only? 2. Mt. says some worshipped but some doubted like Thomas. 3. Mt. 28:7 says "there shall ye see him" in the message to the women. 4. There is reason why Mt. should emphasize the eleven, as to him the ecclesiastical commission was the prominent thing. Notice, they went where they were commanded, hence had an interesting meeting. A fortuitous gathering is inconceivable. A general summons was necessary. The 21st of John gives us the probable occasion of the command. Compare the second or great commission in Mt. with John. 1. This (Mt.'s) makes no mention of suffering or of the reality of his resurrection body. 2. It is fuller than the previous one. 3. Sets forth the completed authority of Christ as its basis. In Acts we have only the story of this work. This Commission is the basis of the Christian sacrament of Baptism.

§171. *Our Lord is seen of James, then of all the Apostles.* Which James? More likely James of Jerus. than the son of Zebedee, but it cannot be determined. Luke in Acts implies manifestations which are not recorded. Several facts are gathered from Acts 1, e. g. that Christ's mother and brethren accompanied him to Gal. Additional evidences of continued false expectations on part of the Apostles. Again they are to tarry in Jerus. till they be "baptized with the Holy Ghost not many days hence." Also the order of the conversion of the world is given : "In Jerus. and in all Judea, and in Samaria and even to the uttermost parts of the earth." From the climactic advance in the proofs of the resurrection, we find a final argument against the subjective visionary theory. No such thing could have arisen from merely accidental visions to different persons.

§172. *The Ascension.* At the end of the 40 days our Lord once more appears. It is at Jerus. He ascends in sight of the disciples. This is the proper conclusion of the record. The Ascension is necessarily associated with the resurrection for there could be no more *death* to Christ. He must ascend, and in presence of the disciples. They had seen him appear and disappear for 40 days. If this then was no more formal than those, they would be continually looking for him to return. Even as it was they expected him to come again in their own day. Also gives a definiteness and location to our ideas of a risen Lord and a Christian heaven. We cannot now enter into the difficulties suggested by the Lutherans and others. Concerning the sacraments—local limitation, &c., can only touch on critical objections. *Place of the Ascension:* An apparent contradiction : Bethany (Lk.), Mount of Olives (Acts). But they are so near to each other that there is no real difficulty. Was it visible to others than disciples? Hard to conceive that it was. John and Mt. don't mention the ascension at all. Only Mk. and Lk. tell of it, and Tisch. rejects $ανεφερετο$ from Lk. Then Acts is our only authority for a visible ascension. But Tisch. is not followed by most critics. At any rate, it is in Acts which is by Lk. Mk. and Lk. had a special object in recording it. Both show Christ as the Savior of the world and look to the future history of the church. And though Mt. and John omit it, yet they refer to it in the Gospel. The going away is not the final point, for he is to come again.

Mk. seems to connect the ascension immediately with the first interview with the eleven on the resurrection Sunday. Lk. seems to imply the same thing. It is after the report of the two from Emmaus. (Though in Acts it is "after 40 days)." Upon this is based the theory of repeated ascensions. Baur says Evangelists teach that Christ's abode after the resurrection was in heaven. So some Harmonists. The sceptics say there were two traditions of his Ascension. One on the first Sunday—and another (Galilean) after an interval of 40 days. But notice, the difficulty cannot be so great, or Lk. is at discord with himself. He records it in *both* forms; and a sufficient explanation is found in the intention of the two passages. The mode of ascension was exquisitely appropriate. His speaking with them—blessing them, and then rising from them till a cloud enfolds him, concealing him from their sight. The words of the angels, also, to the gazing disciples sanction the church's attitude of expectation. And *he* said that true waiting is to work as well as to wait.

www.ingramcontent.com/pod-product-compliance
Lightning Source LLC
Chambersburg PA
CBHW022110290426
44112CB00008B/626